The English Historical Novel

Avrom Fleishman

The English
Historical Novel

WALTER SCOTT TO VIRGINIA WOOLF

The Johns Hopkins Press
Baltimore and London

71–19454

This study of the historical imagination

is dedicated to the memory of

the Jewish community of Amsterdam

Contents

Fiction is history, human history, or it is
nothing. But it is also more than that; it
stands on firmer ground, being based on
the reality of forms and the observation
of social phenomena, whereas history is
based on documents, and the reading of
print and handwriting—on second-hand
impression. Thus fiction is nearer truth.
But let that pass. A historian may be an
artist too, and a novelist is a historian,
the preserver, the keeper, the expounder,
of human experience.

JOSEPH CONRAD

"Henry James: An Appreciation"

Preface

The rhetorician would deceive his neighbours,
The sentimentalist himself; while art
Is but a vision of reality.

YEATS

Art is "but" a vision, yet it is very difficult to fix the belief that historical novels are but works of art. The form tempts its practitioner to play the rhetorician, to justify or deride the crimes and follies of the present by linking them to the past—as in that most successful of historical novels, *Gone with the Wind*. More frequently, the genre is used for self-intoxication, as the close connection of the vogue of Scott and the rise of nationalism suggests. Even when the setting is remote from nationalist aspirations, works like *Pan Tadeusz* and *I Promessi Sposi* can become the focus of inordinate sentiment (often obscuring the novel's true worth). Yet as a vision of historical reality, fictional art is hardly the stuff to further a political animus. There is in it a stronger impulse toward contemplation than the rhetorician or the sentimentalist exhibits. Art is a way of seeing, and the artist's eye is jaundiced like another's; nevertheless it aims to contemplate reality. The adjustment between an esthetically distant perspective and an engagement with the present is a most difficult one for the historical novelist to make. The conflict between these impulses occasionally flares up in a *cause célèbre* like the *Nat Turner* affair.

Readers of best-seller fiction and the literary reviews have recently found themselves exposed to a controversy which few of them could have expected to command their attention. It was the treatment of a sensitive racial theme that brought the issue of the historical novel to life again. Did William Styron slander the Negro race when he portrayed Nat Turner as a fallible human being, or is the novelist entitled to his psychological speculations on a historical figure? The "ten black writers" and others who denounced Styron expressed the assumptions of most readers of historical novels—whatever their brand of parochialism. Even if the reader uses fiction for escapist fantasy, he expects historical novels to be "true-to-life," i.e., accurate in the light of the historical evidence. When Styron defended himself on the grounds that he had created an imaginative reconstruction of a scantily-known phenomenon, he, too, adhered to the assumption that the historical novelist should follow the facts as far as they are known—or the professional historian may censure him when he departs from them. But more, Styron made an implicit claim to be able to discover and express truths that the historian cannot reach: insights into the historical actor, Nat Turner, and into the psychology of the slave, upon which the historian's limited data make it dangerous to generalize. While Styron seems to apologize that a "novel is only a novel," he does not diminish his claim to truth (for a novel *can* tell truths and untruths, as his critics insist), but instead makes a grand claim for credence. A novel can tell a truth otherwise hidden: fiction is a way of knowing. It is the seeming arrogance of this claim that may evoke greatest hostility among his readers, and I propose to give some reasons why it is a legitimate claim.

It would be futile to rehearse the charges and counter-charges in this sad but enlightening controversy. Sticking to the underlying assumptions of the ten black writers (only two of whom are historians by profession), we find the following:[1]

What manner of black commander is this, whose major heterosexual activities—even in fantasy—are with white women? . . . Since this major theme and its supporting scenes are entirely of Styron's creation, the questions belong to him alone. Whose mind has he entered save his own? [Vincent Harding, p. 28]

1. John H. Clarke, ed., *William Styron's Nat Turner: Ten Black Writers Respond* (Boston, 1968); authors and page numbers are placed with the quotations in the text.

Granted, Styron is entitled to his literary license, but black people today cannot afford the luxury of having their leaders manipulated and toyed with. Nat Turner struck a blow for freedom; Nat Turner was a revolutionary who did *not* fail. . . . [Charles V. Hamilton, p. 73]

When a work of fiction is . . . defined for us as "a meditation on history" rather than a "conventional" historical novel, certain questions are forced upon us.

William Styron's *Confessions* is such a work. It straddles two genres; claims, in a sense, to transcend both; and manages to combine the problems of the two while reaping dual dividends as a "novel" which is also "history." Because the book is both "history" and a novel the public mind seems to have invested it with qualities it does not necessarily possess. The events and situations are assumed to be accurate because by being "historical" they must of necessity be "true." And as the "facts" of history are true, so, in a different sense, are the insights (read "symbolic truths") of the novel. [Mike Thelwell, p. 79]

In the first quotation, the subjectivity of fiction is radically asserted. A writer cannot imagine or intuit another man's mind; all he can know and express is himself. In the second quotation, we find a more subtle approach to fiction: Styron has his interpretation; it is not conducive to our ends; we will maintain our own interpretation. Hamilton sees fiction—and history—as myth, and accepts it in competition with political and racial myths propagated by other cultural forces. He merely decides to substitute some myths for others—suggesting both his scepticism as to the myth's truth and his pragmatism as to its usefulness.

Thelwell's is the most interesting view. He is aware that historical fiction is a literary genre; he is astute in seizing on Styron's lapse into something like a claim to be writing history (a "meditation on history"); and he is perceptive of the way in which such a claim might encourage a reader's expectation that a historical novel is simply true-to-life. But Thelwell himself draws an incisive distinction between " 'facts' of history" and "symbolic truths." Most of his essay, and most of the others in this volume, are devoted to challenging Styron's " 'facts' of history." They take up *Nat Turner*'s "symbolic truths" only in the way Harding and Hamilton do in the above quotations: as the personal fantasies of the author or as racist stereotypes. There are other alternatives: the symbolic truth of a historical novel may be an insight into the universal processes of history, a hypothetical explanation of an interstice in historical knowledge (usually a personal motivation), or a vivification of a shadowy period or lost past. There is no guarantee that the his-

torical novelist will succeed in achieving so much; I hold no brief
for Styron's complete success in this novel. But there is at least
that goal, that possible triumph, for the historical novel, and its
difficult beauty has been strongly reaffirmed in this propagandist
debate.

Like all serious historical novels *The Confessions of Nat Turner*
presupposes a concern for the way we know history, and Part 1 of
the novel is taken up with the manner in which the available evidence, Turner's confession, is to be interpreted. For the novelist,
interpretation is necessarily a reliving of the experience of those
involved in history. Styron's highest achievement is to make available what was otherwise unimaginable: the inner life of a slave,
scarcely coming to expression in its own time and lacking the literary resources to transmit its image to the future. A reliving of
past experience invariably evokes the life of the present, for historical life is understood only in its connections with present life,
as a tradition of thinkers from Dilthey down has reasserted. Yet
perhaps the greatest fault of *The Confessions* is its too-ready applicability to the white American temper of the moment, with its
guilty awareness of the historical crime against the Negro, its
acknowledgement of the need for some form of black power to
direct his social evolution, and its scared awakening to the sea of
rage—and frightful violence—that surrounds it. In a sense, *Nat
Turner* is not a historical novel at all, but a parable of the present,
if not a prophecy of the future. A work of historical art generates
an esthetic distance from the present as well as from the past; it
allows us to see not only others but ourselves in history, to adopt the
perspective of ages to come. It is thus a release from the pressures
of the moment, a transformation of history into a permanent object.

One of the finest of current historical novelists—as she is one of
the most under-rated of modern authors—Mary Renault has written
of the epistemological and esthetic problems involved in her enterprise.[2] Her first principle has to do with truth as correspondence
with historical fact:

I have never, for any reason, in any historical book of mine, falsified
anything deliberately which I knew or believed to be true. Often of
course I must have done through ignorance what would horrify me if I

2. "Notes on *The King Must Die*," in *Afterwords: Novelists on Their Novels*,
ed. Thomas McCormack (New York, London, and Evanston, Ill., 1969), pp.
84–86.

could revisit the past. . . . But one can at least desire the truth; and it is inconceivable to me how anyone can decide deliberately to betray it; to alter some fact which was central to the life of a real human being, however long it is since he ceased to live, in order to make a smoother story, or to exploit him as propaganda for some cause.

A second principle introduces an esthetic concept of truth as universal:

We all bring to the past our own temperament, our own pre-occupations, to limit the reach of our insight; our visual field at its widest will be small enough. It seems to me that it is in the struggle to stretch these bonds, to see the universals of human nature adapting to, or intractably resisting, the pressure of life's changing accidents, that the excitement of writing historical novels lies.

A third principle, liberation from provincialism, inevitably follows: "You cannot, as an advertising copywriter would say, enjoy a trip to fifth-century Athens, or Minoan Crete, in the comfort of your own home. You have, as far as your mind will take you, to leave home and go to them." Or, put more ambitiously: "If one could, even for an instant, be anything but contemporary, one would have achieved omniscience. What a triumph of the historical imagination!" These principles of realist responsibility, universality of vision, and imaginative sympathy with the men of the past are those that make historical fiction a continuing and an estimable tradition in English and other literatures.

❦

A further word on history: the present study is also historical in its approach—and not, it is hoped, fictional. A history of historical fiction, like a history of historiography, must heed some of the same norms and pitfalls as the objects of its study. It should have imaginative sympathy with the literary imperatives of past eras, while maintaining a self-consciousness in its own historical milieu that informs its investigations with care and urgency and sometimes with explanatory power. A chronological history would take up *all* the historical novels within its temporal scope, but even a Lukács admits to selectivity, and there already exist extensive bibliographies (see below). I have chosen what I hope to show are esthetically valuable historical novels, and by carefully examining a relatively few texts I hope to sketch the main lines of the genre's development in

England. This is, then, a *critical* history, which proposes standards of value for its subjects of investigation, as well as recording their sequence and relationship. Perhaps this very drive is what distinguishes the historical novel, in the last analysis, from putatively objective history: it unashamedly sees history with sensibility and moral commitment. A critical history of the genre would substitute esthetic norms for the novelist's criteria of evaluation, but it should not relax the intensity of his engagement with history.

Although I have written this book to "fill a gap" in scholarship, I still cannot quite convince myself that there has never been a full-length critical study of the English historical novel.[3] My first principle in writing has been to be inclusive without being exhaustive—accepting a wide variety of novels (on principles to be set forth in the first chapter) as being both historical *and* worth writing about, and briefly passing over certain famous examples of the form as unrewarding for sustained attention. The omissions—and some inclusions—will probably challenge conventional assumptions, and if this book encourages fresh discussion of historical fiction it will have succeeded in its primary aim.

Despite the continuous reading and writing of historical novels, modern critical interest in the genre has gradually declined. Carlyle's preference of fact to fiction ("History, after all, is the true poetry; . . . Reality, if rightly interpreted, is grander than Fiction") shaped most nineteenth-century critical discussions of the subject, while Scott had a consistent chorus of detractors as well as imitators. The very popularity of historical fiction led late nineteenth-century critics like Leslie Stephen to disparage the genre for its inaccurate portrayals of history.[4] Subsequent critical neglect may partially be explained by the fact that the number of items in a catalogue of English historical novels first published at the turn of the century is 2,392.[5] It is the proliferation of popular sensationalism in historical guise that leads—then and now—to the exclusion of the

---

3. Alfred T. Sheppard, *The Art and Practice of Historical Fiction* (London, 1930), comes closest to being one, but is really a professional writers' handbook.

4. See Ernest Bernbaum, "The Views of the Great Critics on the Historical Novel," *PMLA* XLI (1926), 424–41, for Victorian attitudes.

5. Jonathan Nield, *A Guide to the Best Historical Novels and Tales* (New York, 1929 [1902]). Moreover, Nield's listing is not even comprehensive but qualitatively selective, he affirms. See Ernest A. Baker, *A Guide to Historical Fiction* (London and New York, 1914 [1908]), for a more comprehensive list.

form from sustained critical examination. Brander Matthews, for example, spends much of his space apologizing for the imaginative excesses of the genre, and grounds them in the limitations of *any* attempt to write about the past from the perspective of the present. Thus Scott "attempted the impossible," since one can't step outside one's own time, and the "really trustworthy historical novels are those which were a-writing while the history was a-making."[6] The denial of power to the historical imagination is not new.

In the same years that saw a number of modern novelists begin to revive the genre, the historian Herbert Butterfield was writing the most important book on the historical novel before Lukács's. It makes the first clear statement of the idea that the historical novel is "a form of 'history,' a way of treating the past":

With a set of facts regarding the social conditions of England in the Middle Ages the historian will seek to make a generalization, to find a formula; the novelist will seek a different sort of synthesis and will try to reconstruct a world, to particularise, to catch a glimpse of human nature. Each will notice different things and follow different clues; for to the historian the past is the whole process of development that leads up to the present; to the novelist it is a strange world to tell tales about.[7]

If, as I shall maintain, the latter distinction is a false one—if the historical novel, like history, must seek to relate the past to the present with controlled subjectivity—the force of Butterfield's initial comparison becomes even stronger. Both the novelist and the historian are trying to find meaning in otherwise meaningless data, to rethink and complete the rationale of covert and often duplicitous behavior, to reconstruct the nexus of past actions. But the historian's "formula" is distinct from the novelist's "glimpse of human nature." It is their similarities of aim and differences of means that will occupy us in the first, theoretical chapter.

The beginnings of a critical history of the English historical novel are to be found in an essay by Hugh Walpole, written in connection with the Scott centenary.[8] Walpole divides the post-Scott genre into four periods: that of the "simple romancers" (1830–40), the

6. *The Historical Novel and Other Essays* (New York, 1901), pp. 13, 18.
7. *The Historical Novel: An Essay* (Cambridge, 1924), p. 113.
8. "The Historical Novel in England Since Sir Walter Scott," in *Sir Walter Scott Today: Some Retrospective Essays and Studies,* ed. H. J. C. Grierson (London, 1932), pp. 161–88.

"serious Victorians" (1840–70), the "real romantic spirit" (1870–1910), and "modern realism" (1910–30). Apart from the wide reading which allows Walpole to fill these divisions with amplitude, the value of his essay lies in revealing the breadth and complexity of the concept of historical fiction. Walpole suggests that *Vanity Fair* and *Nostromo* may well be considered historical novels, and maintains that the family-chronicle novel in the hands of a Bennett or Galsworthy borders on the genre. Yet it is remarkable that the most thoughtful discussion of the historical novel in English should be written by a non-academic critic, and in too brief a compass to do more than enumerate some of its chief points of interest.

The foremost critic of historical fiction, Georg Lukács, made his interpretation hinge on a special notion of historical process: dialectical materialism.[9] His work has the great virtue of any dialectical approach to literature, in which the relation of an author to his time and of a novel to its setting is a matter not of passive reflection but of ironic tension. Whether we employ the Marxian dialectic or the more general critical concept of irony, a reading of any historical novelist must take up his complicated attitudes toward his own time and toward the period about which he writes. But Lukács admits that his book is not a thorough history of the genre, his principle of selection being based on a particular view of the course of modern history, which the novels chosen are to represent. The course of the historical novel is roughly that of capitalist society since the French Revolution: from nationalist revolutionary stirrings, accompanied by a revived awareness of national history, as exemplified by Scott and his followers; to the class struggle of the mid-century bourgeois revolutions, reflected in the tensions—and often in the confused failure—of such novels as *La Chartreuse de Parme* and *Henry Esmond*; to the emergence of a class-conscious proletariat and its expression in the work of a number of Continental "democratic humanists" or quasi-Marxists.

While the broad outlines of this approach to literary history might be defended, Lukács's judgments of English authors show

9. *The Historical Novel*, trans. Hannah and Stanley Mitchell (Boston, 1963 [originally published, 1937]). For a critique of Lukács's method, see Stephen G. Nichols, Jr., "Georg Lukács: The Problems of Dialectical Criticism," in *Criticism: Speculative and Analytical Essays*, ed. L. S. Dembo (Madison, Milwaukee and London, 1968), pp. 75–92; and Paul De Man, "Georg Lukács's *Theory of the Novel*," *Modern Language Notes*, LXXXI (1966), 527–34.

how necessary it is to modify his Marxian *Weltanschauung* by a knowledge of individual national history, especially literary history. Lukács is concerned to remove Scott, his exemplar of the "classical form" of the historical novel, from any association with Romanticism. But his description of Romanticism as an "ideological struggle against the French Revolution," and as tending to glorify and "romanticize" the past, suggests that he is not susceptible to the variety of English phenomena that go by that name. Moreover, Lukács's class prejudices lead him to miss the revolutionary force of one of the greatest English historical novels after Scott, *Henry Esmond*. Pursuing his special purposes, Lukács omits the plethora of Victorian novels, many of them by major novelists, whose failures might have substantiated his exposé of the capitalist contradictions which mar late-nineteenth-century work in the genre. Finally, the omission of the great modern novelists—Hardy, Conrad, Virginia Woolf (even of such Continental figures as Malraux and Sholokhov) —makes his absorption in Romain Rolland and Heinrich Mann seem arbitrary and irrelevant to a critical history of the genre, let alone its English development. For there are many more values in historical fiction than Lukács's account allows for.

ॐ

Despite the prevalence of *Kitsch* historical novels—the kind which become spectacular movies in the Cecil B. DeMille style—the state of the art of historical fiction is still high. Effective stylists like Marguerite Yourcenar and Zoé Oldenbourg we shall always have with us, but the formally innovative and conceptually powerful exponents of the modern historical novel are to be found elsewhere. Avoiding escapism of the popular type, the serious artist tends to withdraw from the horror of the present to contemplate the horror of the past—particularly in America, where Faulkner and Warren have made Southern history their *métier*. In England, the continued popularity of the genre makes possible the attraction of a number of fine novelists who distinguish themselves from the Georgette Heyers and C. S. Foresters: Renault, Graves, and Golding will be discussed here in their turn. If one wishes to see the genre revived in its former glory, however, one must go outside the

English-speaking world: Spanish bookshops, for example, prominently display paperback editions of Bulwer-Lytton's and Scott's
lesser-known works.

The genre's status has also been enhanced by a revival of the
historians' interest in historical fiction. Not only has *War and Peace*
continued to hold its place at the peak of the art of fiction, despite
its Jamesian detractors, but its historical theory has been the subject
of an influential monograph by Isaiah Berlin (*The Hedgehog
and the Fox*). By the same token, the American historical novel
has gained from the interest of historians in its greatest adepts:
Allan Nevins on Cooper, David Levin on Faulkner, and C. Vann
Woodward on Warren.[10]

Yet what is in my opinion one of the greatest historical novels,
Kleist's *Michael Kohlhaas*, has remained relatively neglected (even
its historical-novel standing called into question), despite renewed
scholarly activity. Even authors who show enthusiasm for history in
art—like John Arden, in his adaptation of Goethe's *Goetz von
Berlichingen*[11]—seem unaware that their themes and methods have
already reached a height of power and discipline in Kleist's short
novel, as well as in his historical dramas. There is therefore some
uncertainty about the future of historical fiction: its past achievement places it near the central line of the novelistic tradition, yet
many of our contemporaries' sheer obliviousness to the past—both
past art and past history—leaves it unachieved as a formative influence on modern literature. When novelists who know themselves to be part of the age of Yeats, Eliot, and Pound recognize that
the historical themes and images of these poets are available to
fiction as well, there is likely to be a recrudescence of the historical
novel as an art form.

10. Nevins has edited for the Modern Library a chronological arrangement
of passages from the five Leatherstocking novels, which forms a continuous
narrative with historical explanations and bridges. On *Absalom! Absalom!* and
other American works, freshly seen as historical novels: Levin's *In Defense of
Historical Literature* (New York, 1967). On Warren's and other Southern
novelists' sense of the past, see Woodward, *The Burden of Southern History*
(Baton Rouge, La., 1960).

11. *Ironhand, adapted by John Arden from Goethe's Goetz von Berlichingen*
(London, 1965). The modern writer's typically ambivalent attitude toward
Scott is expressed by Arden on pp. 5–6: "*Goetz* in many ways foreshadows
Scott's handling of Scottish history in the better of the Waverley Novels. Had
he made his translation [of *Goetz*] at the end instead of the beginning of his
literary life, it is possible that he might have found his way through to the
strength and spirit of the original."

Acknowledgments

Much of this book was written with fellowship aid from the John Simon Guggenheim Memorial Foundation. My research was furthered by faculty summer grants of the University of Minnesota and The Johns Hopkins University. I have profited from discussing special subjects with Duncan Forbes, Jerome Beaty, G. Robert Stange, Maurice Mandelbaum and John Baldwin. Earl R. Wasserman, J. Hillis Miller and Francis R. Hart have read the manuscript with great care and penetration. Mrs. Doris Stude typed it with the patience and skill of a cryptographer. Despite all this help, it's still my book—for better or worse.

To the following individuals and institutions thanks are due for permission to quote from copyrighted works, by Thomas and Florence Emily Hardy: the Trustees of the Hardy Estate and Macmillan and Company Ltd.; by Joseph Conrad: J. M. Dent & Sons Ltd. and the Trustees of the Joseph Conrad Estate; by Virginia Woolf: Quentin Bell, Angelica Garnett, the Hogarth Press Ltd., and Harcourt Brace Jovanovich, Inc. (from *Between the Acts*, and from *Orlando*, © 1928 by Virginia Woolf; renewed, 1956, by Leonard Woolf).

I am grateful to H. E. Gerber, editor, *English Literature in Transition: 1880–1920*, for permission to reproduce a few paragraphs from an article of mine; to James C. Simmons for allowing me to cite material in an article of his, as yet unpublished; and to The National Trust and The British Museum for permitting me to quote from the manuscripts of *Orlando* and *Tess of the d'Urbervilles*, respectively.

The English Historical Novel

Chapter 1   Towards a theory of historical fiction

Everyone knows what a historical novel is; perhaps that is why few have volunteered to define it in print. In such a case, the most persuasive way of defining the subject is not by emphasizing one or more of its manifest characteristics, for these are so widely assumed that it would be foolhardy to legislate among them. Most novels set in the past—beyond an arbitrary number of years, say 40–60 (two generations)—are liable to be considered historical, while those of the present and preceding generations (of which the reader is more likely to have personal experience) have been called "novels of the recent past."[1] Regarding substance, there is an unspoken assumption that the plot must include a number of "historical" events, particularly those in the public sphere (war, politics, economic change, etc.), mingled with and affecting the personal fortunes of the characters.

One further criterion is to be introduced on *prima facie* grounds. There is an obvious theoretical difficulty in the status of "real" personages in "invented" fictions, but their presence is not a mere matter of taste. It is necessary to include at least one such figure in a novel if it is to qualify as historical. The presence of a realistic background for the action is a widespread characteristic of the novel,

1. Cf. Kathleen Tillotson, *Novels of the Eighteen-Forties* (London, 1961 [1954]), p. 91 ff.

and many panoramic social novels are deep in history. The historical novel is distinguished among novels by the presence of a specific link to history: not merely a real building or a real event but a real person among the fictitious ones. When life is seen in the context of history, we have a novel; when the novel's characters live in the same world with historical persons, we have a historical novel.

Whether his preference is for realism or romance, *Kitsch* or high art, the reader of historical novels is also likely to demand some sort of truth from them, if only to praise or blame on the grounds of "accuracy," or faithful recording of presumably established facts. It requires scant sophistication in historiography or esthetics to recognize that such a criterion of value in this genre begs as many questions as does any other mimetic norm for fiction. Granting that historical fiction, like all art, tells some kind of truth, it clearly does not tell it straight. By the same token, history itself does not tell truths that are unambiguous or absolute; even the nature of historical fact is problematic. Yet the value and, almost inevitably, the meaning of a historical novel will stand in some relation to the habitual demand for truth, and it is here that a theory of the genre needs to begin.

As art is of the imagination, the historical novel will be an exercise of the imagination on a particular kind of object. It is an imaginative portrayal of history, that is, of past states of affairs affecting human experience. The historical novelist provokes or conveys, by imaginative sympathy, the *sentiment de l'existence*, the feeling of how it was to be alive in another age. To do this he must describe and interpret—more or less accurately—the states of affairs that called forth personal responses of the kind he wishes to portray. In doing so, he places himself on the same ground as the historian as a recoverer of what actually happened. What, then, is the critical difference between a historical novel and historiography proper? Or to put the question another way, what is the relation between fact and imagination, history and art, public affairs and personal experience in historical fiction?

The most rewarding discussion of these questions is to be found in the work of R. G. Collingwood, the philosopher of history who was most keenly aware of the resemblance between the historian and the novelist:

Each of them makes it his business to construct a picture which is partly a narrative of events, partly a description of situations, exhibition of motives, analysis of characters. Each aims at making his picture a coherent whole, where every character and every situation is so bound up with the rest that this character in this situation cannot but act in this way, and we cannot imagine him as acting otherwise. The novel and the history must both of them make sense; nothing is admissible in either except what is necessary, and the judge of this necessity is in both cases the imagination.[2]

A number of useful distinctions might be made between these two kinds of imagination, necessity, and narrative. But Collingwood prefers to distinguish the two enterprises on the strictness of their adherence to truth and evidence: "The novelist has a single task only: to construct a coherent picture, one that makes sense. The historian has a double task: he has both to do this, and to construct a picture of things as they really were and of events as they really happened" (p. 246). Yet Collingwood's notion that history is both coherent and correspondent with reality, while art is solely coherent, breaks down even in his own terms. He himself argues that the historian exercises imagination, creating a "reconstruction" of the events, not a replica of the events themselves, for these cannot be directly known but are represented by documents, artifacts, and other symbolic equivalents. Since the reconstruction is validated only by "making sense," i.e., being coherent, the correspondence of the historian's facts is not markedly different from the novelist's "coherent picture."

Another account of the historian's enterprise by Collingwood has greater relevance to the working of historical fiction. He defines the historian's role as the mental activity which we have called imaginative sympathy: ". . . envisaging for himself the situation in which Caesar stood, and thinking for himself what Caesar thought about the situation and the possible ways of dealing with it. The history of thought, and therefore all history, is the re-enactment of past thought in the historian's own mind" (p. 215). Under this definition of historiography as a reliving of past experience, the historical novelist has a claim to historical truth, on the strength of his habitual exercise of imaginative sympathy, his personalization of history so that it becomes not a mere movement of forces or sequence of events but the thoughts and feelings of men.

2. *The Idea of History* (Oxford, 1966 [1946]), pp. 245–46. Subsequent quotations are cited parenthetically in the text.

The major resemblance between the historian and the historical novelist lies in their exercise of imagination. How, then, does the historian's imagination differ in operation from the historical novelist's? Collingwood has much to tell us on this point as well:

> The historian's picture of his subject, whether that subject be a sequence of events or a past state of things, thus appears as a web of imaginative construction stretched between certain fixed points provided by the statements of his authorities; and if these points are frequent enough and the threads spun from each to the next are constructed with due care, always by the *a priori* imagination and never by merely arbitrary fancy, the whole picture is constantly verified by appeal to these data, and runs little risk of losing touch with the reality which it represents. (p. 242)

In this influential account of the "web" of historical reconstruction, the chief distinction introduced is the familiar one between imagination and fancy. Collingwood elsewhere maintained that "the historian's imagination is precisely the same thing as the novelist's imagination."[3] Unfortunately he here suggests that the novelist's imagination tends to degenerate into "merely arbitrary fancy." Both the novelist and the historian, however, fill the gaps in the received data with imaginative "threads." So it is not in kind but in degree that their imaginations differ. The historian tries to add sufficient "points" so that only one "thread" or hypothesis can fill the space between. The better historical novels fill in the threads where there is room for alternative hypotheses, but not where the gaps are so wide as to allow *any* hypothesis.

Collingwood insists on a kind of Occam's razor in historical thinking: ". . . if our construction involves nothing that is not necessitated by the evidence, it is a legitimate historical construction of a kind without which there can be no history at all" (pp. 240–41). The novelist goes a bit farther than the inferentially necessary; some of the threads with which he fills the web of historical knowledge are inserted for the sake of the total design rather than for the discrete data to be linked. His web is not a causal chain but a picture, whose meaning is a formal whole. We might compare the historical novelist to the restorer of a damaged tapestry, who weaves in whole scenes or figures to fill the empty places which a more

---

3. *Essays in the Philosophy of History*, ed. William Debbins (New York, etc., 1966 [1965]), p. 48.

austere museum curator might leave bare. But if the insertion is made on the basis of sympathy, experience, and esthetic propriety, it can lend revived expressiveness and coherence to the tapestry.

Moreover, the historian, according to Collingwood's own testimony, may try to tell what *did* happen, but he can only reconstruct what *must have* happened. He must interpret the particular case from generalizations about such cases, or about the kinds of behavior they involve. He must refer to information about reality contained in "covering laws," recognized principles of, e.g., economics, psychology, or warfare, which most philosophers of history—following the so-called Popper-Hempel theory—ascribe to historical explanation (without being at all agreed as to their nature).[4] The historical novelist, too, is bound to make some appeal to general laws when he invents a thread to link the historical actions of his narrative, but he does not claim them from the current stock of knowledge about man and society. Instead, he bases himself on the same kind of premises as artists of every age have employed.

The subject goes back, of course, to the *Poetics*. Aristotle's celebrated (and often misquoted) comparison of poetry and history is translated by Butcher as follows:[5]

> . . . it is not the function of the poet to relate what has happened, but what may happen,—what is possible according to the law of probability or necessity. The poet and the historian differ not by writing in verse or in prose. The work of Herodotus might be put into verse, and it would still be a species of history, with metre no less than without it. The true difference is that one relates what has happened, the other what may happen. . . . Poetry, therefore, is a more philosophical and a higher thing than history: for poetry tends to express the universal, history the particular. By the universal I mean how a person of a certain type will on occasion speak or act, according to the law of probability or necessity; and it is this universality at which poetry aims in the names she attaches to the personages.

4. There is a considerable philosophical literature on the subject. Beyond the primary texts, listed in the bibliography to Maurice Mandelbaum, *The Problem of Historical Knowledge* (New York, 1938), there is a continuing contribution in the journal, *History and Theory*. For those with *l'esprit de géometrie*, Arthur C. Danto, *Analytical Philosophy of History* (Cambridge, 1965), beautifully structures the current debate on general laws in explanation. There are also anthologies of historical theories edited by Patrick Gardiner, Fritz Stern, William H. Dray, and Hans Meyerhoff.

5. *Aristotle's Theory of Poetry and Fine Art*, trans. and ed. S. H. Butcher (n.p., 1951 [1894]), p. 35; the passage comes at the beginning of Chapter IX.

The laws which seem to be invoked here to ascribe a universal validity to poetic truths are clearly not of the sciences or other systems of generalization from particulars; they are the probabilities of character types and the necessities of the human condition. These are the laws which find ready acceptance in tragedy or epic, and which are also present in fiction. The historical novel may be considered a kind of poetry—as permitted by Aristotle when he maintains that the essential qualities involved here are not prose or verse. It engages the universal and may therefore make the philosophic claims of poetry—if not the claim of higher dignity than history, in our unclassical times.

But what is the characteristic of historical fiction that distinguishes it from other kinds of poesis? This must be the particularity of the past which it treats: it is, after all, a novel, filled with named objects which create a virtual world, as populated as the past world it represents. Epic poetry and historical drama, too, may tell stories that happen in a historical past, but they are more intently devoted to telling how a "person of a certain type will on occasion speak or act." But historical novels address a specific past situation in all its concreteness, and often with more domestic detail than a tragic or epic poet would employ. The genre is unashamedly a hybrid: it contemplates the universal but does not depart from the rich factuality of history in order to reach that elevation.

The historical novelist uses the universals of literature—such categories of esthetic experience as romance and satire, tragedy and comedy—to interpret the course of historical man's career. To portray the interiority of a historical actor's conduct, or the impact of a historical situation on an invented personage, the novelist thinks of him as a figure in a universal pattern: not the repetitive patterns of the philosophies of history, but those of literature. The tragic or comic, romantic or satiric modes of portraying human experience in fictional situations have the same universalizing function when applied to historical situations. In the historical novel, the generic properties of plot, character, setting, thought, and diction (in Scott, even song) operate on the materials of history to lend esthetic form to historical men's experience.

The employment of literary modes in historical portrayal necessarily introduces questions on the nature of fictional narrative. From a literary—and, I suspect, from a philosophical and historical—standpoint, the most original and interesting of recent theories of history is that put forward by W. B. Gallie. At one point in his argument, Gallie finds it necessary to remind his readers that he is not a literary critic,[6] for his notions of historical writing are derived from his thinking about literary stories. Only a considerable independence of prevailing assumptions could account for the audacity with which Gallie maintains that historical explanations are introduced for the purpose of writing history—rather than the reverse, as those assumptions maintain. If we ask what is the purpose of writing history, if it is not to explain past events, Gallie's answer comes with disarming simplicity: to tell a story, as the name "history" implies.

Gallie's model is the literary story or novel, but many of his descriptions suggest the atmosphere of myth or children's bed-time story—not inappropriately to the primitive uses and impulses of historical narratives. E. M. Forster distinguished between "story" and "plot" on the criterion of the latter's causal relation between the events narrated—the former being merely a succession of events, a chronicle. Gallie maintains that a story has mere forward propulsion as its essence, and that this temporal rhythm need not be sustained by causal links (although they would help)—that the continuing question for the story-teller and his audience is, how did it come out? Thus the chief elements of history, as of other kinds of stories, are characters distinct and interesting enough to arrest attention and stimulate identification; the presence of unusual rather than run-of-the-mill situations; the characters' response to challenges; a degree of uncertainty, indeterminacy, or unpredictability; and a denoue-ment that leaves things in a definite shape, distinct from the shape in which they began. Gallie's terms are surely too narrow to take in all of history, but they seem to offer a serviceable generic pattern for the historical novel, linking it closely with other continuous prose forms.

As Gallie's comparison of historical with fictional narratives leads us to discover the literary qualities of history, his efforts to distin-guish the two genres lead, like Collingwood's, to an even closer

6. *Philosophy and the Historical Understanding* (New York, 1968 [1964]), p. 104. The quotation which follows is from p. 63. An approach to literary narrative which takes off from Gallie is Frank Kermode, "Novel, History and Type," *Novel*, I (1968), 231–38.

identification of their narrative modes. Gallie raises the question of the historian's relation to traditional interpretations of the past:

Ultimately the historian draws or receives his material from the memories, stories and legends and records of the people or civilization for which he is writing his history. Similarly, to be sure, a novelist or poet may receive his materials from national or personal memory or myth or record. But the novelist or poet will not attempt to improve upon his received material in the way that the historian does, viz. by deriving from them a truer or intellectually more acceptable version of some part or aspect of the human past.

Is it seriously to be believed that a critical relation to tradition—to previous artistic, popular, and even professional-historical stories of the past—is not of the essence in the historical novelist's enterprise? Gallie's indirection finds directions out: in this false distinction from history we can discover the peculiar energy of the historical novel. It retells history in order to make a truer story than has been written by historians, prophets, or other artists. The story is not truer to the facts, as we have seen, but is "intellectually more acceptable"—suggesting a universal implication of the historical particulars. The story means something more in the context of comic, tragic, and other such conceptions of human destiny than it has meant in its previous renditions.

For the historical novelist, if not always for the historian, the structure of a historical story must become a heroic (or anti-heroic) plot: the form of an individual's career. This is not to say that the novelist should acquire a biographical approach to history like Carlyle's, but simply that his conception of a past age will be represented in the development of individuals as well as in that of the group. Their fortunes will be found to have a structure of their own which gives meaning to the apparently random events or blind material forces that impinge upon them. The historical novel is pre-eminently suited to telling how individual lives were shaped at specific moments of history, and how this shaping reveals the character of those historical periods. In doing so it is both a dramatic and a social fiction, but is distinguished from the types that go by those names by the balanced weight it attaches to the personal and the collective experience of men in history.

The individuals selected by the novelist for heroic (or at least specially marked) status are not likely to be world-historical figures, for such figures are by definition exceptional, since they realize in themselves the tensions and direction of history at a particular time. The typical man of an age is one whose life is shaped by world-historical figures and other influences in a way that epitomizes the processes of change going forward in the society as a whole. It is Georg Lukács's great contribution to the study of the historical novel to have made this point and illustrated it in his more successful analyses. We can go further, however, if we see that the relation of the representative hero to the society of his time is not one of statistically-determinable typicality but that of symbolic universality. The heroes of historical fiction represent not only Renaissance man or Edwardian man but man in general, conceived as a historical being who is subject to the forces of one historical age or another. The ultimate subject of the historical novel is, then, man in history, or human life conceived as historical life.

The source of such considerations of the historical novel lies in another theory of historiography—that of Wilhelm Dilthey. Dilthey sees the meaning of history as a symbolic relation between the pattern of historical events and that of the individual life. His work provides a set of terms for the meanings one may find in the careers of fictional, as well as of historical, personages:

> The only complete, self-contained and clearly defined happening encountered everywhere in history and in every concept that occurs in the human studies, is the course of a life. This forms a context circumscribed by birth and death. It is perceived externally in the continuing existence of the person during the span of his life. This continuity is unbroken. But, independent of this, there exist experienceable connections which link the parts of the course of a life from birth to death. . . . The smallest unit which we can describe as an experience is whatever forms a meaningful unit in the course of a life. . . .
>
> Thus we come face to face with the category of meaning. The relation contained in it defines and clarifies the conception we have of our lives; it is also the point of view from which we grasp and describe the coexistence and sequence of lives in history, emphasizing what is significant and meaningful and thus shaping every event; it is, quite generally, the category which is peculiar to life and to the historical world. . . .[7]

Developing this view, Dilthey shows that the form of history, of autobiography (which is under discussion in the above passage), and—by implication—of historical fiction requires of the interpreter

7. *Pattern and Meaning in History: Thoughts on History and Society*, ed. H. P. Rickman (New York, 1962 [1961]), pp. 97–100. See pp. 96–97 ff. for an enumeration of the "categories of life." The quotation below is from p. 89.

the following: a temporal reordering in the line of development or formation, an unfolding of the inner meanings of events in their ultimate outer manifestations, and a discovery of power or causative force in the events themselves. These are among Dilthey's "categories of life," his equivalent of the Kantian categories for experience in the historical realm. It is these relationships that the historical novelist expresses when tracing the career of a historical or invented figure whose fortunes exhibit the characteristic pressures of his times.

It will be observed that this mode of interpreting individual and historical patterns of life recalls the hermeneutic approach to religious and literary texts which is currently in vogue on the Continent.[8] Recently theologians and philosophers have tried to develop historically interpretive principles by taking off from Dilthey's version of the so-called hermeneutic circle: "The significance of an individual existence is quite unique and so cannot be fathomed by knowledge; yet, in its way, like one of Leibniz's monads, it represents the historical universe." This, along with Spitzer's "philological circle" of literary interpretation—one cannot understand the details without grasping the whole, which cannot be known without the details—together create the ironic situation of the historical novelist: he cannot dramatize the individual without seeing his place in the historical context, and yet cannot approach the latter without a concrete sense of its participating members. Yet these paradoxes may prove as fruitful for the historical novelist—and his critics—as have the similar circles found by hermeneutics in other modes of writing.

Dilthey's formulation suggests an extension of hermeneutics to the historical novel: if the meaning of a historical age is present *in nuce* in the careers of historical individuals, then their imaginative portrayal can yield symbolic truths about the meaning of the situations in which they lived. This, then, is the form of historical fiction: to interpret the experience of individual men—both actual or imaginary—in such a way as to make their lives not only felt by

8. See Wolfhart Pannenberg, "Hermeneutics and Universal History," *History and Hermeneutic*, ed. R. W. Funk, *et al.* (Tübingen and New York, 1967), pp. 122–52, for a summary of the recent dialogue as it pertains to history. Richard G. Palmer, *Hermeneutics: Interpretation Theory in Schleiermacher, Dilthey, Heidegger, and Gadamer* (Evanston, Ill., 1969), is the most extensive work on the subject in English.

the reader as he would feel his own existence were he to have lived in the past, but understood as only someone who had seen that life as a completed whole could understand it. Whether we follow Dilthey in making this interpretation through a limited number of philosophically determinable *Weltanschauungen,* or make it through the apparently constant existential conditions in which all men participate (as do the followers of Heidegger), we are led back to the medium in which meaning is embodied: the literary form which expresses historical life. Despite the development of an elaborate terminology of literary hermeneutics, we need go no further than the Anglo-Saxon traditions of literary criticism to acquire a method-ology for analyzing historical fiction. Although the means of inter-preting a historical novel are none other than those of literary criti-cism, they help us grasp those insights into history to which the novelist gave form.

The critical question raised by the historical novel's evocation of the past is the problem of relativism, as it has come down from the historicist tradition. The usual approach of historicists is to expose the compromising of knowledge—especially knowledge of the past—by the historical limitations, cultural forms, or class interests of the interpreter. Yet many historicists, following Ranke, have main-tained the possibility of objective truth if the investigator maintains sufficient self-awareness to criticize his historically-conditioned as-sumptions and motives. The tendency of recent thinkers, including the hermeneutic school, has been to fall in with the historicity of all interpretation and to reject the possibility—and even the desirabil-ity—of breaking free of it. In this view, it is man's placement in a historical situation that gives him the categories by which alone he can interpret past historical men's situations. Relativism is dis-claimed by this approach, yet reappears in an objective form: only the man engaged in the present can interpret the engagements of men in the past.

It will be seen that the ten black writers who responded to William Styron's *Confessions of Nat Turner* are on the side of hermeneutics when they assert that only a historian or novelist in a roughly similar position can understand the inner workings of a historical black man. Their arguments are typical of the widely-held view that the men of the present look back to the men of the past not merely to understand them but to understand themselves.

The past is *relevant*—magical word!—and the specially-favored interpreter not only has access to it but also gains access to himself; understanding what he alone can understand, he gains insight into his special qualities, which allow that understanding. Historical thought is seen here as moving from the present to the past in order to be reflected back to the present with enhanced powers of meeting the problems of life.

Some such reflective movement takes place in historical fiction; only the novelist with a coherent conception of his own world can look back to a past age and see it as a coherent system. The historical novel, like all historical writing, is engaged with—if it is not necessarily compromised by—the present. But the distinction between greater and lesser achievements in historical fiction lies largely in the authorial motive, as it is exhibited in the conduct of the writing itself. The past can only be known by way of the present, but it need not be interpreted for the sake of the present. The present may give a clue to the past, but it need not become a structural model for the reconstruction of the past. The historical novel is an esthetic contemplation of history (what Styron calls a "meditation on history"), and it may be diminished by kinetic or rhetorical aims in the pragmatic, political sphere. The esthetic function of historical fiction is to lift the contemplation of the past above both the present and the past, to see it in its universal character, freed of the urgency of historical engagement. The reflection from the present to the past is completed when the historical novelist reaches not the present from which he began but the constants of human experience in history—however these may appear to him in his time and place.

The standard for genuine historical fiction is its governance by what, from Carlyle to Collingwood, has been called (with varying implications) the "historical imagination." The historical imagination—like the imagination generally, in Coleridge's definition—is *synthetic*: it unifies disparates, creating an order from the vertiginous kaleidescope of temporal experience. The structural source of the unifying activity of the historical imagination is its dual placement in the past and in the present. It must meet the need for reality which Carlyle expressed: the revelation that a given historical personage actually existed, faced human problems, and made decisions toward an open future. But in projecting itself back to the past it must have a critical attitude toward that past. History must be for it both subject-matter and formal control, both an object of study and a way of seeing. The historical novelist writes trans-temporally: he is rooted in the history of his own time and yet can conceive another. In ranging back into history he discovers not merely his own origins but his historicity, his existence as a historical being. What makes a historical novel historical is the active presence of a concept of history as a shaping force—acting not only upon the characters in the novel but on the author and readers outside it. In the course of reading, we find that the protagonists of such novels confront not only the forces of history in their own time, but its impact on life in any time. The universal conception of the individual's career as fate becomes symbolized not by the gods but by history. In several of its greatest examples, the historical novel attains the status of a modern epic in its view of the tragic limits and comic possibilities of man's historical life.[9]

9. The notion that all novels are historical novels, since they are set in historical time and social reality, has the effect of making the term "historical novel" useless in distinguishing a long-recognized activity; e.g., cf. John Lukács, *Historical Consciousness: or The Remembered Past* (New York, Boston, and London, 1968), p. 118 ff. Not all time is historical; not all social life is relevant to historical understanding; novels may refer to a past without thinking of it as a historical epoch, and they may portray social situations without historical significance. Perhaps the best illustration of these possibilities is *La Princesse de Clèves*, though they are even more apparent in the lengthy French historical romances of the seventeenth century.

Chapter 2 Origins: The historical novel in the age of history

The historical novel holds a special attraction for many of the varieties of Romantic imagination, both in its intense response to the given historical world and in its tendency to withdraw to a world of its own creation. A study of the historical novel could become a survey of the modulations of Romantic art throughout the nineteenth century and down to the present. Its origins in Romantic imagination do not, however, relegate historical fiction to the realm of nostalgia for a lost past. The historical novel is not simply a Romantic or period phenomenon but part of a longer literary tradition—that of the novel. Its outstanding characteristic is not to portray a temporalization of eternity, as Georges Poulet has described Romantic time-schemes, but a created world as comprehensive and variegated as the historical world itself—following Roland Barthes' suggestion.[1] To effect this world-design in the form of a novel, more than a Romantic or even a novelistic tradition was required.

---

1. "The Novel and History have been closely related in the very century which witnessed their greatest development. . . . in both we find the construction of an autarkic world which elaborates its own dimensions and limits, and organizes within these its own Time, its own Space, its population, its own set of objects and its myths." Roland Barthes, *Writing Degree Zero*, trans. Annette Lavers and Colin Smith (London, 1967), p. 35. Barthes has written a brilliant and provoking analysis of the structure of historical language, "Le discours de l'histoire," in *Social Science Information* VI (1967), 65–75. See also Wilhelm Dilthey, *Die Grosse Phantasiedichtung und andere Studien zur vergleichenden Literaturgeschichte* (Göttingen, 1954), pp. 309–10, on Scott's creation of a "Welttotalität."

Historical concreteness presupposes the existence of a historiographical attitude of a certain kind, while fictional world-creation assumes the development of a literary tradition that includes realism, romance and satire.[2] To these twin developments—historiographical and literary—in the making of the genre, this chapter is devoted.

The historicity of human affairs is as much the source as the subject of historical fiction. It is no accident that the genre, which had a continuous possibility of emergence from epic tradition and from national chronicle, should have seen its birth in the Romantic era and its establishment and elaboration in the Victorian period. As far as it is possible to speak of the social determination of literary phenomena, the rise of the historical novel may be described as the outcome of the age of nationalism, industrialization, and revolution: the age when the European peoples came to consciousness of and vigorously asserted their historical continuity and identity; the century when widening commerce, population shifts, and factory organization created a new pattern of day-to-day life and consequent nostalgia for the old; the time when the French Revolution and its successors precipitated out what we have come to call the modern world. As in most broad movements of literary culture, however, political-economic influence on the historical novel was effected through a cultural intermediary, in this case, the writing of history itself. Only when the changes in men's predominant activities had begun to reflect themselves in the ways in which they conceived history did the literary expression of a sense of history begin to burgeon, only then did it take the peculiar form of the historical novel.

Despite the emergence of two unquestionably great historians—Gibbon and Robertson—and of an arguably great one, Hume, the English Augustans like their counterparts on the Continent tended to treat the past with condescension for its uncouth "crimes and

---

2. Most of the problems of the mixture of genres, the pressures of realism and romance, and the decorum of mixed fact and fiction were faced by Alessandro Manzoni in his essay, *Del romanzo storico e in genere de' componimenti misti di storia e d'invenzione* (1845). On the basis of his devotion to realism, historical accuracy, and classical decorum, Manzoni concluded that the historical novel was impossible—a contradiction in terms, as seen in its very name. Fortunately, he had already written *I Promessi Sposi*. See Joseph F. De-Simone, *Alessandro Manzoni: Esthetics and Literary Criticism* (New York, 1946), p. 84 ff.

follies," rather than venturing an act of imaginative projection back into the life of the past in order to see its strangeness from the inside and discover its special character.[3] They wanted to gain philosophic wisdom and practical application from the "lessons" of the past, and could with assurance reduce the exotic to rule by virtue of their uniformitarian assumptions about human nature. The Enlightenment was notable for beginning a spirit of critical, objective interpretation, in which the past was to be related to the present and in which the total culture was to be considered, not only its political and military history. But this spirit was still condescending toward the past as merely a stage toward the present; its main interest was in drawing up general laws for rational prediction (rather than in discovering the uniqueness of past ages); and its cultural-history chapters were compartmentalized and did not organically inter-relate intellectual and material development.

The emergence of a new approach constitutes what a monograph on the subject calls "The Transition in English Historical Writing."[4] This transition was propelled by winds of intellectual change from the Continent, beginning with Voltaire's mid-century exercises in cultural history, expanded in the grand historical systems of Vico (whose impact was delayed), Herder, and Hegel, and promulgated by such taste-trend-setters as Chateaubriand and such linguistic pioneers as Jakob Grimm.[5] The new historical outlook, historicism,

3. I follow the generally depreciatory accounts of eighteenth-century historiography in James W. Thompson, *A History of Historical Writing* (New York, 1942), and Harry Elmer Barnes, *A History of Historical Writing* (Norman, Okla., 1937), while aware that they require modification by special studies, e.g., Lionel Gossman, *Medievalism and the Ideologies of the Enlightenment: The World and Work of La Curne de Sainte-Palaye* (Baltimore, 1968), which indicates the complexity and ambiguity of eighteenth-century interest in the Middle Ages, anticipating that of the Romantics. The links between eighteenth century historiography and the growth of historical reference in the novel have recently been filled in by Leo Braudy, *Narrative Form in History and Fiction: Hume, Fielding and Gibbon* (Princeton, N. J., 1970). The implication of this work is that the novel's major uses of history came not in the factuality of social realism but in the self-critical stance of Fielding's narrators, designed to grasp men and events free of the prevailing modes of historical thought: providentialism, didacticism, and great-man theories. In Fielding, the novelist in his approach to truth is the model of an ideal historian, free of the prejudices of traditional historiography—a proto-historicist!

4. Thomas P. Peardon, *The Transition in English Historical Writing: 1760–1830* (New York, 1933).

5. For the return influence of literature on historiography during this period, see Emery Neff, *The Poetry of History: The Contribution of Literature and Literary Scholarship to the Writing of History Since Voltaire* (New York and London, 1947).

has received many formulations in the course of its development, but its chief feature in the Romantic period was its doctrine of organic unity—the unity of historical phenomena in an evolutionary pattern of growth, and the unity of cultural phenomena in the unique identity of the nation.[6] As signalled by Burke's *Reflections on the Revolution in France* (1790), and perhaps best exemplified in this period by Sharon Turner's *History of the Anglo-Saxons* (1799–1805), the past is seen as a peculiarly national affair, as having a direct connection with the present fortunes of the nation, and as an organically intertwined and self-validating system of institutions and values.

Turner is also especially indicative—he was singled out by Scott in his prefatory matter to *Ivanhoe*—for he focused on the Middle Ages, capping a growing curiosity in the late eighteenth century on that remote but ever-visible age. Even in 1818, Hallam could say in *A View of the State of Europe during the Middle Ages* that "we cannot expect to feel in respect of ages at best imperfectly civilized and slowly progressive, that interest which attends a more perfect development of human capacities, and more brilliant advances in improvement. The first moiety indeed of these ten ages is almost absolutely barren, and presents little but a catalogue of evils."[7] But his enlightened, patronizing, and utilitarian attitude had already become atypical, in the wake of a revival of scholarship on "ancient poetry," i.e., medieval romances, Spenser, and "Ossian." With the numerous scholarly collections of ballads, in which Percy, Thomas Warton, and others anticipated Scott's *Minstrelsy of the Scottish Border*, the interest in the Middle Ages became popular, and made possible a new popular–art form. The Gothic novel, which had, by the turn of the century, become the most vigorous of fictional

6. On the rise of this multiform view, see Friedrich Engel-Janosi, *The Growth of German Historicism* (Baltimore, 1944). The term "historicism" is used in the present work in its historical sense, for a movement toward historical considerations in many realms of culture—not in the narrow sense of Popper's anti-determinist attack in *The Poverty of Historicism* (New York, 1964 [1957]). For the later historicism, see Carlo Antoni, *From History to Sociology: The Transition in German Historical Thinking*, trans. H. V. White (Detroit, 1959 [1939]), which divides it into branches: "perspectival" (Michelet, Carlyle, Nietzsche, Collingwood), "metaphysical" (Hegel and other idealists, Dilthey), and "naturalistic" (Weber and other sociologists, including the sociologists of knowledge).

7. In J. R. Hale, ed., *The Evolution of British Historiography: From Bacon to Namier* (Cleveland and New York, 1964), p. 198. For the British historians, see the prefaces in this anthology, and G. P. Gooch, *History and Historians in the Nineteenth Century* (Boston, 1959 [1913]).

modes, marks the entry into fiction of historicist and medievalist trends, and its appearance at this time may be considered the point where the new attitude toward history first found expression in a literary form.

ℰ

Historiography and the novel are, indeed, intimately related both in origin and in nature. In the course of the growing Renaissance awareness that, as one critic puts it, "all history merely pretends to be history"—that historical truth is an imaginative construct open to the irony of experience and comedy of illusion—the modern novel begins. *Don Quixote* establishes itself as a parody of contemporary historians before it develops into a critique of romance. But it is eventually with the self-critical realism of historiography that Cervantes decides to place his art: "This novel, then, is a fake history in which the historian assumes even greater importance than the author in a romance."[8] Ever since this original choice, the novel has tended to debunk rather than dramatize heroic myths of the past. While the concept of romance has gained considerable elaboration in recent critical theory, it is still possible to distinguish the urge toward realism in the novel from the freer play of imagination in the romance. It is with the former that the historical novel remains, although it may employ the imaginative means of romance in its quest for reality.

History enters English fiction as early as the Elizabethan picaresque novels. The rogue-hero of Thomas Nashe's *The Unfortunate Traveler, or, The Life of Jack Wilton* (1594) observes the manners and battles of his time while making his way across Europe, but the relation of the individual to history remains largely spectatorial.[9]

8. Bruce W. Wardropper, "*Don Quixote*: Story or History?," *Modern Philology*, LXIII (1965), 10. The relations between history and fiction in this novel are predictably complex: "*Don Quixote* does not disentangle the story from the history, but points its telescope at the ill-defined frontier itself"; nevertheless, in the "failure to discriminate between history and story, lies the cause of Don Quixote's madness" (pp. 5–6).

9. Another Elizabethan work, Thomas Deloney's *Thomas of Reading, or, The Six Worthy Yeomen of the West* (c. 1598) has some claims to be the first English historical novel. It presents a realistic hero engaged with historical persons and situations, and develops a complicated mixture of past and present perspectives. Although it begins with an encounter of the hero and King Henry

Though occasionally touching historical events, particularly in Defoe and Smollett, the growth of realism in eighteenth-century fiction remains rooted in the contemporary world, until the Gothic novel emerges alongside other pre-Romantic trends in ethics and poetry.

Horace Walpole's *The Castle of Otranto* (1765) took some time to take effect on the novelists' (if not on the public's) imagination, and by the time it did, its specifically medieval evocation was dissipated by mingling with other kinds of exoticism in Beckford, Lewis, and Maturin. Whatever his limits as novelist and historian, Walpole seized (or invented) the past for what was unique in it—if only its antiquity and obscurity. One of Walpole's followers carried his historical vision further, however, and in the process of defining her own fiction took a step on toward the historical novel. In the preface to the third edition of *The Old English Baron* (1780; first published in 1777 as *The Champion of Virtue, a Gothic Tale*), Clara Reeve states her work's literary provenance and mixture of genres with remarkable lucidity:

> This story is the literary offspring of the *Castle of Otranto*, written upon the same plan, with a design to unite the most attractive and interesting circumstances of the ancient romance and modern novel, at the same time it assumes a character and manner of its own that differs from both; it is distinguished by the appellation of a Gothic story, being a picture of Gothic times and manners.[10]

Reeve goes on to describe her work as romance, not novel, because it is an idealization of the past, in contrast to history, which "repre-

---

1 (reigned 1100–35), its atmosphere is that of the sixteenth century and its ethos is the bourgeois spirit celebrated in Deloney's other works. As one editor comments: "Deloney idealizes the past, and to make the action 'seem real,' to make it convincing and believable, he uses a great many 'realistic' details from the Elizabethan present. . . . The result is a new genre, historical romance"; Merritt Lawlis, ed., *Elizabethan Prose Fiction* (New York, 1967), p. 550. This degree of anachronism may create a real difference between historical romances and historical novels. But the term "historical romance" becomes so well blended with "historical novel" in nineteenth-century usage that I have decided to avoid it as a distinguishing mark.

10. In Robert D. Spector, ed., *Seven Masterpieces of Gothic Horror* (New York, 1963), pp. 105–6. Scott's essay on Clara Reeve defends her anachronisms on the same grounds he uses for his own in *Ivanhoe*, i.e., as necessary to encourage sympathetic identification in the present-day reader; see Ioan Williams, ed., *Sir Walter Scott: On Novelists and Fiction* (New York, 1968), pp. 94–101.

sents human nature as it is in real life;—alas, too often a melancholy retrospect!" The distinction of the romance from both history and novel is thus founded in psychological realism; the Gothic novel was not only free to exploit what was awesome in the past, but to do so irrespective of the plausibility of character or incident ("human nature," "real life").

The final stage in the pre-history of the historical novel is that of circumstantial realism, the urge to create a fictional record of an age by using the techniques of regionalist antiquarianism and historical chronicle. The success of the local-color history, dialect, and manners in Maria Edgeworth's *Castle Rackrent*—and Scott's intention to do for Scotland what she had done for Ireland—are well known.[11] Less apparent is Scott's relation to his countryman, John Galt. Galt wrote his *Annals of the Parish or the Chronicle of Dalmailing during the Ministry of the Rev. Micah Balwhidder written by himself* in 1813, and although it was not published until eight years later, it may have been known to Scott before he took up *Waverley* again.[12] The *Annals* is close to being a historical novel, despite its indebtedness to Crabbe's collection of local-color tales, despite its setting partially in the recent past (the hero's ministry exactly spans the active reign of George III, 1760–1810, and despite its discontinuous chronicle of events large and small. For Balwhidder's career and the life of his community are intimately related to

11. On Edgeworth's regionalism, see George Watson's introduction to the Oxford English Novels edition of *Castle Rackrent* (London, New York and Toronto, 1964). Donald Davie, *The Heyday of Sir Walter Scott* (London, 1961), sporadically discusses her regional vitality and its effect on Scott. Davie accounts for the failure of her work to reach historical-novel status on the grounds that she lacked an organicist sense of history (pp. 75–77).

12. The question of Scott's sources is a vexed one. Lieselotte E. Kurth, "Historiographie und historischer Roman: Kritik und Theorie im 18. Jahrhundert," *Modern Language Notes*, LXXIX (1964), 337–62, maintains that the precedents for historicism in German historiography, and the fiction of Benedikte Naubert and Viet Weber, directly influenced Scott's decision to write and his execution of the historical novel; but as in so much source-study, the attributions fail to explain the special features and the enormous success of what must have been felt at the time—and still seems—an innovation. An even more obvious presence was Jane Porter's *The Scottish Chiefs* (1810), which took up the heroic campaigns of Wallace in their strongest colors; but this—like the same author's *Thaddeus of Warsaw* (1803) and her sister Anna Maria's *The Hungarian Brothers* (1807)—could hardly have stimulated the imaginative projection into another age that Scott achieved. See E. A. Baker, *History of the English Novel* (London, 1934), V, 177 ff., on even earlier examples of historical fiction.

historical events, and the connection is established explicitly and substantially in the novel itself. The *Annals* comes down from the palmy days when "a blithe spirit was among us throughout this year [1770], and the briefness of the chronicle bears witness to the innocency of the time";[13] it moves to the days of revolution in America and France, and follows the beginnings of radical and proletarian agitation (Balwhidder's conservatism does not blind him to the arrogance of the anti-Jacobins). Finally, it achieves one of the most powerful passages in historical fiction when it portrays the effects of a mill-closure on the working-force of the town.

༃

At this point there occurs one of the greatest cultural phenomena of this or any other age, a phenomenon that goes by the name of Sir Walter Scott.[14] Scott's achievement has been so amply recorded in literary histories—and so loudly trumpeted by the Scott industry —that it is difficult to say anything temperate about his innovation in the historical novel. The sources of his art have been as well-combed as his influence, yet the uniqueness of his work remains apparent. Whether or not it is true that Scott invented the historical novel as a literary form, he must have thought what he was doing was new. His explanation for withholding his name from *Waverley* and subsequent novels—one of the most piquant of literary escapades and the work of a publicity genius—is that he conceived of his enterprise as an "experiment on the public taste which might very probably fail, and therefore there was no occasion to take on myself the personal risk of discomfiture."[15] Scott was not only wise

13. John Galt, *Annals of the Parish* . . . (London and New York [Everyman edition], n.d.), p. 46. On Galt's historicism, see William M. Brownlie, "John Galt: Social Historian," *Papers of the Greenock Philosophical Society*, 1952.

14. Scott's cultural dictatorship in America is worth a study in itself. For Scott's influence on historiography, see David Levin, *History as Romantic Art* (New York and Burlingame, 1963 [1959]). For his influence on fiction, particularly Cooper's, see George Dekker, *James Fenimore Cooper: The Novelist* (London, 1967). But it is untrue to say, as Mark Twain did, that Scott's notion of chivalry caused the Civil War.

15. I quote the Andrew Lang edition of Scott's novels (Boston, 1892–94), *Waverley*, p. xxv; General Preface to the 1829 Edition. Subsequent citations will be made parenthetically in the text by chapter and page numbers; where a novel is printed in two parts, with two sets of chapter-numbers, the letter A or B is introduced.

after the fact, as in this late comment, but even while publishing *Waverley* was aware of its place among the prevailing types of fiction. In a remarkably self-conscious introductory chapter, Scott distinguishes his approach to history from that of the Gothic novelists, the German romances, and what was to be called the "silver-fork school" of contemporary manners. He emphasizes that the subtitle of the novel, *'Tis Sixty Years Since*, was the mark of a deliberate choice: a period neither too far nor too near the present, whose special characteristics would arouse neither Gothic awe of the remotely exotic, nor the sophisticated contempt bred by familiarity. Scott conceived of history from the outset as a past that allowed itself to be made present without losing its unique character, and this sense of the historical novelist's double perspective helps account for his work's imaginative complexity and great success. It is both an entry into the past—often achieving an interior sense of past life —and a coherent interpretation of that past from a particular standpoint in the present (as I shall try to show in the following chapter).

Another side of Scott's formative view of *Waverley*, from the outset of his writing in 1805, is his mouthing of received eighteenth-century ideas about the nature and study of history. When he declares that "the object of my tale is more a description of men than manners" (A, I, 4), he is trying to get beyond the Gothic romances' absorption with the external trappings of past ages. But when he claims that his greatest emphasis falls on "the characters and passions of the actors,—those passions common to men in all stages of society" (A, I, 5) he risks throwing the historical baby out with the antiquarian bath-water. He goes on to defend this uniformitarian view, but introduces sufficient qualifications to suggest his awareness of historical uniqueness: "Upon these passions it is no doubt true that the state of manners and laws casts a necessary colouring; but the bearings,—to use the language of heraldry,—remain the same, though the tincture may be not only different, but opposed in strong contra-distinction." By the time Scott had finished *Waverley* he recognized in the Postscript to the novel the marked difference even between countrymen sixty years apart: "The gradual influx of wealth and extension of commerce have since [1745] united to render the present people of Scotland a class of beings as different from their grandfathers as the existing English are from those of Queen Elizabeth's time" (B, XLIII, 364). Not only does Scott acknowledge historical differentiation in the midst of national continuity, but goes on, in the time-honored metaphor of the temporal river, to express his double view of the past: ". . . like those who drift down the stream of a deep and smooth river, we are not aware of the progress we have made until we fix our eye on the now distant point from which we have been drifted." We can grasp the present only by looking back to the past, and can seize the past only with the recognition that it is gone.

By the time Scott had written five more Scottish novels, only five years later, he turned a corner in his career, and many of his devotees still cannot forgive him for it. Yet it was the English novels, set mainly in medieval and Renaissance times, that have been his most widely influential—although generally regarded as inferior by the critics. In the prefatory matter of *Ivanhoe*—framed as a "Dedicatory Epistle to the Rev. Dr. Dryasdust, F.A.S." [Fellow of the Antiquarian Society?]—Scott in the persona of Laurence Templeton urged the distinction of his work from "the idle novels and romances of the day" on the grounds of its antiquarian accuracy. But he put forward a defense of his non-antiquarian methods: "It is necessary, for exciting interest of any kind, that the subject assumed should be, as it were, translated into the manners, as well as the language, of the age we live in" (p. xlvii). This translation of the past into the idiom of the present must not become a projection of the present onto the past: "It is one thing to make use of the language and sentiments which are common to ourselves and our forefathers, and it is another to invest them with the sentiments and dialect exclusively proper to their descendants" (p. li). It is still arguable—and argued—that Scott succeeded in toeing this fine line in his English novels, and the intention to combine the twin perspectives of past and present is clear even when he fails.

Scott is the first historical novelist because he is the first to create a fictional world according to these clear historical principles, drawn partly from Enlightenment uniformitarianism and partly from Romantic historicism. He emerges precisely at the time of transition between these ways of looking backward, and gains the power to go beyond both the thin costumery of previous historical romances, which dress up present-day characters in the trappings of the past, and the local-color and Gothic types, which detail or embellish the past for its own sake and without reference to the present. As Karl

Kroeber has said, "He did not merely make it possible to write novels about the Crusades; he made it possible to describe any society in its temporal dimension."[16]

Not only in the form of his approach to the past but in the content of the historical myths by which he interpreted it did Scott shape the course of the historical novel—and the course of a number of parallel cultural movements throughout the nineteenth century. The most important of these is introduced in *Ivanhoe*,[17] and is probably one of the folk beliefs that underlie the popular devotion with which it continues to be read. This is the myth that the historian Christopher Hill has called "the Norman yoke." Scott's Introduction to the 1830 edition of *Ivanhoe* is a classic statement of its assumptions:

It seemed to the author, that the existence of the two races [Norman and Saxon] in the same country, the vanquished distinguished by their plain, homely, blunt manners, and the free spirit infused by their ancient institutions and laws; the victors, by the high spirit of military fame, personal adventure, and whatever could distinguish them as the Flower of Chivalry, might, intermixed with other characters belonging to the same time and country, interest the reader by the contrast, if the author should not fail on his part. (p. xxx)

The contrast between Saxon democracy and Norman aristocracy is, Scott assumes, already implanted in the reader, who is ready to be engaged by its fictional elaboration. If we follow the history of this idea through the centuries down to Scott's time, we can see that this professional novelist had his finger on the pulse of his countrymen.

Hill's outline of the myth reveals the political animus behind Scott's contrast of Saxon and Norman:

Before 1066 the Anglo-Saxon inhabitants of this country lived as free and equal citizens, governing themselves through representative institutions. The Norman conquest deprived them of this liberty, established the tyranny of an alien king and landlords. They fought continually to recover them,

16. Karl Kroeber, *Romantic Narrative Art* (Madison, Wis., 1960), p. 180.
17. He may have taken many of the points of the approach from Sharon Turner, Robert Henry, and Joseph Strutt, whose histories he refers to in the Dedicatory Epistle. He also notes the role his editing of Strutt's *Queenhoo Hall* played in determining him to write a historical novel; see the 1829 General Preface.

with varying success. Concessions (Magna Carta, for instance) were from time to time extorted from the rulers, and always the tradition of lost Anglo-Saxon freedom was a stimulus to more insistent demands upon the successors of the Norman usurpers.[18]

It is easy to anticipate the forms of revolutionary enthusiasm with which such a myth was invested in the seventeenth century, and which it acquired again in the hands of such progressives of Scott's time as Paine and Bentham. But it is not necessary to saddle Scott with their bias: the marvellous power of the notion—what makes it a true myth—is its ambiguity, which enabled conservatives to use it as a defense of the status quo. Since the Glorious Revolution had limited the power of the Stuarts after their attempts at quasi-Norman absolutism, the constitution could be looked on as Blackstone saw it: the continuity of Saxon democratic institutions coming down through English history.[19]

Two other aspects of the myth may unambiguously be found in Scott, and it is they, rather than the above-mentioned political implications, which he bequeathed to the Victorian era. These are the populist and tragic touches in the Norman yoke. The Saxons are the common people, dominated by a small, alien class which always held itself aloof, in manners, culture, even language; England is a Saxon body with a Norman veneer (which might best be wiped away, it was later suggested)—the organic basis of the nation is a Saxon one. Further, throughout its history after the Conquest, England has been an occupied and enslaved nation, never fulfilling its birthright, not yet restored to its true nature. Whatever that true nature might mean in modern terms, it could be expressed as a corollary of the Saxon virtues. From this congeries of racial emotions, political ideas, and plain nonsense derives a major stream of

18. Christopher Hill, "The Norman Yoke," in *Democracy and the Labour Movement: Essays in Honour of Donna Torr*, ed. John Saville (London, 1954), p. 11. Scott quotes a folk rhyme with the phrase, "Norman yoke," in *Ivanhoe*, ch. XXVII.

19. Modern scholarship seems to agree that the Saxons inherited some form of the "Witangemot" or tribal council from the Germanic tribes, but also follows Sir Frank Stanton in tracing the rise of absolutism and loss of traditional freedoms to the Saxon period itself. The Normans, then, merely crystallized and refined a process that had been almost completed when they arrived. See H. R. Loyn, *Anglo-Saxon England and the Norman Conquest* (London, 1962), pp. 199, 291.

historical fiction that has still not subsided; it is from *Ivanhoe's*
Gurth and Wamba, Cedric the Saxon and Friar Tuck, that the
legend-ridden nationalism of popular historical novels descends,
and there are strong traces of the myth in the peculiarly English
populism of Hardy and Lawrence.

℘

With the success of his novels in England, Scott rose to an even
louder acclaim on the Continent and had an enormous vogue in
France, influencing the historical novels of Hugo, Dumas, Vigny,
Mérimée, and Balzac.[20] Scott's conquest of the Continent extends to
Italy, where his tales became the basis of plays and operas that
number into the hundreds in the 1820's and 30's. What this international sensation represents is a grotesque Latinizing of the British
—and often distinctively Scottish—novelist. Scott is a special kind
of Romantic, in whom elements of neoclassicism and the Enlightenment are at least equally strong, but his followers took him to represent a spirit closer to their own. They missed his sense of historical
uniqueness, particularly regarding the richly diversified history of
his own country, Scotland: that is what makes Donizetti's version
of *The Bride of Lammermoor* so silly at times. When foreign
novelists had a vigorous sense of their own countries' specialized
past, they could make the example of Scott an occasion for historical novels that play the role of national epics—as Mickiewicz
did in his verse-novel *Pan Tadeusz*, as Manzoni did in *I Promessi
Sposi*, and as Cooper did in the Leatherstocking novels.

There were, besides Scott, other forces at work in nineteenth-
century England to inspire historical sentiments and their fictional
expression. We may ascribe the rise of nationalistic feeling to the
growth of the Empire, or vice versa; we may explain the increased
reverence for the lost past by the speed of social change under in-

20. See Louis Maigron, *Le roman historique a l'époche romantique: essai sur
l'influence de Walter Scott* (Paris, 1898). On Scott's English influence, see
John H. Raleigh, "What Scott Meant to the Victorians," *Victorian Studies*,
VII (1963–4), 7–34; reprinted in *Time, Place and Idea: Essays on the Novel*
(Carbondale, Ill., etc., 1968). This ascribes modern determinist pessimism in
part to Scott. On his relation to Victorian medievalism—both as inheritor and
progenitor—see Alice Chandler, "Sir Walter Scott and the Medieval Revival,"
Nineteenth-Century Fiction, XIX (1964), 315–32.

dustrialization or by the break-down of Christian cultural hegemony; all helped to make the historical novel popular. The mental climate represented by the Gothic Revival in architecture, the Pre-Raphaelite Brotherhood in art, Disraeli's Young England movement in politics, and the Oxford Movement in religion taken together makes Victorian England the age of medievalism. The variety of Victorian attitudes toward time and history has recently been summarized by Jerome Buckley,[21] who emphasizes the retreat of the poetic mind from notions of publicly-shared historical time to an interest in personal time, private memory and quasi-mystical timelessness. There was also widespread historical activity, both scholarly and antiquarian, which provided a basis for the popular appeal of measured doses of history in fiction. This is the age of the learned society, including the Shakespeare, Philological, Aelfric, Caxton, Hakluyt, Early English Text, Ballad, Chaucer, English Dialect, and Scottish Text Societies, and many others. It is the time of parliamentary action to make the Public Record Office the safeguard of documents that had earlier been left in neglect, and the time of the nationally financed publication of the *Rerum Britannicarum Medii Aevi Scriptores*, the "Rolls Series," of some two hundred and fifty volumes.

It is an age in which minor poets like Walter Savage Landor, Winthrop Mackworth Praed, and Sir Henry Taylor specialized in medieval and Renaissance settings, and in which few major poets could resist at least one venture into historical drama—witness Tennyson's *Harold, Becket,* and *Queen Mary,* Browning's *Strafford,* and Swinburne's *Mary Stuart* trilogy. Not content to revive the Shakespearian history-play, the poets devised new bottles for old wine, e.g., the *Idylls of the King,* the dramatic monologues, and the editions of popular ballads by the last-named poets respectively. The Victorian "prophets" were not the meanest of contributors to this ground swell; indeed, Carlyle's *Past and Present* and Ruskin's *Stones of Venice* may be said to have given Victorian medievalism

---

21. Jerome Buckley, *The Triumph of Time: A Study in the Victorian Concepts of Time, History, Progress, and Decadence* (Cambridge, Mass., 1966). The importance of historical thinking and writing in the Victorian period has been briefly described by Richard A. E. Brooks, "The Development of the Historical Mind," in *The Reinterpretation of Victorian Literature,* ed. Joseph E. Baker (Princeton, 1950), pp. 130–52.

most of its leading ideas. Even Matthew Arnold, the most classical of the Victorians, was caught up in the vogue of Germanic and Celtic mythology and linguistics, although withdrawing from the excesses of "Teutomania."[22] Medievalism was obviously open to satire and the Middle Ages to comic treatment in their own right: Peacock's *Maid Marian* and *The Misfortunes of Elphin*, Frere's "Whistlecraft" mock-Arthuriad, and Barham's *Ingoldsby Legends* were only the top layer of a fund of popular works that responded to the wide public interest in—and amusement by—the romance of the Middle Ages.

Whether the proliferation of historical writing was cause or effect of the widespread public interest in history, it is clear that historiography was a shaping force for the historical novelist. (There were occasional attempts to reverse the process, as in Macaulay's citation of Scott's fictional *Kulturgeschichte* as a model for historians.) The following chapters will enlarge upon the relationships between Dickens and Carlyle, Thackeray and Macaulay, and others, but it is possible to generalize on the relations of historians and novelists by considering the major types of practitioner in each art.

Victorian history may be roughly divided into three groups: the rationalists or Utilitarians, the Liberal Anglicans, and the academic scholars. The first were the descendants of Enlightenment history, who maintained the superiority of modern Western civilization even when considering an advanced culture like India's—as James Mill did—or systematized all history in accordance with a scale of political and technological progress, as Henry Thomas Buckle did. This "Whig" interpretation of history may be muted by scholarly detail, as in George Grote's *History of Greece* or Hallam's *Constitutional History of England*, but it is of the same temper as Macaulay's progressivism, though not as strident. The Liberal Anglicans, on the other hand, were more capable of projecting themselves back into the past, and even employed the stimulus of Vico and Herder in this direction,[23] but their judgments of the past were at least as didactic and value-ridden as those of the rationalists, differing

22. See Frederic E. Faverty, *Matthew Arnold the Ethnologist* (Evanston, Ill., 1951), p. 14 ff., for an account of this type of thought among the Victorians.
23. Duncan Forbes, *The Liberal Anglican Idea of History* (Cambridge, 1952). See also Forbes, "Historismus in England," *Cambridge Journal*, IV (1950–1), 387–400, on the rationalist Victorian historians.

mainly in religious values. Thomas Arnold, H. H. Milman, Connop Thirlwall, Julius Hare, Richard Whately, and A. P. Stanley were, most of them, Anglican divines aiming delicately at religious revival and moral enlightenment through the study of history, and their school represents another broad tendency in Victorian culture that balances its rationalism and liberalism. The third force in nineteenth-century historiography was never entirely free from one or another of these orientations, but managed to subsume them in historical research as an academic discipline. The most explicit of the history-for-history's sake professionals was William Stubbs, whose inaugural lecture as Regius Professor of Modern History at Cambridge in 1867[24] marked the end of a period in which tendentiousness could be carried to the extremes of his predecessor, Charles Kingsley. Stubbs's *Constitutional History* set a new standard in the treatment of sources that made medieval studies for the rest of the century—the work of Freeman, Seebohm, Maitland, and Vinogradoff—the major achievement of British historians.

But the greatest outlet for Victorian medievalist interests was in the dominant artistic form of the age, the novel. Most Victorian historical novels may be readily identified by reference to three sets of qualities: antiquarian, juvenile (for all ages), or tendentious. In the first class, a style was formed by the successors of Scott in the 1830's and 40's: Edward George Bulwer-Lytton, William Harrison Ainsworth, and G. P. R. James. One of the first to make capital of the rich vein that Scott had uncovered was James.[25] In 1829 he sent the manuscript of *Richelieu*, his first historical novel, to Scott, and after receiving what he took to be encouragement to "persevere," he published it with an implicit dedication to the master.[26] He went on to write three books a year for the rest of his writing career, before entering public service on the strength of his standing as Historian in Ordinary to the Queen. Not all these books were novels; the first year's batch, for example, includes *The History of*

---

24. In William Stubbs, *Seventeen Lectures on the Study of Medieval and Modern History and Kindred Subjects* (Oxford, 1886).

25. Even earlier into the field was Horace Smith in *Brambletye House* (1826), set in the Civil Wars; Smith followed up with a long string of imitations of Scott. I owe this suggestion to Francis R. Hart.

26. S. M. Ellis, *The Solitary Horseman, or, The Life and Adventures of G. P. R. James* (London, 1927), p. 45.

Chivalry, which is revealing both of James's motives and of pre-
and early-Victorian taste.

James aimed to satisfy the growing public reverence for the
chivalric ideal as a standard of gentility in an increasingly middle-
class, industrial-commercial society. Much of the Victorian idealization of great men in general and Arthurian knights in particular
is anticipated in James's "solitary horseman," who appears regularly
at the beginnings of his novels. James's position on the uses of history
is clear from the first chapter of *The History of Chivalry*: ". . . there
is scarcely a noble feeling or a bright aspiration that we find amongst
ourselves, or trace in the history of modern Europe, that is not in
some degree referrible [*sic*] to that great and noble principle, which
has no name but the *Spirit of Chivalry*."[27] The emphasis on "spirit"
is the key to the passage: James declares outspokenly that professional historians have gone astray in their attempts to trace the
elements of chivalry to the Romans, Franks, or Normans because
they treat it as an institution rather than as a spirit. By maintaining
this distinction, James is able to ignore the damaging historical
facts about the institution and to portray his heroes not in the light
of their historical situation but in the eternal light of quasi-religious
sanctions for aristocratic norms. This ahistorical view is to characterize much of what passes for historical fiction down to the present:
in place of the universals of literature, we are offered the absolutes
of a social and ethical system.

In the thirties, James was joined in the mass-production of historical novels by Harrison Ainsworth, but the latter did not find his
proper role until 1840 with *The Tower of London*. The principle of
composition in this antiquarian novel is to make narrative provide
the context for description, rather than the conventional reverse.
Given a historical artifact—often, as in *Old St. Paul's* or *Windsor
Castle,* a building—Ainsworth's business is to fill it up with personages both invented and historical, and to decorate it, as it were, with
factual detail. His declared intention was to "contrive such a series
of incidents as should naturally introduce every relic of the old pile
—its towers, chapels, halls, chambers, gateways, arches, and draw-
bridges—so that no part of it should remain un-illustrated."[28]

27. G. P. R. James, *The History of Chivalry* (London, 1830 [second ed.]),
p. 15.

28. Harrison Ainsworth, *The Tower of London: A Historical Romance* (London, Toronto and New York [Everyman ed.], 1909), p. viii; the quotations that
follow are from the Table of Contents.

The critical word here is "naturally," but Ainsworth's contrivances include such a cast of characters as the following: "Of the three Giants of the Tower, Og, Gog, and Magog; of Xit, the Dwarf; of the fair Cicely; of Peter Trusbut, the Pantler, and Potentia, his Wife; of Hairun, the Bearward; Ribald, the Warder; Mauger, the Headsman; and Nightgall, the Jailer. . . ." When grotesquerie fails, the novelist becomes an antiquary in his own right; the fourth chapter of the second book is titled: "Of the Tower of London; its Antiquity and Foundation; its Magnitude and Extent; its Keep, Palace, Gardens, Fortifications, Dungeons, and Chapels; its Walls, Bulwarks, and Moat; its royal Inmates; its Constables, Jailers, Warders, and other Officers; its Prisoners, Executions, and secret murders." A third element used in filling up the Tower—besides the fantastic byplay and the antiquarian trappings—is an indulgence of English sympathy for the long-suffering queens of the sixteenth century. Ainsworth's sentimental account of Lady Jane Grey and his attempt to exonerate Queen Mary in the eyes of his traditionally anti-Catholic countrymen are the beginnings of a motif in historical fiction that continues throughout the nineteenth century and receives a new impetus in the works of Maurice Hewlett, Ford Madox Ford, and others in the twentieth. This affection for noble heroines in Ainsworth and his devotees is the emotional equivalent of their nostalgia for the noble relics of the national past.

Bulwer-Lytton is a more complicated case. There is much juvenile heroics and mechanical antiquarianism in his historical novels, but neither of these should be final ground for critical judgment, for a special relation to the present animates his work. He displays considerable erudition in the prefaces, appendices and notes to his novels, and was perhaps the first to bring Italian history into Victorian fiction, both the Roman period in *The Last Days of Pompeii* (1834) and the Middle Ages in *Rienzi: The Last of the Tribunes* (1835). But the depth of Bulwer-Lytton's historical understanding may be gauged from the following fairly typical interpolation: "The main difference . . . in the manner of life observed among the Athenians and Romans, was, that with the first, the modest woman rarely or never took part in entertainments; with the latter, they were the common ornaments of the banquet. . . ."[29] He does not overindulge in the Victorian tendency to revel in the immorality of

29. *The Novels and Romances of Edward Bulwer Lytton* (Boston [Illustrated Library Ed.], 1895), vol. xxxiii, Bk. iv, ch. iii, p. 332; the quotation that follows is from the Preface to the 1834 edition, p. xiv.

the pagans; he is closer to the Enlightenment detachment that aims at a "just representation of the human passions and the human heart, whose elements in all ages are the same!" But he lacks Scott's complementary sense of historical uniqueness, and in consequence his Romans, medieval Italians and medieval Englishmen are almost indistinguishable from each other.[30]

It is Bulwer-Lytton's tendentious tendencies in his English novels that are of greatest interest. *The Last of the Barons* (1843) and *Harold, Last of the Saxons* (1848) are tracts for the times—the times being the hungry forties, when the condition-of-England question was being raised (especially by Carlyle) in a historical context. In these novels Bulwer-Lytton expresses a political creed, combining Tory nostalgia for the lost nobility of pre-Reform England (it was quickly observed that all four of these novels' titles refer to the last of a race) with Whig satisfaction in the hardy virtues of the progressive English people. As a penetrating study of his fiction concludes:

The fundamental fault is that Bulwer, as even his political career shows, does not know whether he is a Radical, a Whig, or a Tory. Like Cooper and to some extent Scott, he never resolves the conflict in himself between emotional conservatism and intellectual liberalism. Bulwer's great heroes—Warwick, Harold, Rienzi—are reactionaries who seek to stem change or return to the past. . . . His sympathies are with them. Yet Bulwer admits that most really beneficial progress is brought about by strong, unidealistic, practical men well adjusted to their times—men like Edward IV, William the Conqueror, Richelieu, and Napoleon. He believes in Progress but dislikes those who bring it. He holds morality very dear but admits that good ultimately comes out of those who ignore it. He loves liberty but admires strong, almost despotic leaders. He holds that men have moral choice and he values strong personality, but he sees the *Zeitgeist* as the ultimate controlling force.[31]

30. James C. Simmons, in an as yet unpublished paper, "The Novelist as Historian: An Unexplored Tract of Victorian Historiography," discusses the turn toward factual accuracy by Bulwer-Lytton, Palgrave, Harriet Martineau and others—a trend toward making fiction a substitute for historical instruction. Simmons points out that this impulse toward truthfulness was less an importation of Continental historicism than a reversion to Romantic historiography, featuring nationalism, hero-worship, and vivid portraiture and narrative. These authors used romantic methods to tell historical truth, and avoided the new quasi-scientific methods of doing so. See also Simmons, "Of Kettledrums and Trumpets: The Early Victorian Followers of Scott," *Studies in Scottish Literature*, VI (1968), 47–59.

31. Curtis Dahl, "History on the Hustings: Bulwer-Lytton's Historical Novels of Politics," in *From Jane Austen to Joseph Conrad*, eds. Robert C. Rathburn and Martin Steinmann, Jr. (Minneapolis, 1958), p. 71. Although Dahl's

Dahl suggests that Bulwer-Lytton might have gone beyond Scott, in his contrast of the ideal values of the past and the pragmatic values of the present, by focusing on the difference between the anachronistic idealist and the world-historical man of his age. But the critical conclusion must be that in these novels the two types are not distinctly controlled by an ironic view of the limits of idealism in historical action, but remain ambivalent commitments of the author's confused sensibility.

If Bulwer-Lytton's mixture of nostalgia and progressivism reflects the transitional character of the first half of the century, by the time of Charles Kingsley's heyday, similar ambivalences are overwhelmed by a note of stridency. Kingsley began to write fiction addressed to the condition-of-England question at the time of the Chartist near-revolution just before the mid-century, but after the Chartists' defeat and the cooling-off of the fifties, his reformist tendencies gave way before the mood of an increasingly self-satisfied imperialist nation. The most blatant of his historical novels, *Westward Ho!* (1855), gains part of its power to arouse jingoistic emotions by the intrusion of Kingsley's disturbed sexual psychology (the same kind of disturbance that led him to make his famous attack on Newman[32]). Where Englishmen and Spaniards are putting each other to the sword in the struggle for the New World, we are not far from the reduction of the historical novel to primitive saga (which Kingsley much favored). When he follows Bulwer-Lytton in the classical line, in *Hypatia* (1853), his presentation of fifth-century Alexandria becomes a moralistic exposé of sensuality and religious hysteria, while his veneration of early Christianity is expressed with enough personal selectivity to exclude the monastic variety, which is shown to fall in with the barbarism of the pagans. But it is in *Hereward the Wake* (1866), in a medieval setting, that Kingsley comes into his own: the Norman yoke, the Teutonic berserker, the hero's fall through sexual self-indulgence, all the elements of a personal—but apparently widely-shared—view of history are there. The conception of the hero is indicative: "His face was of extraordinary beauty, save that the lower jaw was too long and

---

analysis of Bulwer-Lytton's political motives is convincing, it is too much to say, as he does, that the directly tendentious use of historical fiction constitutes "a new form . . . the political historical novel" (p. 61).

32. See Walter E. Houghton, "The Issue Between Kingsley and Newman," *Theology Today*, IV (1947), 81–101; reprinted in David J. DeLaura, ed., *Apologia Pro Vita Sua* (New York, 1968), pp. 390–409.

heavy, and that his eyes wore a strange and almost sinister expression, from the fact that the one of them was grey, and the other blue."[33] Kingsley wrote from his eminence as Regius Professor of Modern History, an appointment as revealing of his contemporaries' historical values as it was insulting to the fraternity of professional historians.

At the close of the novel, when the hero lies dead in Wagnerian gloom, "those who had the spirit of Hereward in them, fled to the merry greenwood, and became bold outlaws, with Robin Hood, Scarlet, and John, Adam Bell, and Clym of the Cleugh, and William of Cloudeslee; and watched with sullen joy the French robbers tearing in pieces each other, and the Church who had blest their crime." Kingsley leads us to the brink of another world, if he does not actually keep us there throughout: it is the playful, legendary world of juvenile fiction. If Bulwer-Lytton is the great disseminator of Scott's impulse in the early Victorian period, Kingsley is a major stimulus for the inundation of late Victorian historical novels. It is these latter that fill the lists of Baker and Nield; their perennial progeny still make the best-seller lists. There was Charlotte M. Yonge, who filled a half-century with an oeuvre in which it is difficult to distinguish the juvenile from the adult fiction. There were G. A. Henty and Howard Pyle and Sabine Baring-Gould and a host of other prolific commercial writers. There are even juvenile novels which verge on genuine art, like Stevenson's *The Black Arrow* (1888) and Conan Doyle's French and English tales. This was also the period in which almost every major Victorian novelist felt called upon to attempt the historical novel; perhaps because the standard of their contemporaries was so poor, these attempts were for the most part unsatisfactory and were not repeated. But they nevertheless saved the genre from falling into utter bathos, before a number of major modern writers brought it renewed life.

33. Charles Kingsley, *Hereward the Wake* (London and New York [Everyman ed.], 1966), p. 21; the quotation below is from p. 420.

Chapter 3 Scott

I. SCOTTISH SPECULATIVE HISTORY

If it is to the nineteenth-century intellectual tradition known as "historicism" that the modern imagination owes its sense of the unique character of past epochs, no historian helped spread the notion more effectively than Walter Scott. Yet, by a curious paradox, Scott has lost much of his impact in his own realm, fiction, in part because of a critical tendency to judge him in modern terms, without attention to the historically special qualities that make him the novelist he is. When Scott is placed within his proper intellectual milieu, his work is seen to be alive with historical concerns which, while they are not, indeed, precisely our own, are expressed in esthetic forms that can stand as an example to the fiction of any time. To begin by placing Scott within the history of ideas, then, is not to assign him a narrow and outmoded interest; instead, we may come to see his achievement as offering a challenge to the art of our own day.

Scott has not been lacking in historical-minded critics. He has been fortunate in having a succession of Scottish readers who remain in touch with their country's past and are thereby enabled to see his novels within a tradition. In the present century, it was Edwin Muir[1] who revived this interest by noting Scott's position as a man

1. Edwin Muir, *Scott and Scotland: The Predicament of the Scottish Writer* (New York, 1936). For a more somber view of Scott's divided situation, see David Craig, *Scottish Literature and the Scottish People: 1680–1830* (London, 1961).

of letters in early nineteenth-century Edinburgh, caught between antiquarian affection for Scottish national and folk traditions and pragmatic satisfaction in the commercial progress that was making Scotland one of the first modern countries in the world—a leader in the industrial revolution and in the development of a dominant middle class. Scott's problem has subsequently been described as typifying the ambivalence of Scottish writers toward the transition between agrarian tradition and capitalist modernity, as though this was a peculiarly Scottish phenomenon. The condition is a pervasive one that has found responses throughout the great tradition of the novel: it can be seen in Balzac and Dostoyevsky, in Faulkner and Lawrence. If, however, Scotland was in advance of the times economically, it is no accident that Scott should have been in advance of his literary compeers in response to the new cultural forms. One of the reasons, it may be concluded, that the historical novel begins with Scott is that the tension between tradition and modernity first achieved its definitive form in Scotland.

Scott's ambivalence toward the values of Scotland's past and those of its present has been summarized by David Daiches:

. . . Scott's attitude to life was derived from his response to the fate of his own country: it was the complex of feelings with which he contemplated the phases of Scottish history immediately preceding his own time that provided the point of view which gave life—often a predominantly tragic life—to these novels. For underlying most of these novels is a tragic sense of the inevitability of a drab but necessary progress, a sense of the impotence of the traditional kind of heroism, a passionately regretful awareness of the fact that the Good Old Cause was lost forever and the glory of Scotland must give way to her interest.[2]

Although one might qualify some of the descriptive terms in this account, Daiches' thesis has the virtue of putting its finger on the source of dramatic tension in the novels themselves. However much they are brought to happy endings by melodramatic plot involutions, Scott's novels are set in motion by conflicts that are universal and real, polarities not only of the time but of all periods of transition.

The values of the past are those of the folk or *Gemeinschaft*, of ritualized religion and nuclear family ties, of the absolute ethics of

2. David Daiches, "Scott's Achievement as a Novelist," *Nineteenth-Century Fiction*, VI (1951–52), 84; the essay has been collected in Daiches' *Literary Essays*.

relatively primitive societies, and of personal motivation by inherited mores—for the individual has not yet differentiated himself clearly from the group. On the other side stand the values of modern life, not moral pragmatism or economic improvement alone, but also the values of the Enlightenment: rational freedom, liberation from the dead weight of the past both intellectually and politically, a new world abuilding for the fulfillment of all members of society. Scott's inability to choose between them reflects not a vacillating temperament but a comprehensive vision, for both are absolute and eternal value-systems, like those which Coleridge found at work in *Waverley*—the instinct for conserving the past and the instinct for progress and freedom. Taken together, these universals structure the repeated historical drama of past and present in Scott's fiction, and give esthetic scope to his otherwise provincial absorption in the concrete details of national life.

The fulness of Scott's absorption in his own time is reflected not only in his work but in his career, which has attracted almost equal attention. Much in evidence are the close ties which this lawyer and professional writer maintained with the leading intellectuals and professional societies of his Edinburgh. There is a fund of squirearchical scepticism of all intellectual activity—particularly of the abstrusely philosophical—in Scott's personal tone, which has led even astute critics to believe that he was an unspeculative man and artist. A portrait has emerged of a business-like and unreflective Scott whose sense of the past proceeded from chauvinistic prejudice, and whose politics was thoroughly Tory, inspired by Burke's passionate beliefs in the primacy of the non-rational bonds of society and the permanence of its organically-evolved institutions. The evidence of Scott's complex attitudes belies this widely accepted view and places him closer to an intellectual tradition in some respects opposed to Burke.

Lockhart's *Life* gives abundant evidence of Scott's enduring friendship with the family of the philosopher Adam Ferguson and his education at the University of Edinburgh under the tutelage of Ferguson's successor, Dugald Stewart. The balance of Scott's attitudes toward contemporary philosophy is indicated in his memoir of his former teacher: "The celebrated Dugald Stuart is also dead, famous for his intimate acquaintance with the history and philosophy of the human mind. There is much of water-painting in all metaphysics, which consist rather of words than ideas. But Stuart was most impressive and eloquent. In former days I was frequently with him, but not for many years."[3] Scott's contempt of airy metaphysics was itself an echo of one of the Scottish schools of thought, and his affinity for Stewart's pragmatic restatement of his predecessors' thought was an affinity for the current of empiricism best suited to his own temperament. That Scotland was able to provide an intellectual choice of this sort was no accident but another reflection of the cultural development that went hand-in-hand with the country's economic progress.

Scott's relation to Scottish philosophy has been traced by Duncan Forbes in a series of articles that opens up new vistas for criticism. Forbes portrays Scott as a conscious sociologist dealing with many of the objects of study and governing theories of the Scottish school of speculative historians: "He accepted the leading principle of conjectural history: the law of the necessary progress of society through successive stages, and used it . . . as a weapon,"[4] that is, as an encouragement to further progress by his contemporaries. To the Enlightenment concepts of determinism, progressivism, and uniformitarianism, the "conjectural" or "speculative" approach allows some value to be added for the uniqueness of nations at various stages of the past. Forbes concludes: "The result is a unique blend of sociology and romance, of 'philosophical' history and the novelist's living world of individuals, of the general and the particular, in which lives the peculiar genius of Sir Walter Scott."

In his fledgling years as a novice attorney and passionate antiquarian, Scott joined an Edinburgh debating society, The Speculative.[5] As its name suggests, its meetings were designed not only to give young lawyers practice in forensics, but to air the philosophical, historical, and other interests that absorbed the Scottish Enlightenment. Quite aside from topical issues and conventional debating points, the Society's interests ran to the broad questions of social formation that had been raised by the speculative historians. Thus Scott read papers not only on literary issues like "The Authenticity

3. *The Journal of Sir Walter Scott*, ed. J. G. Tait (Edinburgh, 1939–46), II, 263.

4. Duncan Forbes, "The Rationalism of Sir Walter Scott," *Cambridge Journal*, VII (1953–54), 27.

5. J. G. Lockhart, *Memoirs of Sir Walter Scott* (London and New York, 1900 [1837–38], I, 150–52, gives the basic facts; these are expanded in Edith Batho, "Scott as Medievalist," in *Sir Walter Scott To-day*, ed. H. J. C. Grierson (London, 1932), pp. 133–57.

of the poems of Ossian," involving questions of folklore related to his own research in the ballads, but also on the early stages of institutions and cultural forms in the past: "On the Origin of the Feudal System" and "On the Origin of the Scandinavian Mythology." There is no need to suppose the determination of the content of these essays by the speculative historians to sense the close relationship of Scott's intellectual formation to the universe of discourse they created.

A clear statement of Scott's prevailing ideas about primitive societies is to be seen in his Introduction to *Rob Roy*. He there takes pleasure in debunking traditional myths about romantic folk heroes: e.g., he holds that the MacGregor clan sided with the Stuarts not because of chivalric loyalties but because loyalism gave them license to harry the Lowlands in the name of the Good Old Cause. This insight does not dispel Scott's curiosity about the historical individual, Rob Roy—an interest that extends down to the details of his extraordinarily long arms, which could tie his stocking-bows without his bending over. Ultimately, however, the colorful history of Rob Roy's clan constitutes "an interesting chapter, not on Highland manners alone, but on every stage of society in which the people of a primitive and half-civilized tribe are brought into close contact with a nation in which civilization and polity have attained complete superiority" (p. lxi).[6] The forms of culture, manners, etc., are for Scott differentiated not only according to the local conditions of each group or period, but also according to their place in a regular pattern of social evolution, the growth-pattern of civilizations. There are stages of human progress; these stages are fairly uniform among various societies—e.g., the Highlanders are compared by Scott to American Indians—and their peculiar strengths and weaknesses are explainable by their place in an evolutionary sequence. This approach to the past is not unique, of course; in our own time it is the province of theories of history like Toynbee's and Spengler's, and features of it go back to Vico. In Scott's time, it was the hallmark of the speculative historians, so called because their picture of the past was a reconstruction of the major stages in the course of civilization, often without hard data, but deduced from generalizations about the forms of all social phenomena. One might want to call these thinkers theoretical sociologists, seeking

6. My procedures for citing Scott's works are given in Chapter II, footnote 15.

the laws of social change and the necessary stages of all societies'
development, but we had best stick to the term "speculative historians," as closest to their contemporaries' parlance.

What welds Scott's emphases on both the uniform and the unique
aspects of history into a coherent view of the world (a view reflecting
more than a confused transition between eighteenth- and nineteenth-
century attitudes) is their mutual implication in a philosophy of
history. The speculative school to which I have referred includes
both constancy and change in its very definition of history: there is
progress, or at least novelty, as between past and present, but it proceeds along rationally predictable lines and is similar where conditions are similar. These principles of historical evolution may be
traced in the writings of William Robertson, Adam Smith, John
Millar, and others but the version of the theory most appropriate to
Scott is that of the philosopher closest to his own circle, Adam Ferguson.[7]

Ferguson's *Essay on the History of Civil Society*[8] is a general
theory of the origin and development of institutions, and as such
has been hailed as a forerunner of modern sociology. But one of its
aims is to bring Enlightenment theory of history to bear on the
problems of Scotland in the latter half of the eighteenth century.
Ferguson's description of the general laws of development strikes a
warning note for his own time, as suggested by his section-headings:
"On the Decline of Nations" (Book v) and "Of Corruption and
Political Slavery" (Book vi). Much of this account is reminiscent
of the commonplaces of the pre-Romantic movement's invective
against excessive refinement in England and, prospectively, in Scotland:

> Ill fares the land, to hastening ills a prey,
> Where wealth accumulates, and men decay.

Ferguson's warning against the dangers of progress is closer to
modern terminology than to Goldsmith's neo-classical terms, for it
is not to the enclosure movement and the consequent depopulation

---

7. See David Kettler, *The Social and Political Thought of Adam Ferguson*
(Columbus, O., 1965), for a survey of Ferguson's place in the intellectual and
other movements of the time. For a useful collection of excerpts from these
figures, see Louis Schneider, ed., *The Scottish Moralists on Human Nature
and Society* (Chicago and London, 1967).

8. This work has been freshly edited and introduced by Duncan Forbes
(Edinburgh, 1966). The lengthy quotations below are from pp. 221–22, 219,
and 271–72.

of the countryside that he draws attention but to the industrial revolution that was already gaining momentum in his time. Where eighteenth-century primitivism tended to see a threat in any deviation from an agrarian economy dominated by a landed aristocracy, the speculative historians greet urban and commercial society as a necessary stage of progress, but warn against its less savory consequences.

With the growth of Scotland to commercial eminence and with the general (though slow) rise in the standard of living and of national wealth, a widespread character-change occurred which we are still experiencing today, in a more articulated but recognizably similar form. This phenomenon has been called *anomie* by Durkheim, and has received other titles and considerable elaboration from modern sociologists, but the term "alienation"—as it descends from Hegel and Marx into the vocabulary of literary criticism—has perhaps greatest force. This is how Ferguson in 1767 describes the consequences of political liberty and economic abundance:

If to any people it be the avowed object of policy, in all its internal refinements, to secure the person and the property of the subject, without any regard to his political character, the constitution indeed may be free, but its members may likewise become unworthy of the freedom they possess, and unfit to preserve it. The effects of such a constitution may be to immerse all orders of men in their separate pursuits of pleasure, which they may . . . preserve without any attention to the commonwealth.

The root of this notion is to be found in a nascent assumption that the social ties of the individual are like the ties of part to whole in an organic body, and in a footnote Ferguson comes close to expressing this assumption in the metaphorical language that was to characterize nineteenth-century organicist theories.

The consequences of such a view of the individual and society are spelled out in Ferguson's historical paradigm: "rude nations" (which we would call "primitive" or "folk" societies) are organized on the close identification of individual and community, and this holds them together despite their lack of freedom, order, and peace. The growth of states into "polished and commercial nations" does away with the simple virtues of loyalty, patriotism, and blood-brotherhood, along with the barbaric vices; men become absorbed in an elaboration and refinement of the arts—both the industrial and the fine—and with the enjoyment they derive from them. Finally, such a nation becomes weakened by a decline in the heroic fiber of the individuals who compose it, and becomes prey to despotism through the indifference of its citizens. In summary, Ferguson writes:

> The manners of rude nations require to be reformed. Their foreign quarrels, and domestic dissensions, are the operations of extreme and sanguinary passions. A state of greater tranquillity hath many happy effects. But if nations pursue the plan of enlargement and pacification, till their members can no longer apprehend the common ties of society, nor be engaged by affection in the cause of their country, they must err on the opposite side, and by leaving too little to agitate the spirits of men, bring on ages of languor, if not of decay.

One special feature of this theory needs to be noted. Although Great Britain was, even as Ferguson wrote, embarking on a "plan of enlargement and pacification" that would encompass the globe, it is probably not colonialism that he or his Scottish reader would refer to with these words. Rather it is the extended state of the dual sovereignty—formally an equal union but in effect a dependent Scotland controlled from a remote London—that would come to mind:

> In proportion as territory is extended, its parts lose their relative importance to the whole. Its inhabitants cease to perceive their connection with the state, and are seldom united in the execution of any national, or even of any factious, designs. Distance from the feats of administration, and indifference to the persons who contend for preferment, teach the majority to consider themselves as the subjects of a sovereignty, not as the members of a political body. . . .
> The disorders to which a great empire is exposed, require speedy prevention, vigilance, and quick execution. Distant provinces must be kept in subjection by military force; and . . . dictatorial powers. . . . Among the circumstances, therefore, which in the event of national prosperity, and in the result of commercial arts, lead to the establishment of despotism, there is none, perhaps, that arrives at this termination, with so sure an aim, as the perpetual enlargement of territory.

Ferguson's description of alienation, rebellion, and repression can readily be applied to Scotland after the Act of Union. It serves as an introduction to the dramatic tensions of some of Scott's major fictions, preeminently *The Heart of Midlothian*, which portrays not only the popular reaction to an imposition of force by a distant and unassimilated authority, but also the contrast between the anomic individuals who succumb to the new conditions of life, and those who respond with traditional values and come eventually to master those conditions.

Ferguson was as ambivalent about the rise of commercial civilization in Scotland as Scott himself, and he asserted a set of socio-
political views that are remarkably similar to Scott's. These include
an exhortation to sociability, not merely in the form of Shaftesburian
personal benevolence but with the specific burden of engagement
in political and community affairs; the imperative of effort—"effective beneficent action"—in behalf of social improvement, without
waiting for Providence to distribute rewards and punishments;
sympathy with the "Moderate" wing of the Scottish Church against
the traditionalist, "Populist" faction; and a watchfulness with regard to the laissez-faire faith that commerce can only help the nation, believing instead that "interest alone can never hold a society
together." Ferguson had a theoretical predilection for a republic,
the ideal of Montesquieu's forms of statecraft, grounded as it was
on the free exercise of virtue in its citizens without the constraint
that forces men to be virtuous in spite of themselves. This ideal
was accompanied in him by a healthy scepticism as to the realizabil-
ity of the ideal: he is speculative but not utopian. On more topical
matters, his fear of the French Revolution and the ground-swell
of social discontent at home expressed itself in an acceptance of
evolution within the *status quo* as the best available form of government. In Ferguson and others of his school, Scott had precedents
for retaining a commitment to material progress and political
liberty while growing hostile to the forces of capitalist expansion
and of revolutionary class conflict.

It is not only in moral sentiments or political temper that Scott
resembles Ferguson and other speculative historians but also in his
attitude to the pattern of history. The key-note of the Scottish
approach is the "law of the heterogeneity of ends," which may be
formulated as follows: "the progress of civilization is not the result
of conscious planning; men pursuing their own selfish interests are
led by an invisible hand to promote an end which was no part of
their intention."[9] The most obvious application of this thesis lies in
the economic principle that "private vices make public virtues"
which Adam Smith inherited from Mandeville, i.e., that the free
pursuit of a variety of selfish individual ends leads to a maximal
social benefit, economic prosperity. But the attitude is given a broader

9. Duncan Forbes, "Scientific Whiggism: Adam Smith and John Millar,"
Cambridge Journal, VII (1953–54), 653.

application in Ferguson's and other speculative historians' vision of historical change in all periods: from the varied devices of historical actors, certain necessary and often beneficial results follow which were not intended and could not have been predicted by them. Despite their warnings of the anarchic degeneration of modern societies—which in Scott sometimes appear as tragic awareness of human failing, irrespective of the state of social development—these philosophers follow the eighteenth-century mode of substituting rational order for divine benevolence in their vision of history. For these "scientific Whigs," history was a complex process of myriad forces, which nevertheless obeyed scientifically ascertainable laws; it was neither the design of a deity nor the direct unfolding of an absolute, rational system, but a steady stream of tendency, good on the whole. Thus beliefs in the orderly progress, predictable stages, and large consistency of historical events were disengaged from theistic assumptions and were made available to the secular world-view which is found writ large in Scott—despite his occasional lip-service to Providence.

ౘ

Leslie Stephen summarized a Victorian view of Scott that shows remarkable persistence among literary historians of our own day, to the effect that he was a fine historian because he was a reactionary antiquarian:

What Scott did . . . was precisely to show by concrete instances, most vividly depicted, the value and interest of a natural body of traditions. Like many other of his ablest contemporaries, he saw with alarm the great movement, of which the French Revolution was the obvious embodiment, sweeping away all manner of local traditions and threatening to engulf the little society which still retained its specific character in Scotland. . . . And this is, in fact, the moral implicitly involved in Scott's best work.[10]

The movement of Stephen's prose is itself typical of the Romantic attitudes to history which he is describing: from a sympathetic emotion toward the past, to a reminder of social forces detested in the present, to the erection of the values of the past into political and literary norms for the present. The theory is, of course, Burke's even when he is not named, and the appeal of the view is to those

10. Leslie Stephen, "Sir Walter Scott," *Hours in a Library* (London, 1907), I, 222.

who would erect Burke into a prophet for contemporary politics. But the enlistment of Scott in this cause must prove more of an embarrassment than his prestige is worth.

That Scott found value in the past, in tradition, and in particular elements of the British constitution is undeniable; that he was as furious an anti-Jacobin as Burke is one of the few unambiguous facts in his biography. What is often lost sight of in bringing Burke to bear on Scott is that Burke was a Whig on American, Irish, and Indian issues, and a theorist on the best methods of obtaining political progress. If Scott is to be seen as Burkian, he must be acknowledged in his progressive as well as his conservative commitments. But a wider view of British thought in the period of the French Revolution shows that a mixture of tradition and progress is to be found in many political writers, and that it is almost taken for granted by the Scottish school. Dugald Stewart, for example, has been described as being "inclined to the view that social institutions represent a kind of deposit of wisdom, a heritage of the community that has put into them, over time, sagacity and reflection on much experience, transcending by far that of any individual".[11] On the other hand, the writer continues,

. . . Stewart could contend that while the danger of "sudden and rash innovations" could not be stressed enough, yet "it is possible also to fall into the opposite extreme, and to bring upon society the very evils we are anxious to prevent, by an obstinate opposition to those gradual and necessary reformations which the genius of the times demands." And he could write of "bigoted attachment to antiquated forms," "principles borrowed from less enlightened ages," and "reverence for abuses sanctioned by time."

This is the Whiggish spirit rampant, the spirit of contempt for traditionalist obscurantism, for selfishness pretending to divine sanction, and for the plain laziness that bolsters the conservative love of stasis. It is also Scott's paternal heritage, whatever his heated responses to topical affairs may have led him to; he is a born Whig and a Tory by acclamation. The mixture in him of these partisan positions only goes to further the tensions dramatized in his work.

It is my contention that Scott's novels are grounded in a theory of history which approximates that of the speculative historians rather than in one that derives from the conservative strain in Burke. There can be no question but that Scott was interpreted as a conservative

11. Schneider, *op. cit.*, p. xliii.

by his successors in the writing of historical fiction, but as has long
been seen, Victorian medievalism made a misinterpretation of Scott's
sceptical distaste for the obscurantism and hypocrisy of medieval
society, particularly in religion.[12] Further, the ascription of Burkian
sentiments to Scott is usually expressed with a vagueness as to its
fictional application that blunts it as a critical tool.[13] Scott's vision
of history is not a static one, which glorifies the stability of any
social order, but a dynamic picture of constant change, emphasizing
growth, the development of the present from the past, and even
the broad principle of progress.

The difficulties of the Burkian reading of Scott are amply illustrated in the case of a concerted effort to show the working of
Burkian principles in the novels themselves. Alexander Welsh
erects a portrait of a Tory Scott based not only on the *Reflections on
the Revolution in France* but on Blackstone's *Commentaries on
the Laws of England*, which he characterizes as the expression of
conservative self-satisfaction: "the optimism which may well be
called Blackstonianism . . . led in the sphere of law to contented
acquiescence with the existing state of things."[14] Similarly, Welsh
notes that by converting the Glorious Revolution into "a final
settlement, not a precedent" Burke raised the British state, legal
code, and property distribution to absolutes. Welsh then makes a
series of fascinating readings of the major Waverley novels in an
attempt to show them as a series of struggles for property, ending
uniformly in a systematic, legal distribution which affirms the
value of the traditional social order. However much we gain
from Welsh's account of *Rob Roy* and *Old Mortality* from this
standpoint, in the case of the novel which I have chosen for detailed examination below, a conservative optimism regarding British
law will be found alien to *The Heart of Midlothian*, where
Jeanie Deans symbolizes a new legality instead of affirming the old.

The array of points-of-view on Scott has recently been helpfully
set out by Francis R. Hart in an attempt to reconcile the Burkian
reading by Stephen, Davie, and Welsh with "the tradition stretching
from Coleridge to Lukacs and David Daiches of finding the subject

12. The classic statement is A. W. Benn, *The History of English Rationalism
in the Nineteenth Century* (New York, 1962 [1906]), pp. 309–10.

13. E.g., Donald Davie, *The Heyday of Sir Walter Scott* (London, 1961),
pp. 17–19.

14. Alexander Welsh, *The Hero of the Waverley Novels* (New Haven and
London, 1963), p. 103. Welsh is quoting A. V. Dicey here, and goes on to
apply the account to Scott.

of the Waverley Novels in an ambiguous vision of human history."[15] The special interest of Hart's remarks on history lies in his attempt to bridge the "Romantic-Antiromantic" controversy by reminding us that "Dilthey, and after him Cassirer, long ago challenged as Romantic myth what Cassirer calls 'the popular error concerning the unhistorical and antihistorical spirit of the eighteenth century'. . . ." By mentioning the eighteenth-century historians and philosophers in whose wake Scott stands—Hume, Robertson, Gibbon, Montesquieu, and Ferguson—Hart suggests that the Enlightenment had its own brand of historicism, tied to its non-Romantic doctrine of nature and metaphors of growth and change. This makes it possible to place Scott's mixture of tradition and progress, without adopting Romantic organicist metaphors with their conservative thrust.

Society in Scott's fiction is constantly changing, often for the better in a long-range estimate of stability and convenience. But this Enlightened sense of progress goes together with a nostalgic sense (resembling Ferguson's) of the lost values of simpler social forms, the tribal virtues of loyalty, honor, and military skill, and the heroic heritage of aristocratic family-lines. As Scott develops this double sense, especially in the theme Hart calls "the falls and survivals of ancient houses," we see that the aristocratic age is doomed, not only by its vices but by its very virtues. As did the speculative historians, Scott saw the past as fulfilled and outlived, while the main question for the present was to recall its virtues—discriminating them from its vices—so as to meet the challenges of the new social order and changed tenor of personal life.

Historical tradition is the subject but not the norm of Scott's fiction. The temporal dimension of his novels is necessary to trace the historic course of certain values, e.g., those of chivalric heroism, but it is not an absolute guarantor of any one set of values. This argument cuts two ways: it not only excludes the Burkian interpretation but also the Marxist progressivism found in Lukács's reading. Scott's fiction can stand in justification neither of a traditionalist *status quo* nor of a revolutionary historical trend—which Lukács holds up as the inner meaning of these works. The only affirmation Scott makes is of the historical process—of the workings of history itself, which make it certain that no political or social group can make an unqualified claim to credence, though they may

15. Francis R. Hart, *Scott's Novels: The Plotting of Historic Survival* (Charlottesville, Va., 1966), p. 5. The quotation below is from p. 182.

conditionally stand for social progress. Thus the appropriate context for Scott is neither Marx nor Burke but Scottish intellectual life—including the speculative historians, who were more concerned to define the form of historical progress than to insist upon a set of ends already achieved or to come. Scott's vision of history is open-ended and free, neither a validation of the past nor an invocation of a necessary outcome on the horizon. Scott was not an ideologist but a dramatist of ideas, and his historical thinking is closer to being an esthetic contemplation of change than it is to being a celebration of any society, past or present.

It may seem, however, to be merely a matter of convenience to link Scott so closely to Ferguson, for they lived amid a fairly large society of intellectuals who maintained many of the same presuppositions as theirs on society and history. Such a view is reinforced when we consider the similarity of Ferguson to the more influential Adam Smith:

There is, with all his individualism, the same insistence on society as a fundamental fact in life, the same natural and historical psychological union, if we may so say, of the individual and society, the same refusal to accept the distinction between the natural and the artificial, the same organic conception of society, the same impatience with attempts either to explain the state as an artificial construction or to reconstruct its institutions on purely rational patterns in defiance of sentiment, custom, and the deep roots of centuries of intertwining, the same sense of the sway of custom and fashion in taste and morals, the same insistence on the "instinctive," the unreflective, the uncontrived, the same radical denial of the hegemony of abstract reason as the arbiter of life and the sole principle of scientific analysis.[16]

But if Ferguson is like Smith in these respects, he is also like Scott. Ferguson, then, provides us with a point of reference for Scott's attitudes, although other contemporaries like Lord Kames, Gilbert Stuart, and John Millar dealt in greater detail with some of the periods of history—particularly the medieval—in which Scott worked. Rather than assembling a catalogue of the specific points of correspondence in their writings, I prefer to clarify the processes of social change in Scott's fiction by tracing one central theme down through his work, as it spans the ages of European history.

16. W. C. Lehmann, *Adam Ferguson and the Beginnings of Modern Sociology* (New York, 1930), pp. 117–18.

II. THE CONTINUITY OF THE WAVERLEY NOVELS

While a number of recent studies have carefully considered the cultural sources of Scott's fiction, and while others have advanced our understanding by close readings of individual novels, there is yet a third perspective that may fruitfully be deployed over the corpus of Scott's work. This is to read the Waverley novels together as a sustained history of certain institutions—though not, of course, as one continuous record of European or even of British history. The caveats of such an approach are obvious: Scott did not write his novels in the order of their historical chronology and did not set out as a comprehensive historian in his fiction (although he wrote both a children's and an adults' history of Scotland, and a massive history of the French Revolution and its aftermath in his biography of Napoleon). Moreover, the novels do not cover the span of European, or even of Scottish, history, beginning only with the Crusades and leaving imposing gaps in the aftermath. Yet to adopt a chronological arrangement of these novels is not artificially to juggle the materials in order to see them in a new light. Scott does have a consistent attitude toward history, and it is possible to see this attitude operating esthetically by showing its coherence on an extended scale. When this scale is adopted, the working premises of the Scottish speculative approach to history are seen to come subtly into play in the shaping of Scott's narratives. In this light, Scott's vision of history emerges as an evolutionary and guardedly optimistic one, in accordance with the speculative historians' double sense of the patterned advance of institutions (as well as of entire societies) and the dangers created by their new forms.

The speculative historians' view of the past had specific reference to the condition of Britain in their own time, and their concern was charged with political and economic implications for the conduct of the governing classes—broadly speaking, the aristocracy and, increasingly, the bourgeoisie. Dugald Stewart, for example, addresses himself to the role of the aristocracy in the modern body politic:

I before took notice . . . . of that natural aristocracy which we find in every community arising from the original differences among men in respect of intellectual and moral qualities. That these were intended to lay a foundation for civil government, no man can doubt. . . .
As the possession of power, however, is to the best of men a source of corruption, the general utility requires that some checks should be

imposed on the pretensions of the aristocracy; and the only effectual checks may be easily perceived to be a *popular assembly* on the one hand to secure the enactment of equal laws, and a *single magistrate* on the other possessing the sole executive power to prevent the competitions and rivalships among the order of nobility.[1]

In such a passage we feel the presence not only of Montesquieu, standing behind the speculative historians' principle of the separation of powers, but also an inkling of the attitudes of the rising bourgeoisie toward the ancestral masters of Scotland and England. The historical record of the aristocracy is one of "pretentions," unequal laws, and "competitions and rivalships"—it is a record of class privilege and a flamboyant style of life modeling itself on outdated norms. Distinguished from this historical aristocracy there is a "natural aristocracy," only partly overlapping it and marked by its innate "intellectual and moral qualities." The requirement that these latter should be the leaders of the state—the "foundation of civil government"—is therefore only partly fulfilled by the traditional dominance of the historical aristocracy. One implication, beyond the democratic and monarchial checks which Stewart mentions, is that the way must be opened to natural aristocrats, of whatever class origin, to come to the fore in order to serve the "general utility."

Scott was aware of this distinction between the natural and the historical aristocracy, and throughout his poetry and fiction may be said to have worked toward a refinement of the aristocratic ideal. By showing the shortcomings of the historical figures in his novels, and by leading his heroes through a pattern of education in moral and political values, Scott was adumbrating a *paideia* for modern life, filling the same social function that the heroic tales and epics of antiquity had played for their times. A number of recent critics have perceived that Scott carefully analyzes the idea of a gentleman, but it has not been clearly seen that this is his ulterior social motive in his choice of historical subjects. History for Scott is the history of the Western European aristocracy from the early middle ages to his own time, and the Waverley novels may be read in relation to the sequence of stages in the historical growth and decline of this master class.

In the "Essay on Chivalry," written for the *Encyclopedia Brit-*

1. In Schneider, *op. cit.*, p. 113.

tanica, Scott shows himself aware of the varied historical fortunes of the chivalric norms of that class. Although chivalry may be a set of artificial conventions embodying a fund of natural "intellectual and moral qualities," the efficacy of this ideal has been strictly tied to political and social changes:

> The Civil Wars [of the fifteenth-century] not only operated in debasing the spirit of Chivalry, but in exhausting and destroying the particular class of society from which its votaries were drawn. To be of noble birth was not, indeed, absolutely essential to receiving the honour of knighthood, for men of low degree frequently attained it. But it required a distinguished display of personal merit. . . . The noble families, therefore, were the source from which Chivalry drew recruits; and it was upon the nobles that the losses, proscriptions, and forfeitures, of the Civil Wars chiefly fell. . . . And, thus, Providence, whose ways bring good out of evil, laid the foundation of the future freedom of England in the destruction of what had long been its most constitutional ground of defence, and, in the subjugation of that system of Chivalry, which, having softened the ferocity of a barbarous age, was now to fall into disuse, as too extravagant for an enlightened one.[2]

From this mélange of observations, we may derive a number of propositions governing Scott's treatment of the aristocracy in the Waverley novels: a) the manners and morals of chivalry are historically tied up with the aristocracy, and a concern for the fortunes of those virtues involves a history of that class; b) these virtues are not necessarily confined to the aristocracy, and are to be found in members of other classes, but the ruling class kept the attendant honors to itself except in remarkable cases; c) the aristocracy as a class suffered a change in fortune in the course of history—whether one locates it largely in the fifteenth, seventeenth, or nineteenth century; d) the decline of the aristocracy was an "evil" but produced "good" results, i.e., Scott's attitude toward the passing of this major phase of the past is ambivalent; e) chivalry had a civilizing social effect, but it was tied to a class that restricted as well as defended English freedoms, and the loss of chivalric values in the modern world is compensated by greater political liberty; f) in the later stages of social development, earlier forms of refinement appear "extravagant," but there is a note of self-congratulation in

2. "Essay on Chivalry," *The Miscellaneous Prose Works of Sir Walter Scott, Bart.* (Edinburgh, 1847), I, 551.

the word "enlightened" that may carry Scott's irony—i.e., the modern world is not truly enlightened and may stand to gain by the revival of the morals, if not the manners, of the chivalric ideal. Many of these leading motifs are sounded by Scott in the course of telling his tales of chivalric aristocrats of the past, and in bringing the passing of the class and its values to the attention of his contemporaries.

❦

Scott's penultimate novel, *Count Robert of Paris* (1831) takes up the medieval aristocracy at the point of its articulation as a class. This point is the First Crusade, when the chivalric ethic was expressed—and more honored in the breach than in the observance, as we are to see in *The Talisman*—by pursuance of a holy war. One of the subsequent acts of the Crusaders was to sack a Christian city, Constantinople, but *Count Robert* does not have to reach that episode to reveal the divisiveness and self-interest of the European war-lords who assemble there in 1097. Much of the plot is taken up with the petty intrigues of noblemen from all Europe, but only the conflict of the titular hero and the actual one—of Robert and Hereward, symbolically Norman and Saxon—seems based on any principle that transcends egoism.

Chivalry and the knightly order are tied up with a caste system: Scott believes, according to the researches of his time, that the Normans, acquiring it from the Franks, introduced feudalism into England after the Conquest, instead of finding the so-called "free" Saxons already well subordinated. Hereward, the natural aristocrat and libertarian Saxon, has nothing but contempt for the "artificial" titles of the aristocracy with which he is confronted on the entry of the Crusaders. Much of our sympathy is engaged by the upright man of the people who contemns the haughty aristocrat, Count Robert, but after being defeated and spared by him in a duel, Hereward accepts the role of a squire of low degree to the Count in their subsequent campaigns. The natural and at least one of the titled aristocrats are seen at this first stage to be brothers-under-the-skin in their heroism.

Scott wrote two novels in a series called *Tales of the Crusaders* which pick up these themes. In the 1832 Introduction to *The Be-*

trothed (1825), he described his "wish to avoid the general expectations which might be formed from the title [i.e., a history of the Crusades]. . . . The story was, therefore, less an incident belonging to the Crusades than one which was occasioned by [them]. The confusion among families was not the least concomitant evil of the extraordinary preponderence of this superstition" (p. xvi). Aside from the rationalistic dismissal of the Crusades as mere "superstition," Scott makes the point that the key effects of this foreign adventure were on the social structure at home—and particularly in the consequences for aristocratic houses.

The Betrothed is an exemplary tale of the revolutionary chaos of the Border Wars which was occasioned by the absence during the Crusades of the loyal, Norman aristocracy, represented in the novel by Sir Hugo de Lacy. This implied critique of the aristocracy's failure to fulfill its duties at home is capped by Scott's treatment of the baronial Welsh revolt. King Henry settles the issue by releasing the Flemish weavers from feudal obligations in order to encourage them in manufacturing and trade, thus erecting them as a loyal counterweight to the power of the barons. For all its absorption in the local color of Welsh chronicles and the primitive aura of Bardic poetry and passion (represented by the minstrel, Cadwallon), the historical perspective of the novel is to see its period (1187) as a transitional phase to a more settled monarchial system which will curb the divisive tendencies of the aristocracy and further the creative impulses of the middle class. But this evolution will brook no direct threat to the ruling class by the peasantry: "A large force had been sent into the country to subdue the insurgent peasants; and the knights and nobles despatched for that purpose failed not to avenge to the uttermost, upon the wretched plebeians, the noble blood which they had spilled during their temporary triumph" (XXIX, 394–95).

In the other "tale of the Crusaders," *The Talisman* (1825), Scott's intentions are equally clear from his Introduction: ". . . Richard I, wild and generous, a pattern of chivalry, with all its extravagant virtues, and its no less absurd errors, was opposed to Saladin, in which the Christian and English monarch showed all the cruelty and violence of an Eastern sultan, and Saladin, on the other hand, displayed the deep policy and prudence of a European sovereign . . ." (p. xvii). The Enlightenment motif of the wise Moslem or Jew, which Scott may have derived from Lessing or others, is here not simply an embodiment of a rationalist philosophical ideal against which to set the follies of the author's professedly Christian countrymen. It is also a standard of political authority against which the European monarchs are found wanting. Not only is the school-boy legend of Lion-Heart exploded, but the political relations between Richard, Philip of France and Leopold of Austria are shown to be of the most tawdry sort. Here Scott extends the Enlightenment standard of moral and intellectual excellence to the political realm, and finds the noble leadership of the medieval nations at a low ebb.

The transfer of the healing talisman to Europe at the end of the novel has been seen as a symbolic transferral of Saladin's political and moral norms to a sick society. But in practice the talisman does not work very well at home: ". . . though many cures were wrought by means of it in Europe, none equalled in success and celebrity those which the Soldan achieved" (xxviii, 458). Indeed, the Crusades represent a high-water-mark of international unity, for after the homecoming, the nations return to a state of *bellum omnia contra omnes*:

> The period also preceded that when the grasping ambition of Edward I. gave a deadly and envenomed character to the wars betwixt the two nations; the English fighting for the subjugation of Scotland, and the Scottish . . . for the defense of their independence. . . . The same disunion had begun to show itself betwixt the French and English, the Italians and the Germans, and even between the Danes and Swedes; but it is only that which divided the two nations whom one island bred, and who seemed more animated against each other for the very reason, that our narrative is principally concerned with. (vii, 103–5)

Thus the closing reconciliation between the King of England and the Crown Prince of Scotland (as the hero Kenneth turns out to be) is only a temporary settlement of the plot through Saladin's intervention, while the normally divided state of the medieval nobility is both the cause of the Crusades' failure and the condition of Europe to which they return.

A more detailed picture of England in the early middle ages is given in *Ivanhoe: A Romance* (1819), which completes the tale of the Crusaders' return in 1194. Back home in his domain, Richard finds the prevailing lawlessness so attractive that he joins in with

Robin Hood and his merry band. Following on his portrayal in *The Talisman*, the anti-chivalric judgment stays with Lion-Heart even after he has been held up as a principle of humanity and kingship. He intervenes as Ivanhoe's tutelary spirit at the tournament of Ashby and directs the conquest of Front-de-Bœuf's castle, but the final judgment of him is of "a generous, but rash and romantic monarch." Though his return brings England back its rightful king, there seems no warrant for confidence that the condition of society we see throughout the novel will be much altered. (Historically, of course, Richard soon departed for the wars.)

On the state of law and government, from the usurping King John down to the Norman villains, on the insecurity of the merchant class (particularly when Jewish), and on the status of the grumbling peasantry represented by Gurth and Wamba, there is little need to enlarge. *Ivanhoe* is not a romantic idealization but a thorough-going critique of medieval civilization, akin to the Enlightenment view and anticipating that in *A Connecticut Yankee in King Arthur's Court*.[3] That it also serves up slices of the roast-beef of old England and dramatizes the myth of the Norman yoke made it a constant reference for Victorian medievalism. But we can read it today as Scott's considered judgment on the unviability of the times for any but the heroes of romance.

Scott wrote two novels of the fourteenth century, both set in Scotland and striking notes of Scottish nationalism, but for all their patriotic nostalgia the age they portray is an unattractive one. *Castle Dangerous* (1831) closes with the English surrender of Douglas Castle to the Scots in 1307, among the first in the series of Bruce's victories leading up to the liberating Battle of Bannockburn. But the point-of-view from which the tale is told is English, the main characters' motivations are those not of ardent patriotism but of a chilly chivalric honor, and the penultimate chapter closes with a deflating dialogue in which the Bishop of Glasgow recommends "forbearance and peace" to a Scottish warrior. Moreover, the donnée of the novel—the heroine's vow to marry the man who can hold the castle for a year and a day—is taken straight from the realm of romance. Despite the lack of historical realism in this last-

3. Cf. J. E. Duncan, "The Anti-Romantic in *Ivanhoe*," *Nineteenth-Century Fiction*, IX (1955), 293–300.

completed novel (which closes with Scott's envoi to his readers), its
jaded sense of things medieval comes consistently through.

The failure of medieval social order is even more acutely portrayed in *St. Valentine's Day, or The Fair Maid of Perth* (1828),
which takes up the condition of Scotland at the end of the fourteenth century. Here the war of each against all is organized into a
class struggle, the burghers of the "fair city" having their *con-
dottiere* in Sir Patrick Charteris to protect them against the exac-
tions of the nobility. The comic situation of an aristocrat's man
pushing around the foolish bourgeois, Oliver Proudfute, turns
sombre when Proudfute is later ignominiously killed. But by this
time, all Scotland has been declared to be uninhabitable by the
King himself—the weak Robert III, who is being manipulated by
the most powerful of the nobles, Douglas.

Besides the personal misery (traced in the romantic plot) which
Douglas's scheming generates, there are the calamities of permanent
feuding among the Highland clans, brought into the story by the
touching coward, Conachar. The "civilized" and "primitive" states
are equated in their perpetual conflicts, but civilization seems even
more vicious when the aristocrats stage a trial by combat between
the warring tribes, and watch them kill each other off at the
climactic Palm Sunday massacre of 1396. The pacifist spirit of the
incipiently Lollard middle class is given an attractive spokesman
in the titular heroine, but the most durable townsman is the
armorer Henry Smith, who has learned to use his weapons in an
ugly world. Catharine recognizes this in the event: ". . . she had
reflected that men rarely advance in civilisation or refinement beyond the ideas of their own age, and that a headlong and exuberant
courage, like that of Henry Smith, was, in the iron days in which
they lived, preferable to the deficiency which had led to Conachar's
catastrophe" (B, XIX, 336–37). The historical relativism expressed
here does not exclude an implicit judgment of the medieval past as
an age of iron.

The tenor of life in the later middle ages remains constant in
Quentin Durward (1823) and *Anne of Geierstein, or The Maiden
of the Mist* (1829), despite the addition of a new element. Society
is still ravaged by predatory forces, both external—like the band
of mercenary *Landsknechten* led by William de la Marck—and
internal, like the Duke of Burgundy, Charles the Bold, who op-

erates in both novels. But a new force distinguishes the later medieval period from the earlier, and brings it to within a step of the Renaissance. This is the emergence of strong monarchy in the person of machiavellian rulers, who are represented in these novels by Louis XI of France. Scott's account of *Durward*'s anti-hero states precisely Louis' point of departure from previous self-aggrandizing monarchs: "Brave enough for every useful and political purpose, Louis had not a spark of that romantic valour, or of the pride generally associated with it, which fought on for the point of honour, when the point of utility had been long gained" (A, I, 3). Charles is, on the other hand, the image of the traditional aristocrat—cholerically egoistic, proud, and principled—and these novels follow the conflicts between their personalities and life-styles from 1468 to Charles's death in 1477.

In both novels, king and duke are not only mutually opposed but are also set against another social force, just coming to political prominence: the new middle class, represented in *Quentin Durward* by the townsmen of Liège and in *Anne of Geierstein* by the Swiss Cantons, fighting for independence from Burgundian domination. Louis' role is to capitalize on the Duke's troubles by supporting his enemies, and he therefore puts himself on the side of the forces which receive Scott's approbation, in the portrayal of the Swiss leader, Arnold Biederman.

Not that Louis emerges as a progressive monarch or enlightened consciousness in advance of his time; in conversation with the astrologer, Galeotti Martivalle, he is alarmed by the proto-Humanist's prediction of an age of scientific progress that will transform the world, "erecting and destroying kingdoms." "Let futurity look to what concerns them," he interrupts; "we are men of this age, and to this age we will confine our care. Sufficient for the day is the evil thereof" (*Durward*, A, XIII, 224). In a later conversation with his courtier, Philip des Comines, Louis steps out of character in his outrage at the Duke of Burgundy's disavowal of feudal loyalty to the king, but the historian brings him abruptly out of his confusion: "Your Majesty is aware, that the strict interpretation of the feudal law is becoming obsolete even in the Empire, and that superior and vassal endeavour to mend their situation in regard to each other, as they have power and opportunity" (B, XIII, 231). Louis is a sophisticated political thinker compared with

Charles the Bold, whose response to the murder of the Bishop of Liège by de la Marck's band is to propose to make the canals run red with the townsmen's blood for their alliance with the Boar of the Ardennes and their revolt against the Bishop.

In the same vein, Charles passionately wages war against the plebian Swiss Confederacy, seeking to avenge their victories over the flowers of chivalry—as well as to extend his dominions in order to fulfill his dream of taking up royal status. That the war is fought between classes rather than between peoples or nations is insisted upon in the historical briefing which Biederman gives the nominal hero, Arthur Philipson (another exiled Briton, like Durward). Biederman has not only led the citizens of the cantons against their feudal lords but has disclaimed his own title and lands, preferring to become an elected Landamman. (It is for this reason, and not for "Gothick" taste, that Geierstein, the former Biederman castle, is in ruins, adding to the picturesque descriptions of the Alpine landscape.) The community of free citizens that emerges is not an anticipation of the modern bourgeoisie, however, but a revival of the classical ideal of the Roman Republic (an ideal shared by the speculative historians): "May Heaven continue among us the homebred virtues of the Romans, and preserve us from their lust of conquest and love of foreign luxuries!" as Biederman expresses it (A, VII, 123).

The hero and his father, the Earl of Oxford, fire one token shot in support of Burgundy, but after fulfilling their minimal obligation to a fellow nobleman, they retire to the republican virtue of Geierstein (although the novel closes by foreseeing their eventual return to England in the train of Henry VII). Scott's critique of feudal society becomes explicit when he comments on the convention of the Estates of Burgundy, which refuses Charles taxes for his wars: ". . . in all feudalized countries (that is to say, in almost all Europe during the Middle Ages) an ardent spirit of liberty pervaded the constitution; and the only fault that could be found was, that the privileges and freedom for which the great vassals contended did not sufficiently descend to the lower orders of society, or extend protection to those who were most likely to need it" (B, IX, 169). The heroic virtues of the aristocracy are affirmed, but require to be exercised in behalf of the entire body politic. Scott laments not so much the passing of the class that represented the aristocratic ideal as its failure to apply it in its relations with all classes of the nation.

❦

The next grouping in Scott's fiction may be called his Renaissance novels, set in the Tudor period (with the addition of one Jacobean novel, which is continuous with them). Of these, two follow the religious wars: *The Monastery: A Romance* (1820) beginning with the English domination of Scotland after the battle of Pinkie in 1547, and *The Abbot: Being the Sequel to The Monastery* (1820) ending with the defeat of Mary Stuart at Langside in 1568. The most serious omission in Scott's view of the medieval period—a sense of the religiosity of its culture—is made up for in these works. Scott's lack of sophistication in Catholic doctrine allowed him only a sporadic sense of the power of medieval religion, but it did not inhibit his sentiments for the dissolved monasteries. The monastery is seen as an integrative socio-economic force, governing its vassals well enough to insure that many of them remain loyal to it after the disappropriation. In the ensuing border wars, the tenant community of "the Debateable Land" becomes a cross-section of the entire nation, divided in loyalties and exhausted by conflict. In the course of the wars, when "every man's sword was directed against his neighbour's bosom" (A, I, 1), all sides tend to be discredited and we are left, with relief, on the threshold of the Elizabethan peace. The only regret expressed for the departing world of chivalric loyalties is focused on the pathos of Mary Stuart as she embarks for imprisonment in England.

Scott was aware of the special difficulties of presenting British Reformation history to a modern (and prevailingly anti-Catholic) audience. In the fortunes of two families, the Glendinnings and the Avenels, these novels explore the influence of religious ideology as it operated on the formation of the gentry. By the close of *The Abbot*, Edward Glendinning (as Ambrosius) has become the last of the abbots, a saintly defender of the church in which he had once been a worldling. The last in the train of chivalric heroes, Roland Graeme—after his earlier devotion to the defense of the Church and of Mary—returns to Protestantism and becomes a loyal follower of the new regime. Thus the Glendinnings, traditional vassals of the monastery, and the Avenels, traditional aristocrats, issue in Sir Halbert Glendinning and Roland Avenel, Protestant members of the new gentry, while the staunch Catholics in these families—Edward/Ambrosius and Roland's grandmother—die in exile or retirement. The Reformation novels can be seen, then, as tracing the transition from a Catholic to a Protestant, from a chivalric and feudal to a pragmatic and expansive aristocracy.

Elizabethan England, the scene of *Kenilworth: A Romance* (1821), presents a less complicated social conflict than the transitional Britain of the Reformation novels. From the outset, the new men and manners of the time are pointedly described: the nouveau-riche religious trimmer, Foster; the Machiavellian courtier, Varney; the factotum equipped with a "blunt conscience," Lambourne. Equally, the culture of the aristocracy begins to take on the features of the international Renaissance; Cumnor Place is furnished with Spanish foot-cloth, Italian salt-cellar, Flemish tapestry, cushion "in the Moorish fashion," Venetian mirror, etc. When the reader (with the heroine) reaches the castle which gives the novel its title, the spirit of Renaissance art and courtiership is shown at its highest pitch. This is a society of high ostentation and wilfull repression, dangling on the whims of a rather foolish woman yet bouyed up by its self-propagated myth of imperious strength. It is given to the loyal servant, Wayland Smith, to confer judgment: ". . . I would rather shoe colts on the coldest common in England, than share in their gayest revels" (B, IX, 138). In such a realm, the tragedy of Amy Robsart is to be taken as a yardstick of the frivolous weakness of the aristocracy, represented by Leicester, and its manipulation by unscrupulous courtiers like Varney, which the blindness of the queen allows.

Perhaps the most peculiar yet characteristic feature of the Elizabethan world symbolized by Kenilworth is its effort to create a *summa* of the nation's history, in order to justify itself as its authentic and permanent outgrowth. The first sight of Kenilworth's battlements reveals Arthurian soldiers (represented by real men as well as by dummies); the castle itself presents "on its different fronts magnificent specimens of every species of castellated architecture, from the Conquest to the reign of Elizabeth" (B, IX, 134); and the pageant given to celebrate the queen's visit includes scenes from the ancient Britons and Romans down through the Saxons and Normans—all of whom are held to endow the English with their special qualities. But this proud heritage is belied by the moral state of the aristocracy in the period of its highest ostentation.

Much the same style of life persists at the court of James I, as seen in *The Fortunes of Nigel* (1822), set during the preeminence of the Duke of Buckingham. Scott's James is a much more interesting figure than his Elizabeth—or his vastly overpraised Mary Stuart—both as a political actor and as a psychological individual. The "wisest fool in Christendom" combines Scottish folksiness with Renaissance sophistication, provincial miserliness with learned Humanism. Unfortunately for the hero and for the nation, he also combines unmanly pliability in the hands of his son and his son's favorite, Buckingham, with stubborn assertion of his personal prerogatives. As a result, his refusal to render elementary justice to Nigel by repaying his debts leaves the young-man-from-the-provinces at the mercy of courtiers like Dalgarno and, ultimately, Buckingham. The former's role in furthering his master's designs on Nigel's property is revealed to be only an instance of the courtiers' moral degeneracy—which is made even more explicit when Buckingham taunts Dalgarno with having prostituted his sister for the sake of personal advancement. Scott points a contrast in the upright aristocrat Lord Huntinglen, Dalgarno's father, and in George Heriot, the "new man" of economic affairs who maintains a high standard of mercantile integrity. But both men are too old and ineffectual to protect the innocent in a London that bears a striking resemblance to Dickens's—complete with debtors' prisons, slums, and other elements of a society rotten at the base.

Not only do the characters of the Renaissance novels lack the chivalric ideals and rugged loyalties of the figures of the medieval tales; their dominant motivation is now simply money—or, in the case of the crown prince and the royal favorite, land. The number of misers populating the novel is Balzacian, from the King down to the proprietor of Nigel's refuge in the sanctuary at Whitefriars. The economic background to this change in character-formation is sketched in Scott's description of the London scene: "All that was passing around, however, marked the rapid increase of a capital which had long enjoyed peace, wealth, and a regular government. Houses were rising in every direction; and the shrewd eye of our citizen already saw the period not distant, which should convert the nearly open highway on which he travelled, into a connected and regular street, uniting the court and the town with the city of London" (A, v, 79–80). *The Fortunes of Nigel* treats the new wealth of London in the sardonic style of Jacobean comedy (*A New Way to Pay Old Debts* is mentioned by the hero, applying it to his own case). As the passage continues, it anticipates the conflicts which the next Stuart regime was to foster with the new men of wealth: ". . . although his reign appeared calculated to insure to Great Britain that lasting tranquillity and internal peace which so much suited the King's disposition, yet, during that very reign, were sown those seeds of dissension, which, like the teeth of the fabulous dragon, had their harvest in a bloody and universal civil war."

❧

Scott's novels of the Commonwealth and Restoration periods focus on the struggle between the two classes wielding power—we may call them, broadly speaking, Cavalier and Roundhead. As his subject matter approaches the tensions of modern politics, Scott's discrimination of social classes becomes more subtle and his characterization of them more profound. It is this sociological specificity that accounts for the general judgment that the "Scottish" novels are superior to the "English," the (relatively) modern to the medieval. Some of the novels of the modern group are, indeed, set in England, but share the Scottish novels' concreteness in differentiating the classes and interests engaged in the civil wars and their aftermath, the Jacobite revolts.

All the colors are arrayed in *A Legend of Montrose* (1819), which deals with the Civil War in Scotland, climaxing in the Battle of Inverlochy in 1645. The gathering of Montrose's Royalist forces provides an occasion to display the variety of motives enlisted in the revolt against the Scottish Parliament. There are the aristocrats, like the Earl of Menteith, who are fearful of the growing power of certain of their number—in particular, the Marquis of Argyle, whose loyalty to Parliament has allowed him to become a dictator in western Scotland. There are the debased gentry, like the justly famous Dalgetty, the mercenary who joins the campaign not simply for pay and loot but because his style of life contemns the bourgeois and the Puritanical. There are the Highland clans, who are moved by loyalties like those of Menteith, and by love of gain like that of Dalgetty, but whose political sophistication is on the level of the blood-feuds and personal rivalries which thicken the plot and hasten the defeat of Montrose's political cause.

By characterizing the elements of Montrose's campaign, Scott assembles the elements for a social history of Scotland, but his novel is not a neat historical schema. In telling the story from the point-of-view of Montrose's followers, Scott seems to be taking a partisan view of history from the Cavalier side. But the real force of the novel lies in conveying the complexity of Scottish politics, with northern aristocrats ranged against western (while allowing for the exception of certain northern Presbyterian families); with Highland clans placed on both sides in the war; and with Lowlander and Presbyterian forces on the fringes of the action, suggesting a broad range of unexplored life. Even in the scope of a short novel like *A Legend of Montrose*, Scott makes it impossible for us to think in simple categories of Highlanders vs. Lowlanders, or of aristocracy vs. bourgeoisie, when considering the historical life of a nation—or to assign monolithic terms to a class as variegated as the aristocracy of Scotland.

Scott's assurance as a historical sociologist is less marked in his two English novels of the Civil War, *Woodstock, or The Cavalier* (1826) and *Peveril of the Peak* (1823). In *Woodstock*, to be sure, there is a consistent effort to distinguish the variations within the contending parties. To contrast with the "royal martyr"—whose spirit hovers even in Cromwell's study, in the form of a Van Dyke portrait—there is his son, whose libertinism generates the later complications of the plot. To contrast with the quintessential cavalier of the novel's subtitle, Sir Henry Lee, there is his nephew, Markham Everard, the hero whose moderatism in politics and conduct points up the limitations of his inflexibly traditionalist class. To contrast with the movingly human Presbyterian minister, Nehemiah Holdenough, there is the ranting Independent who steps out of the ranks to cast him from his pulpit in the novel's dramatic opening scene. Despite or because of all his criticism both of Royalist frivolity and ineffectuality and of Puritan opportunism and fanaticism, Scott's political judgment seems closest to Everard's trimming. He passively supports Cromwell's regime as long as it is "too firmly fixed to be shaken by any plots which could be formed against it" (b, xx, 350), and quickly turns to support the Restoration, in the belief that "a settled government could not be obtained without the recall of the banished family." His own position, Scott acknowledges, "will please neither Whig nor Tory" (A, XI, 192).

While *Woodstock* is set in the decade of the 'fifties, between the Battle of Worcester and Charles's Restoration, *Peveril* spans the much longer period from the start of the Restoration to the closing phase of the Popish Plot (1660–80). The shift between the opening scenes of the novel and those with which it is mainly occupied is a significant one. At the outset, the Cavalier Peveril and the Cromwellian Bridgenorth—representing the aristocracy and untitled gentry, respectively—are united by deeper bonds than their political conflict can annul. (Bridgenorth has interceded with Cromwell for Peveril's life, and Peveril has sheltered Bridgenorth's daughter at his castle.) But the atmosphere of intrigue and corruption which permeates the London of Charles II is a more divisive force than the Civil War itself. Bridgenorth becomes a fanatic engaged in Fifth-Monarchy plots against the regime, while Julian Peveril is involved in his aunt's ultramontane Catholic circle and, with his father, implicated by Titus Oates in the Plot.

Personal life at this time is so keenly dependent on historical trends, that the novel allows the Peverils to be reprieved when the court finds Oates's influence fading and can dare to challenge his absurdity. The grotesquerie of the personages of the Duke of Buckingham's court—indeed the grotesquerie of most of the characters of the novel, from the arch-Catholic Countess of Derby to the Arabian-Nights heroine, Zarah-Fenella—is Scott's expression of the quality of life under the Restoration. This is not a moralistic judgment of its libertinism but an esthetic embodiment of its deracination.

Just as *Peveril* shows the lasting difficulties of reconciling Cavalier and Roundhead, the opening scene of *Old Mortality* (1816) suggests the artificiality of the Caroline effort to draw the Covenanters into the orbit of a secular society by inviting their participation in a *wappen-schaw* and country games. Not only are the ascetic Puritans put off, but the gentry has so far declined that its charade of chivalric forms ends in a comic fiasco. As the novel develops, the aristocratic manners displayed, e.g., by Evandale and Claverhouse when they arrange Morton's reprieve on the basis of gentlemanly obligations, come to assume a spurious look in the context of the real historical drama being played out by the Covenanters.

Not the Jacobites but the Covenanters provide the subject of Scott's closest approach to tragedy. The comic postures and maniacal politics of the Covenanters become submerged in the high passion of their rhetoric; even the afflatus of their Biblical language comes to invest their rebellion with greater dignity than the relatively minor skirmishes of Drumclog and Bothwell Brig would justify.

The hero Morton's career shows the waverings of a typical gentleman of the time: his father had tried both sides in the Civil War, and the example of trimming, as well as the revered memory, is imparted to the son. Although both sides claim him he feels greatest amenity in the genteel society of his beloved, but the passion and high seriousness of the Covenanters—even of such an opportunist as Burley—draw him into rebellion. When William III's policy of moderation leads all but the extremists of both camps back into the mainstream of national life, Morton can return to society—to expiate his rebellion, in one sense, and to claim his role in the new life of the nation, in a larger sense. In tracing the transition from the rebellion of 1679 to the establishment of peace in 1689, Scott leads Morton from the view that the land holds "nothing but violence and fury," to a sense of its openness to the future. *Old Mortality* is remarkable, then, not only for its portrayal of the tragic memory of the Covenanters—kept alive by the title-figure of Old Mortality—but for its indication of the capacity of the gentry, in the person of the hero, to renew itself and regenerate the nation.

The more pessimistic strain in the post-Revolution state of mind is rendered in *The Bride of Lammermoor* (1819). Although not strictly speaking a historical novel, it tells more about the structure of society at a given historical moment than many of the other Waverleys. The events on which the novel is based took place around the year 1669, according to a considerable body of extant historical evidence: deeds, contracts, and authenticated reports of the time. The central family was not called Ashton, as in the novel, but Dalrymple, and the head of the family, James Dalrymple, was one of the most important figures of his age. He was Viscount Stair, Lord President of the Court of Session—the equivalent, say, of Supreme Court Chief Justice—and author of "Stair's Institutes," the standard work on Scottish law, comparable to Blackstone's *Commentaries*. He was also a member of the new Whig aristocracy that took control of the country after the defeat of James II in the Glorious Revolution. Scott could not copy the exact names, partly because descendents of the Dalrymple family were still living; in fact, they gave him some difficulty after he wrote of their ancestors' acts even in a disguised form. But he went beyond the necessary disguise in transforming Viscount Stair into a baronet, Sir William Ashton. He is characterized not as an aristocrat but as a subtle, small-minded, ultimately hapless bourgeois who remains an interloper, though he has risen to Lord Keeper of the Seal.

It is given to the old aristocracy to possess the chivalric virtues, the heroism, free spirit, and moral integrity which Scott recalls for his modern readers. He represents this chivalric survival in the person of the hero, the Master of Ravenswood, whose historical equivalent in the Dalrymple affair was Archibald, Lord Rutherford. The latter did not fall into quicksand while riding to a duel against his beloved's brother, as does Ravenswood in the novel, but died rather unremarkably in his bed in 1685. The most interesting change from the received story which Scott makes is to transform a man who was in reality only the third lord of a relatively new aristocratic house, into the last scion of an ancient family. Scott emphasizes that the Ravenswoods have been masters of their domain for centuries, that their title has the sanctions of age and heroic deeds in the past. Their class is the traditional master-class of Scotland, but in the course of the Glorious Revolution the Ravenswoods have supported the Stuarts and in consequence have lost their lands and become economically defunct.

The Ashtons, representing the new aristocracy, have bought up the Ravenswood estates, successfully vied with them at law, exercised their pragmatic finesse in business dealings, and taken over entirely from the old masters. Scott sets up the novel as a conflict of families which embodies a major social transition, and thereby captures one of the critical moments in the history of the classes which concern him most.[4] He attempts, of course, to propose a

4. Scott's attitude toward this transition is—like all ambivalent attitudes— by no means clearly determined. Andrew D. Hook, "*The Bride of Lammermoor* Reconsidered," *Nineteenth-Century Fiction*, XXII (1967), 111–26, modifies the extreme position in Robert C. Gordon, "*The Bride of Lammermoor*: A Novel of Tory Pessimism," *Nineteenth-Century Fiction*, XII (1957–58), 110–24; also in *Under Which King? A Study of the Scottish Waverley Novels* (Edinburgh and London, 1969). In weighing these heated views it should be noted that the old aristocracy is given little moral advantage over the new forces in Scott's estimation; see the sexton's complaint to Ravenswood not only against the harshness of the Ashtons, but also against the ineffectuality and errors of omission of the Ravenswoods. This debate has been renewed in *Nineteenth-Century Fiction*, XXIII (1968), 493–99.

reconciliation between these two classes—or their descendants in the time at which he was writing. Speaking in the person of his hero, the Master of Ravenswood, he voices a desire for "the day when Justice shall be open to Whig and Tory"—to the new and old aristocracies, respectively. But the ineffectual heroism of even an enlightened aristocrat like Ravenswood and the fatuity of the Ashtons suggest the difficulties that stand in the way of reconciliation in the present.

꒯

Scott wrote a novel on each of the Jacobite rebellions of the eighteenth century, and this group—generally considered his most characteristic and finest works of art—also shows him at his most accomplished as a social historian. Together these novels constitute a history of the major trends in the transition from a pre-industrial and semi-feudal society to a recognizably modern, commercial one. That this society happens to be Scotland's should not blind us to the novels' relevance to the broad pattern of modern European development.

Rob Roy (1817) has always been highly favored for its pictures of Highland landscape and personality, as well as for its robust burgher, Bailie Nichol Jarvie, but has never won much admiration for its structure. Yet the social situation of its characters does much to lend significance to the novel's otherwise desultory plot. It has also been seen that both Rob Roy and Jarvie play a tutelary role toward the *Bildungsroman* hero, Frank Osbaldistone, the one drawing him away from the propriety of his English background toward the romance of free Highland ways, the other confirming him in his civilized prudence in face of lawless Highlanders and Jacobites. But the hero's education is not only a moral one: he develops a general view of an entire social world in the course of vast changes. It is his exemplary—and explanatory—role in relation to the forces of change that gives Jarvie his central position in the novel and justifies the apparently excessive imaginative power which one critic has found in him.

The Scotland of 1715 which Jarvie unfolds to Osbaldistone is, in the Highlands, just emerging from the archaic social order of the clans and, in the Lowlands, gearing itself to take advantage of the commercial possibilities opened up by the Act of Union, which ended trade barriers with England and allowed for rapid commercial growth in Glasgow—although not as quickly, as Jarvie points out, in the more conservative Edinburgh. When Osbaldistone first comes to Glasgow, it has not yet begun to take advantage of its new role, and we are treated to a projection of its future glories while seeing it in the maiden state. Scott draws from this pleasant irony the satisfaction which the progressive Scotsman of his day felt in looking back on the economic miracle of the previous century. As Jarvie enlarges on the problems of the day—unemployment, primitive agricultural methods, aristocratic support of clan lawlessness—the hero is brought to see that Jarvie's hope for economic progress, and not Rob Roy's nostalgia for primitive freedoms, is the true heroism of the modern world.

The relevance of economic factors to the novel's action does not stop there; nor are they merely instrumental when they provide the initial motivation which sends Osbaldistone to his uncle's estate and ultimately to Scotland. As Jarvie explains to the naïve hero, all the machinations of the plot come down to economic factors: his father has bought, on credit, large tracts of Scottish forest lands; the Highland landholders have used these credits to float large loans (presumably for the conspicuous consumption that characterizes this stage of the aristocracy's development); the Jacobite Rashleigh Osbaldistone has pursued his obscure, Jesuitical plots in order to prevent Frank's father from paying his debts, in the expectation that when he reneges, the landholders, his creditors, will lose their lands to the Glasgow financiers who have advanced them funds; and Rashleigh's hope is that this will so infuriate them that they will join the Jacobite rebellion which he is contriving. Although this plot (Rashleigh's and Scott's) may seem rickety, Jarvie's ascription of Jacobite discontent to the precarious economic position of the Highlands gives it greater depth: "the stopping of your father's house will hasten the outbreak that's been sae lang biding us" (B, IX, 124), because the clan chiefs have been driven to the wall by the Hanoverian government's stopping payment of the protection-money that has kept them quiet during the previous reigns. Thus the complicated movements that occur in *Rob Roy* reflect the economic pressures and social changes going on at the outset of the century, when government policy shifted to the furtherance of commercial interests and the traditional sources of Highland wealth were dried up. " 'It is very singular [says Frank] that the mercantile transactions of London citizens should become involved with revolutions and rebellions.' 'Not at a', man, not at a',' returned Mr. Jarvie,—'that's a' your silly prejudications' " (B, IX, 126).

While *Rob Roy* points toward the emergence of a new type of pragmatic modern man, *Waverley, or 'Tis Sixty Years Since* (1814) shows the process of change at work in the traditional aristocratic man. The hero's assimilation of chivalric romances in his uncle's library and his revelling in legends of his heroic ancestors, going back to the Crusades, provides the novel with a youthful Don Quixote to be disabused of his follies by confrontation with reality. Like the Don, Edward Waverley is a member of a declining aristocracy, living by an outdated set of chivalric standards in a world that has radically changed. Even the arch-chivalrous Fergus Mac-Ivor sees the folly of Waverley's letter challenging his former commanding officer to a duel for ordering him to obey his military duty. But the anachronistic Waverley is made much of wherever he goes simply because he is an aristocrat, highly eligible as a match and potentially useful as a political tool. We can read the novel, then, as a description of the readjustment the aristocracy must go through to bring it out of its medieval, chivalric forms and fit it to be a responsible class in the new society amaking.[5]

Only part of this readjustment is political. Waverley must, of course, learn that the Jacobite attempt to turn the clock back in 1745 is as arcane as the antiquarianism of the Baron Bradwardine or the Tory fustiness of his uncle, Sir Everard. The main action of the novel—which traces Waverley's desertion of a military career under the Hanoverians, his joining the Pretender's expedition into England, and his imprisonment for treason and ultimate reprieve by the victorious regime—provides a firm structure in which to place the various kinds of cultural learning that go to educate the new aristocrat. Perhaps the most powerful lesson is that of blighted love. When Flora Mac-Ivor rejects him, she does so not because of his personal short-comings but because of the way of life of his class:

I will tell you where he will be at home, my dear, and in his place,— in the quiet circle of domestic happiness, lettered indolence, and elegant

---

5. See S. Stewart Gordon, *"Waverley* and the 'Unified Design,'" *ELH: A Journal of English Literary History*, XVIII (1951), 107-22, for a fuller treatment of this development.

enjoyments of Waverley Honour. And he will refit the old library in the most exquisite Gothic taste, and garnish its shelves with the rarest and most valuable volumes; and he will draw plans and landscapes, and write verses, and rear temples, and dig grottoes; and he will stand in a clear summer night in a colonnade before the hall, and gaze on the deer as they stray in the moonlight, or lie shadowed by the boughs of the huge old fantastic oaks; and he will repeat verses to his beautiful wife, who will hang upon his arm,—and he will be a happy man."

(B, XXIII, 190)

Flora's devastating portrait is, of course, rendered from the point of view not of the modern age but of the heroic: she wants *her* aristocrat to be a chivalric warrior gallantly laying down his life— in a lost cause, for preference. Flora's passion—politically sub- limated sexual passion—overwhelms Waverley; he needs a woman who, like Rose Bradwardine, can welcome the picture of a conven- tional aristocrat which Flora draws. From Flora, Waverley learns that he is no chivalric knight but a genteel modern given to anti- quarian tastes—somewhat like Sir Walter himself.

If Waverley must divest himself of ancestral anachronisms, he can receive little guidance in the present way of the world from his father, for Richard Waverley was, for all his defection to the Whigs and subsequent trimming, a duffer at the game, losing his place and hounded to his death after allying himself with a cabal against Walpole's government. It is Waverley's guidance by Colonel Talbot that becomes the means by which he sees his Jacobite folly and the prudence of setting his course within the Hanoverian world. Talbot provides not only political realism but moral tough- ness as well. It is he who affirms the necessity of sending the un- regenerate Mac-Ivor to the gallows, and this necessity prevails despite Scott's lament for the severity of an act of purely political justice—despite Waverley's, and the reader's, awe at the heroism of Mac-Ivor's unflinching defiance to the last. Indeed, Mac-Ivor himself has predicted that the government has been "too heartily frightened" to allow the Jacobite leaders to get off with another set of light punishments and pardons, and that it will make "root- and-branch-work" of the Highland aristocracy especially. The death of Fergus Mac-Ivor is a climactic moment in the transition from the old to the new aristocracy, and Waverley's survival is a token that the new ruling class will be a more tractable and realistic one. Scott indicates the ambivalent but firm conclusion to be drawn from the transition in a pictorial image:

> It was a large and spirited painting, representing Fergus Mac-Ivor and Waverley in their Highland dress, the scene a wild, rocky, and mountainous pass, down which the clan were descending in the background. . . . Beside this painting hung the arms which Waverley had borne in the unfortunate civil war. The whole piece was beheld with admiration, and deeper feelings.
>
> Men must, however, eat, in spite both of sentiment and *vertu* . . .
> (B, XLII, 359–60)

and the company falls to, enjoying the fruits of the Augustan peace.

The transformation of the aristocracy, and of Scotland with it, is completed in *Redgauntlet: A Tale of the Eighteenth Century* (1824), which centers on an abortive Jacobite conspiracy of about 1765. Commentators seem to have missed the irony of the title, assuming that the novel is named for its most imposing, though not its central, character.[6] In fact, the title applies to the entire family of Redgauntlets—to its latest scion, Darsie Latimer, as well as to his demonic Jacobite uncle. The novel is rich in family history, not only in the chivalric traditions communicated from uncle to nephew but in the famous tale which stands at the thematic center of the work. "Wandering Willie's Tale" is a folk parable of the Redgauntlets' splendid past, their decline in fortune (till it plumbs bottom at a revel of the devil and his assorted Jacobite followers), and their comic defeat by the crafty peasant, Willie's forefather. The tale resumes the sequence of stages by which a typical aristocratic family is seen moving, after the Glorious Revolution, from feudal indolence to economically-pinched harshness, and finally to temperate adherence to the new order of modern life. Sir Robert Redgauntlet "began to be keener about the rents than his tenants used to find him before," and "made men sometimes think him a devil incarnate," but his successor Sir John "had been bred an advocate, and afterwards sat in the last Scots Parliament and voted for the Union" (A, letter XI, 153, 156).

---

6. E.g., David Daiches, "Scott's *Redgauntlet*," in *From Jane Austen to Joseph Conrad*, Martin Steinmann, Jr. and R. C. Rathburn, eds. (Minneapolis, 1958), pp. 46–59—otherwise a ground-breaking article.

In this sequence, the events of *Redgauntlet* mark the family's struggle to break clear of its past in order to confront the future. After the execution of Darsie's father in the '45, his mother has spirited him away from his uncle and the rest of the family, and has given him over to an Edinburgh solicitor to be raised according to the ethics of bourgeois professionalism. It is significant that Darsie does not gain from this education the same personal prudence that is much more easily inherited by his friend Alan Fairford, the solicitor's son. It is part of Scott's plan to raise Darsie into the image of a new aristocratic hero, not into another unheroic Fairford. Neither the extreme, romantic lawlessness of the smuggler Nanty Ewart, nor the extreme, commercial law-abidingness of the Quaker Joshua Geddes will predominate in Darsie; both these protective father-figures do not really teach him anything. Darsie will emerge as Sir Arthur Darsie Redgauntlet, a spirited aristocrat, to be sure, but one who has freed himself from the illusions of an outdated heritage.

In the family's history of collective delusion, it is Darsie's uncle (called Herries of Birrenswork and other pseudonyms) who has brought his political principles to the pitch of mania. When his sister describes their uncle's feverish dissatisfaction, "bewailing the downfall of the cause, and wishing for the bullet of Dundee, and the axe of Balmerino," Darsie says: "A strange delusion, ... and it is wonderful that it does not yield to the force of reality" (B, XII, 223). That this is not a mere psychological observation but expresses an awareness of the broad outlines of the family's career in history, is borne out by Darsie's following remark on his uncle and his followers: "Whatever these people may pretend, to evade your uncle's importunities, they cannot, at this time of day, think of subjecting their necks again to the feudal yoke, which was effectively broken by the act of 1748, abolishing vassalage and hereditary jurisdictions." Darsie, the new Sir Darsie, is more at home in the modern world than in visions of the medieval, and in him the aristocracy has completed its transformation into its contemporary form. Further, Darsie's sense of justice is a specifically British (not merely Scottish) one, which is outraged by the high-handed, class-prejudiced administration of justice by his uncle's client-squire; his principle is, "Every British subject has a right to know why he suffers restraint" (A, VI, 286). Here, in legal, political, and social attitudes, the old aristocracy has given way to a new image of heroism for Scott's own time.

ॐ

Scott's other eighteenth-century novels do not show the aristocracy in any significantly new light. *The Black Dwarf* (1816), with its Gothic expansion of the disorders of Jacobite fanaticism, and *Guy Mannering, or The Astrologer* (1815), with its introduction of a gypsy and seer element in a story of aristocratic pride, span the century at its beginning and end. Two novels, *The Antiquary* (1816) and *St. Ronan's Well* (1824), have a more contemporary flavor, the former set "near the end of the eighteenth century," and the latter "about twenty years since" the writing. But none of these is truly a historical novel, any more than are *The Pirate* (1821) or *The Surgeon's Daughter* (1827), though the former has some interesting reflections on English racial origins and the latter partakes of the exoticism of colonial warfare in India. *St. Ronan's Well* does, to be sure, convey a sustained critique of modern society, first by setting up the contrast of the "Auld Town" of St. Ronan's with the new town of St. Ronan's Well, and then by erecting a series of satirical portraits of the beau-monde assembled at the watering-spot. But the satire runs thin, while the plot—which reflects the decline of the established gentry in a story mingling madness, incest, and other signs of decadence—leaves social reality behind for bizarre Gothicism.

The Antiquary, on the other hand, has the makings of a historical vision of the present, and almost survives its meanderings of plot and multiplication of secondary characters. Its basic contrast is drawn between the local aristocrat, Sir Arthur Wardour, and the local gentry landholder, the antiquary Jonathan Oldbuck, Laird of Monkbarns. Although both are exposed to satirical treatment on account of their differing antiquarian hobby-horses—the knight's predilection for Gothic demonology and the squire's dedication to almost every variety of historical scholarship—their class values and economic motivations provide additional distinctions. One of the strands of the plot hinges on Sir Arthur's investment in a copper-mining enterprise which he believes can be conducted through the magic powers of the charlatan, Dousterswivel. We sense that the

aristocracy has been caught at the moment when it has been forced
to interest itself in modern forms of money-making, but has not
yet left behind its medieval mental furniture.

Oldbuck, on the other hand, though he has financially supported
his friend in the scheme (partly out of antiquarian curiosity), is a
model of middle-class financial prudence and—where his researches
are not concerned—of worldly sagacity. His background is carefully established as German Protestant bourgeois (his grandfather
having been exiled for printing the Augsburg Confession). To be
sure, he has refused a career in business, but not in favor of the
genteel dissolution of his elder brother. Rather, Oldbuck is a form
of middle-class intellectual, a Foxite Whig who approves the initial
aims and excuses the later excesses of the French Revolution (in
contrast to Sir Arthur and Lord Glenallan, who breathe fire at
the very mention of republican democracy). The fact that Oldbuck
is Presbyterian and Hanoverian, or that Sir Arthur is Anglican and
Jacobite, has by now become irrelevant; the new political forms of
the nineteenth century have come to dominate political sympathies.
But the frequent discussions of France and the pervasive, hysterical
alarm at a supposed invasion are the only ways in which current
affairs impinge on the characters' lives. The other strand of the
plot, having to do with the real identity of the hero, Lovel, becomes entangled with the destructive pride of a Catholic aristocratic family, but has little implication for the new status of the
aristocracy. That "Lovel" emerges as Lord Geraldin is, however,
some guarantee that the next generation of aristocrats will be more
humane and rational than its predecessors. We are left with the
sense that the hereditary guilts and internecine struggles of the
Wardours and the Glenallans will be permanently put aside as
relics of a bygone age, after the marriage of Lord Geraldin and
Isabella Wardour.

❦

The approach to the Waverley novels chosen here necessarily emphasizes their individual fragmentariness as well as their collective
continuity. By focusing on single novels, it is possible to see their
plot resolutions as organically completing at least some of them;
by treating them as briefly as I have done here, their lack of an
image of social equilibrium, their transitional quality, is more
marked. But these varying conclusions are not merely reflections
of an arbitrary choice of method. There is at work in Scott the

tendency of the organic artist to resolve his themes and ravel up his plots, but there is also the tendency of the broad-viewed historian to see the energies of each period dissipated, the impulses to reconciliation in its best men unsatisfied, and the nation's passage to its next crisis as at once a repetition of previous patterns of conflict and a confrontation of new and unique elements. The continuity of the Waverley novels is established by a consistent interest in the aristocratic classes of Britain, in their constant and sometimes tragic transformations, and—as we shall see in the following chapter—in the gradual emergence of a natural aristocracy in the life of modern Scotland. It is a continuity reinforced by Scott's absorption of the strain of speculative history which sees both the adherence of historical events to certain constant laws of social development—in the eighteenth-century mode—and also their continual production of novelty, of new forms and vivid individuality —in the mode of the Romantics and the historicists of the nineteenth-century.

The striking fact about the succession of the Waverleys—given the patterns of conflict and reconciliation that emerge so clearly in Hart, Welsh, and Daiches—is that the same social tensions occur again and again, in different guises and situations. Nor does this repetition imply a simple Enlightenment view of the constancy of human nature and the relative unimportance of historical differentiation. There is a pattern in the history of human institutions, but it is not made up of progressive reconciliations nor of providential fulfillments.[7] Rather it is the movement from primitive clan society, with its nuclear ties and absolute commitments; to aristocratic society with its elaborate codes, expressing the dominance in an undeveloped economy of a military caste over weak middle and lower classes; to a modern world in which the survivals of medieval forms are shown—even to the bearers—to be anachronistic, while a reinterpretation of traditional virtues by the ruling class is required. This is the historical pattern worked out by the speculative historians, and it helps us to see the pattern of development in purely secular terms, without undue satisfaction in progress, and with attention to individual variations. The working-out of this development may be observed in detail in an individual novel, *The Heart of Midlothian*.

7. Cf. P. F. Fisher, "Providence, Fate, and the Historical Imagination in Scott's *The Heart of Midlothian*," *Nineteenth-Century Fiction*, x (1955–56), 99–114—which sees providence at work in individual lives, if not on the historical scale.

III. *THE HEART OF MIDLOTHIAN*

If, as I have maintained, the course of history in Scott follows the pattern marked out by the speculative historians—in which some of the strengths along with some of the weaknesses of the aristocracy, in common with their societies, are lost in the progress or "refinement" of civilization—we should expect his greatest novels to bear the imprint of this pattern in their dramatic form. A number of recent critics, Arnold Kettle and Robin Mayhead among them,[1] have perceived that *The Heart of Midlothian*'s theme is the shifting relationship between justice and law, but they have not been able to ground this eternal drama in the historical transition which the novel traces. When this ethical-political theme is seen in historical development, the novel's centrality in the tradition of historical fiction emerges in a new light.

Other critics have contented themselves with skeptically rejecting any claim for the novel's thematic unity by adducing the variety of interests at work in *The Heart of Midlothian*—as well as in other, less celebrated, Scott novels. What theme indeed could bind together a novel with so large a number of activities, which seem never fully integrated into its meandering plot? The novel begins with a historical situation, the Porteous riots, that only tangentially touches the main action in which the Deans family is engaged, and the main action itself slips into two parts, focusing on twin climaxes: the courtroom scene and the appeal for the Queen's mercy. Furthermore, what are we to make of the numerous apparent irrelevancies in the novel's structure: the Gothic, pseudo-supernatural atmosphere of Madge Wildfire and her forest band, or the protracted conclusion, which takes the action outside its previous scenes and sets it apart in a "Highland Arcadia"?

We cannot easily make use here of the usual terms for describing novels of loose but socially comprehensive form: the eighteenth-century picaresque and the nineteenth- and twentieth-century panoramic modes. Neither of these typologies will serve to classify the relation of the heroine, Jeanie Deans, to her world—although she does move through several strata and regions of both Scotland and England, observing much along the way. *The Heart of Mid-*

---

1. Robin Mayhead, "*The Heart of Midlothian*: Scott as Artist," *Essays in Criticism*, VI (1956), 268 ff.; Arnold Kettle, *An Introduction to the English Novel* (New York, 1960 [1951]), I, 113 ff. Joan H. Pittock, in her rejoinder to Mayhead—*EC*, VII (1957), 477–79—exhibits the dangers of assuming that Scott's treatment of his philosophic themes was unstudied.

lothian does not seek comprehensively to set out a detailed picture of a social background; nor is its chief historical incident, the Porteous riots, extensive enough to account for its status as a historical novel. Instead, the keenest historical sense in the novel is provided by the drama of what Jeanie becomes, both as the embodiment of a previously aristocratic ethical ideal and as a symbol of her society's progress from a lower to a higher stage of civilization. Jeanie, I shall maintain, grows in stature until she attains the proportions of epic heroism: she becomes the incarnation of Scottish society in its development in and beyond the eighteenth century. Genuine nobility is here found and developed in a woman of the peasantry, while the offspring of the gentry decline in successive generations into crime, effete sophistication, barbarism, and exile. There is a historical parable here, and it is a parable of modern history as the speculative historians conceived it.

The first chapter introduces a number of tangible evidences of Scott's historical viewpoint. One is the position of the Tolbooth as a palimpsest, a series of layers of history underlying the surface action. Just as the Introduction and Postscript on Helen Walker, the prototype of Jeanie Deans, form a set of screens through which the reader passes to the central action, so the topographical setting of the novel becomes a series of concentric circles radiating out from the Tolbooth, the "Heart of Midlothian," to the City of Edinburgh to the county of Midlothian to the whole of Scotland and ultimately to all Great Britain. Here the novel's title is set at work: *The Heart of Midlothian* concerns a subject as central to the life of the nation as the heart is in the functioning of an organic being. Moreover, this image-pattern will become symbol, capable of reconciling opposites and of functioning on several planes of reality, for the *heart* of Midlothian will come dramatically to be Jeanie Deans, whose heart or *Gemüt* will both reaffirm the value of law and social order represented by the Tolbooth, and also qualify it by values which social institutions generally lack, i.e., "heart."

The second aspect of history that is set out in the first chapter is an ambivalent sense of the value of the past, which an examination of such antiquities as the Tolbooth inevitably arouses. Such relics of the past generate not only nostalgia but a complementary recognition that they have been superseded in the present— that the time of grand crimes and grand punishments has passed. One of the young lawyers of the opening chapter speaks of the "many extraordinary and daring crimes [induced] by the long civil dissensions of Scotland—by the hereditary jurisdictions, which, until 1748, rested the investigation of crimes in judges, ignorant, partial, or interested—by the habits of the gentry, shut up in their distant and solitary mansion-houses, nursing their revengeful passions . . ." (A, I, 17). But this aristocratic heritage of lawlessness and privilege is now mercifully of only antiquarian interest.

The development of Scotland since its union with England has diminished the brutality and injustice of the aristocracy, and other elements of the modern scene bear witness to the march of progress. The very subject of discussion in this first chapter, the Tolbooth, is at the outset described as having recently been torn down,[2] and insofar as it is a symbol of historical misery, it recalls the fallen Bastille, with a muted suggestion of the inevitability of such change. The lawyers' antiquarian discussion, therefore, takes the form of a reminiscence on the horrors of the past, while the present is assumed to be established on a more stable, rational, and civilized basis. As a comic underscoring of the note of progress, the chapter begins with a road accident that creates the occasion for telling the novel's tale. At the time of the story's recitation the mails and carriage transportation have been vastly improved and the accident to the new coach is due to excessive speed—a reminder that progress is not an unmixed blessing, but also that it provides opportunities to take stock of the past.

Beyond providing images of the historical view which we are to take in the novel, the opening chapter acts as a framing device to establish the story transmitted by the lawyers as instinct with legal interest—thereby anticipating the legal theme of the novel. The protagonists of the episode, Halkit and Hardie, are drying out in an inn after their coach accident and—being internally as well as externally warmed by the hospitality—fall to discussing the favorite subject of young professional men: the philosophic grounds of their profession. Their immediate provocation is the mention

2. Scott himself acquired some of the doors and stones of the Tolbooth at its destruction in 1817, and used them at that architectural Waverley novel, Abbotsford. A footnote to this passage suggests the balance of his mind on past and present values: ". . . it is not without interest that we see the gateway through which so much of the stormy politics of a rude age, and the vice and misery of later times, had found their passage, now occupied in the service of rural economy" (note 10).

of the Tolbooth, which is currently threatened with destruction by a forward-looking municipal government. Hardie is led to define the nature of prisons as an image of the world—"a prison is a world within itself, and has its own business, griefs, and joys, peculiar to its circle" (A, 1, 13)—and then proposes the subject of "The History of the Prison of Edinburgh" as one of the "real records of human vagaries," a legal archive "where every now and then you read new pages of the human heart, and turns of fortune far beyond what the boldest novelist ever attempted to produce from the coinage of his brain" (A, 1, 15). There is present here not only the well-worn rhetorical convention that truth is stranger than fiction and that the story to follow is no fiction at all but truth. There is also Scott's commitment as a novelist to embody in art the truths of human life which he has discerned in his own career as a lawyer and antiquarian. Indeed, it is difficult to resist the impression that it is Scott himself speaking through a persona to express his view of his two professions—novelist and lawyer—in their intimate relations with historical life.

The relevance of the frame-chapter to the novel's legal theme does not end here. After further discussion of the richness of legal history in dramatic subjects, Halkit offers as an instance the sad tale of one of his clients (who is, by an unaccountable coincidence, a fellow-passenger and who subsequently enters the conversation). Dunover's career is a Micawberish one of constant efforts at commercial success followed invariably by financial ruin, legal distress, and the debtor's prison. The "sort of ill-luck or fatality attached to the hero," Dunover, comes to an end, however, with the recital of his misfortunes. In the course of putting the record of an individual's sufferings at law into a narrative form—composing a history, as it were, of Dunover's career—the somewhat flippant lawyers are inspired to do something for their previously discarded client, and set him on his feet again. For this act of mercy, they are to be rewarded by a supramundane court with glittering professional success. The reader, too, gains a boon from Dunover's experience, for the novel which is thereupon presented is a tale narrated by Dunover to the lawyers—he has heard it during one of his stints in the Tolbooth. (It is set down by a listener at the inn, Peter Pattieson, who forms part of Scott's narrative machinery in this and other *Tales of My Landlord*.)

We have in this frame-story, then, a series of parables of the large historical themes of *The Heart of Midlothian*: social change, legal refinement, and the emergence of the modern. But the chapter as a whole also serves as an illustration of the ways in which a given historical event, such as the Porteous riots, is best transmitted to the present: not as an antiquarian relic but in the form of a personal drama, the story of Jeanie and Effie Deans. By taking up a true tale (the story of Helen Walker described in the Introduction), further historicizing it by grafting it to a true tale of the Tolbooth (the Porteous lynching), and then developing it through fictional episodes, Scott indicates the way in which merely factual material is made into symbolic history by fiction.

❦

The theme of legal evolution is the link that connects the personal drama of the Deans family with the public event of the Porteous lynching. The connection of these two cases in the Tolbooth prison is not merely a matter of coincidence—a coincidence secured by Scott when he makes the romantic villain in Effie's case become the chief instigator of the riots. The abolition in 1809 of the law of circumstantial evidence for child-murder, like the destruction of the Tolbooth in 1816, was a step in the march that the progressive side of Scott saw as his country's destiny. (He cites the repeal of this "severe" law in the notes to the novel.) Moreover, the legal and ethical issues raised in the two plots run parallel to each other: Is the mob justified in lynching Porteous for an act of murder which the legal system is unwilling or unable to punish? Is Jeanie justified in upholding an excessively severe law on the basis of religiously-grounded moral absolutes (themselves also of a legalistic kind)? Both issues raise the question, when the law is either too lenient or too harsh, should it be corrected by the individual acting on his sense of justice? The novel is poised on the traditional distinction between a humane, common-sense justice traditionally linked with the divine realm (*la loi, das Recht*) and an institutional, historically evolved system of law which always falls short of the ideal (*le droit, das Gesetz*).

Scott seems to resolve the legal issues of the Porteous lynching rather simplistically by making the leaders of the mob out to be criminals, who desire only their personal ends in "springing" one of their cohorts,[3] and by ascribing to the Edinburgh mob the words of the mob that urged Pilate to crucify Christ (A, VII, 96: "Away with him—away with him!"). Yet the narrative emphasizes the good discipline and conscientiousness of the entire assemblage in constituting themselves not enemies but upholders of the law. In his ambiguous treatment of the event, Scott poses the problem of revolution: men in need of elementary social justice express their indignation in demands for vengeance and thereby compromise the values they seek. If justice is shown to be above the law here, then mercy is shown to be above justice. The situation exemplifies the same scale of values as figures in the main plot of the novel: the growth of Jeanie's convictions from the arid legalism of her family's Covenanter tradition to a more civilized, more complex ethic based on both mercy and justice.

Besides its general historical setting in the age of the French Revolution and the industrial/social transformation of Scotland, *The Heart of Midlothian* is the product of a period which saw a major movement for legal reform.[4] Stemming from a parliamentary committee of 1770, which recommended the repeal of the death penalty for a large number of offenses, including situations similar to Effie's, the movement for legal reform was furthered by Sir Samuel Romilly's parliamentary campaign, which reached a climax in 1818, the date of the novel. (Romilly failed to get his measures through the House of Lords, yet public opinion was so effectively aroused that a committee set up in 1819 made recommendations that were partly put into effect during the period which followed.) In the very years in which Scott meditated and wrote this novel, then, fundamental questions of the law were on the public mind.

The novel catches up the contemporary debate on capital punish-

---

3. Scott's long footnote on the government investigation of the Porteous affair attests that no designation of the leaders could be made. His identification of them with the Wilson-Robertson band is, then, a conscious invention.

4. The standard history of the legal change is Leon Radzinowicz, *A History of English Criminal Law and Its Administration from 1750*, volume I: *The Movement for Reform* (London, 1948); see especially p. 430 ff. on the laws governing murder of bastard children by their mothers. A more specific discussion of the laws involved in the novel is David Marshall, *Sir Walter Scott and Scots Law* (Edinburgh and London, 1932), pp. 127–28, which gives the dates and terms of the revisions of the child-murder laws. For a formulation of the reasons for the law that makes it sound almost plausible, see J. H. A. MacDonald, *A Practical Treatise on the Criminal Law of Scotland* (Edinburgh, 1877), p. 149 ff.

ment and its traditional concomitant, the royal reprieve. The usual recourse of judges who could not induce their juries to acquit or to lessen the charge, when required to apply capital punishment for such crimes as petty theft, was to frame an appeal for royal pardon. The large number of royal intercessions into a legal system that was widely recognized as excessively severe built aristocratic *noblesse oblige* into the institutional structure of the law. By setting up his novel to reach its climax with the Queen's exercise of mercy, Scott was taking a position on a lively issue of the day. His own approach to legal reform was not the clean sweep of the reformers but was still of a progressive sort: it implies the need to build mercy into the workings of the law instead of leaving it an exceptional recourse, subject to cavalier temperament.

Scott's interest in the resolution of these legal issues in the present does not minimize his sense of historical specificity: he shows the influence of historically conditioned motives both in the execution of the law and in the revolt against it. The Edinburgh mob requires vengeance not only against Porteous but against the entire system of London-based, quasi-colonial rule which Porteous represents. By the same token, the intervention of the English government is intended to prevent any Scottish challenge to its authority, and creates a deviation from legal form: the postponement of Porteous's legally-prescribed execution for murder. Mercy is put to the service of political repression, while the demand for rigorous justice becomes an expression of nationalism.

When the minor hero of the novel, Reuben Butler, makes a vain effort to halt the lynch mob, the eternal philosophical problems of justice, mercy, and the law acquire further historical references. Picking up a theme that has been previously sounded—"Let us mete to him with the same measure he measured to them" (A, VII, 89)—Butler raises the question, "what hath constituted you his judges?" (A, VII, 96), echoing the maxim, "Judge not that ye be not judged."[5] The debate between Butler and the mob does not simply

---

5. The relations of this theme to its obvious source have been carefully studied in D. Biggins, "*Measure for Measure* and *The Heart of Midlothian*," *Études Anglaises*, XIV (1961), 193–205; but the analysis does not reach the underlying ethical issues, which go beyond the structural roles of Jeanie and Isabella in their devotion to absolute norms. The conflict of justice and mercy in both the play and the novel is best described in Hegel's theory of tragedy; see *Hegel on Tragedy*, ed. Anne and Henry Paolucci (Garden City, N.Y., 1962), especially p. 70 ff.

affirm the Christian values of mercy above the savage lust of the community for vengeance. "We are not his judges," comes the reply to Butler's question; "he has been already judged and condemned by lawful authority. We are those whom Heaven, and our righteous anger, have stirred up to execute judgment, when a corrupt government would have protected a murderer" (A, VII, 96). From the standpoint of contemporary politics, Scott might have rejected the revolutionary implications of the people's taking the law into their own hands, because it takes it out of the hands of the state. But as a defender of legal institutions and their integrative social function, Scott might have been swayed by the appeal to "lawful authority"—the mob is defending Scottish national rights and Scottish courts. Even more: it is affirming the foundation of the state itself. Although the convicted murderer claims to have acted "in the lawful exercise of my duty" (A, VII, 96), he has unleashed a chaos of police violence in Edinburgh, and the city rises in an anger that reflects the spirit of the community. By recalling the Porteous affair, Scott suggests not so much the political danger of revolution in the present as the achievement of greater autonomy and maturity in the administration of modern Scotland.

The Porteous episode is, then, a thematic as well as a dramatic introduction to the story of Jeanie and Effie Deans. Dramatically, it provides some of the conditions which complicate the main plot, such as the subsequent disinclination of the Queen to pardon Effie after her pardon of Porteous has been contravened by other Scotsmen. Thematically, it sets in motion an ethical dialectic which gives *The Heart of Midlothian* a specifically historical relevance, relating it to the emergence of a non-aristocratic heroic ideal in modern Scotland, responsive to the need for social justice but anxious to avoid the specter of revolution. Moreover, it frames these historical considerations within a universal perspective by taking up the timeless absolutes of mercy, justice, and the law.

%

In this, as in any, Scottish historical situation, religious issues find a large place. Scott's religious position has never been satisfactorily defined, for it was personal, shifting, and self-contradictory. But the implications of *The Heart of Midlothian* are related to a contemporary religious phenomenon: the rise of evangelicalism in the early years of the nineteenth century. John Buchan has summed up the general position: a primary element of Scott's world-view was "a sense of community, of society as an organic thing where every man's life was linked with that of his fellows. For this reason he disliked the intense preoccupation of a man with his own soul which he thought had been the weakness of Scottish Calvinism, and which the imported evangelicalism from England was reviving north of the Tweed."[6] In the novel, Scott's social attitude is critically applied to the historical roots of this revival: the radical individualism of the Covenanter tradition (whose latter-day exponent is Davie Deans). That it also exposes one aspect of Jeanie may be more difficult to accept. But the kind of religious conscience that is more interested in principles than in situations—that is ready to see human life go down in order to maintain a dogmatic consistency—is precisely the kind Scott's strain of pragmatic humanism could not brook. His ability to see Jeanie as something more than her principles—and as capable of learning by experience to incorporate them in a more humane moral view—is token of his own tendency to modify traditional attitudes for a viable response to the present.

Scott belongs in the tradition of the Moderate party in the Scottish church, along with philosophers like Ferguson (and artists like Burns). It is they who resisted the efforts of the orthodox to make the church central in national life. After Scott drew the fire of the orthodox for his portrayal of the Covenanters in *Old Mortality, The Heart of Midlothian* immediately followed, and was designed to make up for the slight by portraying an old Cameronian in a more sympathetic light. In the event, the novel took the form of a skillful moral re-education for the orthodox—teaching the lesson of charity in dramatic action. But it also portrays a greater strength in the religious culture of Scotland than Scott's moderate views on religious matters might have suggested.

It is only after the Porteous affair that the Deans family is introduced and we at last come to the protagonists of the major action. The third of the introductory chapters devoted to them (VIII, IX, and X) does not merely provide a quaint character sketch of Davie Deans and a mechanical filling-in of Jeanie's background, but establishes

6. John Buchan, *Sir Walter Scott* (London, etc., 1932), p. 365.

the socio-cultural force of Puritanism—or its Scottish equivalent in the Presbyterian church—as the source of some of the operative norms of justice in Scottish national life.[7] Given the Calvinist emphasis on radical evil, God emerges as a stern lawgiver and avenging sword. Jeanie refuses to lie to save her sister largely because of her belief in the Ninth Commandment, which she insists on interpreting as prohibiting the bearing of false witness *for* a neighbor—despite her father's seductive urging to follow the letter of the law and save his daughter's life.

It is generally overlooked in our liberal age, however, that Effie Deans, while innocent of the crime of child-murder with which she is charged, is guilty of breaking the Seventh Commandment. While she is not formally accused of vice, she herself feels the charge strongly enough to project it on Jeanie, sensing she finds her punished for guilty passion: "ye are angry because I love Robertson" (A, xx, 307). Critics who do not admit this as an element of Jeanie's values will find it difficult to accept her failure to lie to help her sister,[8] and are unlikely to appreciate the denouement, in which Effie's tainted moral condition has its appropriate issue in a life of rootlessness, frivolity, and conscience-ridden misery. Scott's treatment of the effects of moral laxity on personality is considerably more complicated than the orthodox idea of the matter, but her career makes us aware of a core of truth in the extreme religious position. Effie is the bearer of the

7. The narrow interpretation of Jeanie's religious burden is given in Winifred Lynskey, "The Drama of the Elect and the Reprobate in Scott's *Heart of Midlothian,*" *Boston University Studies in English,* IV (1960), 39–48, in which Jeanie is described simply as a symbol of the elect and Staunton of the reprobate—as though Scott were merely a religious moralist, and a Calvinist at that! A more historical account of Scott's relation to religious tradition is David Craig, "*The Heart of Midlothian*: Its Religious Basis," *Essays in Criticism,* VIII (1958), 217–25, where Jeanie is seen as the product of a Scottish religious upbringing, with all its inadequacies and historical limitations. The view that Jeanie's experience represents a progressive stage of Scottish culture is suggested in A. O. J. Cockshut, *The Achievement of Walter Scott* (New York, 1969), p. 191: ". . . she, without thought, by the sheer power of her truth and love, working on inherited tradition, guides the covenanting tradition back into a form which is viable in the new age, but more gentle and no less intense than the original form."

8. Dorothy Van Ghent in *The English Novel: Form and Function* (New York, 1961 [1953]), denigrates Jeanie largely for her sexually jealous hostility toward Effie—a position surprising in a critic so sophisticated in the complexity of human motivation.

modern *anomie* that is the greatest threat in the progress of Scottish society, and her story acquires a historical as well as an ethical implication.

In *The Heart of Midlothian,* Scott may be seen taking a hand in reaffirming his country's native strength but also stirring it out of its dogmatic slumber into more supple, more humane ways of dealing with moral issues. Yet Scott was not inventing but expressing a cultural trend, for the country was already on the way to legal reform and ethical relaxation; as we have seen, the very law which is the prime example of excessively severe justice in the novel had already, only nine years before its publication, been repealed. The novel is then rather a celebration of progress achieved than the work of a voice crying in the wilderness. Like other Scott novels, it works by a dialectic of opposed historical values, each of which is given credence in its proper time or domain, but each of which is found to be historically limited and therefore wanting. Out of this array of limited positions Scott projects a universal value, formed by a synthesis of the best in the partial truths. In this novel, the values of tradition and of modernity are brought together: Calvinist justice is to be modified by secular mercy, Scottish communal spirit by loyalty to British authority, while the present age is to be strengthened by rediscovering the moral vigor of its cultural antecedents, of whom Jeanie Deans is the living exemplar.

ॐ

Sooner or later, any critique of *The Heart of Midlothian* must come to an estimate of Jeanie Deans's heroism. It has been well observed by recent critics that Jeanie's famous act at the trial, so forbidding by today's standards, is rooted in a cultural tradition that gives it a meaning larger than the individual—without mitigating its austere chill. Although this position discovers a greater historical depth in the action than had previously been plumbed, it fails to consider its universal literary models—which are in turn wider than the historical reference. Jeanie is in the position of Antigone and other tragic figures confronted by absolute alternatives, each of which has a degree of validity in theory but which are mutually exclusive in practice. The dramatic action takes the form of a process of bringing the heroine to acknowledge the limited validity of her choice, to learn the value of what she has more or less blindly rejected, and thereby to find place for both moral impulses in an enlarged moral vision.

The attitude we are to take toward her action is further defined by Jeanie's answer to the defense attorney's questions about what Effie had told her of her pregnancy (the chief point in the case, on which conviction is predicated). "Nothing," she replies. The lawyer catches up the word: "Nothing? True; you mean nothing at *first* . . ." (A, XXIII, 346). The formal interrogation, the deathly pale and unmovable heroine, the obsessive repetitions of the negatives, gather together to recall the opening scene of *King Lear*. Given this further Shakespearian motif in the novel, it becomes possible to detect the kind of heroine with whom we have to deal. She is a figure of high idealism and unvarying dedication to moral principle, but since that principle excludes all others that conflict with it, her consistency becomes inflexibility, her high principle priggishness, and her idealism destructive pride. Like Shakespeare and (at least by implication) Sophocles, Scott will lead his admirable but limited heroine to a broader conception of morality, one that admits of greater human sympathy than absolute principles usually allow.

The first stage of her development occurs on the trip to London, the next significant stage of the plot. It occurs by means that Scott had only occasional recourse to in his other writings and which here operate with wonderful effect: symbolism derived from literary allusion. Amid the improbable but imaginative adventures with the robber-band in the forest near Grantham—which lies suggestively close to Sherwood Forest—the educative relationship that springs up between Madge Wildfire and Jeanie goes beyond Gothic grotesquerie. Madge here reveals herself to be George Staunton's first sexual victim, then leads Jeanie a Puckish chase through the forest—landing her at the rake's sick-bed to get the full story of her sister's seduction. In the educational process, Madge painfully embarrasses Jeanie at church, and this otherwise comic irrelevancy may be seen as the first stage of taking her down from the high plane of her principles and humanizing her religion with laughter.

Moreover, Madge creates a mad charade whose implications have never been fully explored: "Did ye never read the Pilgrim's

Progress? And you shall be the woman Christiana, and I will be the maiden Mercy—for ye ken Mercy was of the fairer countenance, and the more alluring than her companion—. . ." (B, VI, 89). The pages describing their visit to the Stauntons at Willingham are filled with allusions to *The Pilgrim's Progress*, and give the episode the character of a scene in Bunyan's parable.[9] Madge goes on to sing one of Bunyan's hymns to make the point yet more forcibly:

> He that is down need fear no fall,
>   He that is low no pride;
> He that is humble ever shall
>   Have God to be his guide.
>
> Fulness to such a burthen is
>   That go on pilgrimage;
> Here little, and hereafter bliss,
>   Is best from age to age.
>   (B, VII, 95)

We must take Jeanie to be the target of these lyrics, even if their source is only Madge's reflections on herself. While we need not accuse Jeanie of specific sins of pride, the evidence of her narrowness continues to pile up: e.g., she has never read Bunyan because he was a Baptist and her father had excluded him from his library. Jeanie, we see again, is not to be identified with Davie Deans's orthodoxy, but she is made in her father's image. Her trip to the Queen, so purposive in the plot, comes to assume the nature of a pilgrimage—the word having been added to the context in the second of Bunyan's stanzas. It is a voyage through the Valley of Humiliation to the state of loving-kindness, beyond the toils of law and even justice.

The immediate result of these symbolic associations is to make Jeanie a much more complicated moral being than she has been. She begins to modify her attitude to the law and even her own principles of truth-telling in her response to the worst offender

---

9. For Scott's pleasure in Bunyan and for his approving view of allegory, see his review of Southey's *The Pilgrim's Progress: With a Life of John Bunyan*, in Ioan Williams, ed., *Sir Walter Scott on Novelists and Fiction* (New York and London, 1968). See also Steven Marcus, *Dickens: from Pickwick to Dombey* (New York and London, 1965), p. 73 ff. for a discussion of Bunyan's relevance to other nineteenth-century novels.

—moral and civil—in the novel, Staunton. After Staunton's confession of his past undoing of Madge and Effie, he urges Jeanie to make use of her power to betray him as a means of obtaining a reprieve for her sister. She thereupon engages in a more complex train of reflections than she had previously been capable of:

> The question how far, in point of extremity, she was entitled to save her sister's life by sacrificing that of a person who, though guilty towards the state, had done her no injury, formed the next earnest and most painful subject of consideration. In one sense, indeed, it seemed as if denouncing the guilt of Staunton, the cause of her sister's errors and misfortunes, would have been an act of just, and even providential retribution. But Jeanie, in the strict and severe tone of morality in which she was educated, had to consider not only the general aspect of a proposed action, but its justness and fitness in relation to the actor, before she could be, according to her own phrase, free to enter upon it. What right had she to make a barter between the lives of Staunton and of Effie, and to sacrifice the one for the safety of the other? His guilt—that guilt for which he was amenable to the laws—was a crime against the public indeed, but it was not against her. (B, X, 153–54)

The paragraph catches up one of the novel's moral themes: justice against the offender is renounced in an onset of situational considerations. While employing the introspective sophistication of her religious heritage, Jeanie has dropped its egoism and censoriousness: "What right had she" to judge Staunton. She betrays her underlying hostility to Effie in refusing to consider his crime against her sister as a crime against herself, but she also reveals a new sentiment of mercy toward the penitent sinner.

The morality of mercy is accompanied, however, by a weakening of Jeanie's obedience to the civil law: she reflects in the next paragraph that to betray one of the leaders of the Porteous lynching is to betray a national hero, and this thought excludes any hint of her duty to aid in the apprehension of a criminal. Partly from her father's tradition of preferring the law of God to the law of the state, and partly from a new independence born of her sense of mercy, Jeanie is led to become a withholder of the truth rather than its staunch proclaimer, an emergent individualist rather than a devoted citizen. In her development beyond a simple Protestant ethic, we can trace the growth of new cultural modes in modern Scotland: it has lost its governing religious absolutes, and needs to develop new sources of obligation to a secular social order.

Considered in the course of the dramatic development we have been tracing, Jeanie's great speech to the Queen becomes the crowning event in a process of ethical transformation. To recognize its moral power is not to deny its rhetorical formality (although denigrators of its stock sentiments would do well to compare it with its model, Portia's mercy-speech). This power lies in Jeanie's ability to awaken the Queen's sense of mercy—as well as her anxieties about eternal rewards and punishments:

"Alas! it is not when we sleep soft and wake merry ourselves, that we think on other people's sufferings. Our hearts are waxed light within us then, and we are for righting our ain wrangs and fighting our ain battles. But when the hour of trouble comes to the mind or to the body—and seldom may it visit your Leddyship—and when the hour of death comes, that comes to high and low—lang and late may it be yours —O, my Leddy, then it isna what we hae dune for oursells, but what we hae dune for others, that we think on maist pleasantly. And the thoughts that ye hae intervened to spare the puir thing's life will be sweeter in that hour, come when it may, than if a word of your mouth could hang the haill Porteous mob at the tail of ae tow." (B, XIII, 199)

The Queen's first words of reply are perhaps the only ones possible to a cultured aristocrat after such an emotional onslaught: "This is eloquence." It is indeed, eloquence, but not of the classical kind; it is the eloquence of the pulpit, expounding, for the special benefit of those in high places, not only the virtue of charity but also the remission of the desire for vengeance (in this case, against the Porteous mob). This is the climactic moment in the gradual shift in Jeanie (and, at least temporarily, in the Queen)—from an ethic of justice to an ethic of mercy. At this point, Jeanie herself becomes the "heart" of Midlothian and, by extension, the symbolic spirit of Britain, making its entry into the modern age by modifying its traditional authoritarianism, whether political or religious.

❧

The formal order of the novel—Jeanie's development from a traditional into a modern Scotswoman—contains more than the pattern of the *Bildungsroman*, the novel of education which follows an individual's growth. If Jeanie sums up in herself a period of Scottish history, we should expect to find in her career a record of the successive layers of civilization through which Scotland has passed. In her character can be found the Covenanting tradition of her father, the more broadly based Christian tradition of which Reuben Butler is the spokesman, and the modern pragmatic attitude summed up in the figure of the Duke of Argyle.

Argyle's position as the king-maker who insured the Hanoverians the loyalty of Scotland lies behind his dramatic importance in the novel. A nobleman of Scotland who has nonetheless accepted the English crown—and an imported German version of it, at that— Argyle serves as the cosmopolitan intermediary who brings pure Scots Jeanie into relation with the powers that be in modern Britain. When Jeanie is given a new situation by Argyle on his estate at Roseneath, she not only inherits the rewards of virtue and long suffering but takes her place in the modern Scotland of which Argyle is a leading proprietor. Argyle represents the forces of Scottish economic growth as well as its cultural and political maturation. His interest in advanced scientific farming is the motive that leads him to bring Davie Deans to Roseneath as an adviser in animal husbandry, while his religious moderation—along with his interest in Jeanie—leads him to import Reuben Butler as its Minister. This willingness to assimilate Scottish tradition, whether agricultural or religious, into the new world being created under the symbolic governance of Argyle marks Scott's attempt to portray a new Scottish national community. Roseneath is a symbolic landscape of modern Scotland.

Despite the widely-held view that the fourth volume of *The Heart of Midlothian* is an unnecessary appendage, when Jeanie completes her career at Roseneath the novel comes full circle geographically and resolves its historical and ethical themes. Starting as she does from the east of Scotland near Edinburgh, she makes her way down almost through the length of England, pausing in her travels at Grantham to learn some of the lessons of English low-church piety and aristocratic malaise. After her success in London she makes her way back to the north, by the western route, pausing at Carlisle to witness the destruction of another source of her education: the lynching of Madge Wildfire (and execution of her mother). When she settles down at Roseneath on the Firth of Clyde, she all but completes the circle, roughly on the same latitude as the region of the Firth of Forth from which she began. That her new position is both parallel to yet distinct from her origin suggests the inner quality of Jeanie's development. *The Heart of*

Midlothian is, then, an image of Scottish history in symbolic space as well as in dramatic time, and it expresses its themes in its characters' movements through the world.

The setting of Roseneath is well calculated to provide a total view of Scotland, for it stands at a meeting-point of Lowland civilization and Highland primitivism. Several of the characters in the Roseneath episodes represent the problem of these cultural elements in the new Scottish dispensation. The most dramatic of them is, of course, the Whistler, the child of Effie and Staunton, who reaches an extreme of savagery. If we consider the Whistler's career in other than moralistic terms—although Scott himself is partly responsible for the latter—the Whistler's presence implies a continued tendency toward regression, which remains a possibility even in a rapidly expanding civilization. His parents, on the other hand, mark the movement toward luxury and corruption that the Scottish speculative historians saw threatening a civilization under economic development. Extremes meet: the over-developed sophistication of the Stauntons issues in a reversion to the primitive in the "natural" son, the Whistler.

Throughout the Waverley novels we have seen the "wild spirit of chivalry" at odds with and occasionally schooled by the modern spirit, in the form of bourgeois prudentialism. That wild spirit derives from the folk institutions and aristocratic castes which have dominated societies up to the modern age, and it therefore continues to exercise its colorful but destructive influences in the medieval and Renaissance novels. The novels of Jacobitism suggest that Jacobite chivalry is the last gasp of a social type that has finally run its course, and that the transition in values from anachronistic loyalties to constructive sociability can be made permanent. The new order at Roseneath is the fullest visualization of the character of the new society that Scott gives us: it is not as bourgeois-industrious as the Glasgow of Baillie Jarvie, nor as genteel a retired country life as that which other Waverley heroes inherit, but it represents a productive agricultural community inhabited by dutifully (but not fanatically) traditional families like the Butlers.

How do the characters who are excluded stand to this imagined community? Staunton, who has risen to titled status, is the image of the chivalric hero gone bad: not only in his decadent aristocratic sphere but in his descent into the criminal world, he exhibits the lust for adventure and propensity to bring trouble in his wake that have characterized Scott's medieval knights and Jacobite intriguers. In modern times, the adventurous hero has lost his occupation, and the only outlet of his flamboyant energies is crime: smuggling, seduction, and insurrection (the lynching of Porteous). As Scott set out in the "Essay on Chivalry," the tendency of the chivalric ideals is to fall into their opposites: courtly love into licentiousness, freedom into turmoil, gallantry into mannered absurdity. From Scott's standpoint, then, it is no accident that the Stauntons convert to Catholicism: this is no arbitrary piece of prejudice but a suggestion that Staunton's true era was the Middle Ages, and that in modern life his anachronism is likely to express itself in a reversion to the cultural forms of that time. The age of chivalry is indeed gone, but as it leaves it explodes once more in a pathetic emulation of the past.

Staunton's ejection from life and from history is at the hands of his son, and there is more than retributive justice in the slaying of an errant father by his own bastard. The Whistler is the true son of his father, but at the same time distinct in his historical implications. He reverts not to mere criminality like his father but still further back, to the primitive life of the Highland clans which habitually harry the Lowlands—here, the Roseneath farm. He is the latter-day version not of medieval aristocracy but of the prior stage of heroic values, the clan society. Scott saw the values of the Scottish clans as clearly as he saw the virtues of the chivalric ideal, and he often bursts into his narratives to express his sense of how badly they are needed to uplift the calculating manners of modern, business-minded Scotland. In this his most comprehensive vision of modern Scotland he sets out a drama of the last vestiges of both primitive and medieval heroic values and social norms. In the clear light of the present, they can only strike the beholder as stages to be passed through on the way to modern civilization.

It is, ultimately, the sons of Jeanie and Reuben who shall inherit the future and uphold society in war and in peace—the one destined to be a soldier, the other a lawyer. These are the professions with which the life of Jeanie and, indeed, that of Scotland have been most concerned in *The Heart of Midlothian*, from Porteous's bad soldiery to Jeanie's forensics. Roseneath emerges as an image of a revitalized British society fruitful in its sons who will take charge of the future. And, in a kind of symbolic justice, Jeanie serves as the spiritual queen of this realm in Argyle's absence—the image of Caroline's regency of the larger realm of Britain.

But the Roseneath scenes do not provide images of bounty alone, and the fourth volume—which has been scorned as a fatuous idyl—instead incurs the danger of dissipating its symbolic force by its realistic qualifications. The novel becomes a considerably more complicated vision of history by the addition of its final volume, and our respect for an author who has given us this much must express itself in a faith that he knew what he was about in drawing out the story to its final consequences. For the remaining chapters do not merely confirm Jeanie in the rewards of virtue; they describe the challenges which the new social structure and moral authority will be called upon to face. To end on the note of a Highland Arcadia would have been to create an apocalyptic realm outside of history; to add the Captain of Knockdunder and the Whistler is to bring that realm into the world of politics, crime, and the continued historical experience of Scotland.

It is remarkable that life at Roseneath has been generally considered as an idyl of simple Highland virtues. It is true that, in keeping with comic and romantic conventions, Jeanie's rewards are considerable: there is much stock-taking of material possessions in the burgerly, Robinson Crusoe manner and the mood at meal-times is festive, not stinting the copious listing of delights and dishes. But the effective governor of this utopia is a tyrant; for all his grotesque comedy, the Captain of Knockdunder presents a reminder of the unjust world of history from which the heroine had presumably been withdrawn. In every phase of Knockdunder's administration, the insolence of office proceeds unchecked by the absentee landowner; the Duke's absence resembles that of *Measure for Measure* and other dramas in which the just ruler withdraws in favor of a corrupt governor.[10] When it is a question of installing

10. Several suggestions for Scott's picture of an absentee landlord's high-handed governor may have been provided by the clan chieftan Cameron of Lochiel; as Adam Smith describes him:

It is not thirty years ago since Mr. Cameron of Lochiel, a gentleman of Lochabar in Scotland, without any legal warrant whatever, not being what was then called a lord of regality, nor even a tenant in chief, but a vassal of the Duke of Argyle, and without being so much as a justice of peace, used, notwithstanding, to exercise the highest criminal jurisdiction over his own people. He is said to have done so with great equity, though without any of the formalities of justice; and it is not improbable that the state of that part of the country at that time made it necessary for him to assume this authority in order to maintain the public peace. That gentleman . . . carried, in 1745, eight hundred of his own people into the rebellion with him. (Quoted in Schneider, *op. cit.*, p. 195.)

Reuben Butler as minister, and the Presbyterian-influenced Butler asks for the parish's election ("call") to validate the Duke's award of the living, Knockdunder replies: "Never fash your peard about it, man . . . Leave it a' to me.—Scruple! deil ane o' them has been bred up to scruple ony thing that they're bidden to do" (B, XX, 289). The liveliness of the diction should not blind us to the reality portrayed, nor should Butler's high-mindedness obscure his willingness to accept the way of the world and his living under these conditions. It is with equal acquiescence that the spiritual arm accepts the facts of secular illegality, when Butler inquires about Knockdunder's obvious connivance in smuggling and is bluntly told off. The very situation with which the novel began—the smuggling of Wilson and Staunton—is thus built into the image of new Scotland, as it was historically.

Not only is criminality a constituent element of the regime, but the normal administration of labor suggests its economic character:

The gracious Duncan [Knockdunder], finding matters were at a stand among the workmen, summoned before him the delinquents, and impressed all who heard him with a sense of his authority, by the penalties with which he threatened them for their delay. Mulcting them in half their charge, he assured them, would be the least of it; for, if they were to neglect his pleasure and the Duke's, "he would be tamn'd if he paid them the t'other half either, and they might seek law for it where they could get it." (B, XXI, 295–96)

This legal system, even more than the British government that reprieved Porteous, is based on a negation of law, on the use of legally-vested authority for the perpetration of injustice. The conclusion of the episode shows Knockdunder smoking in church, secure in his legal power to be above the law. The discussion which follows brings out some of the main issues of political philosophy with which the novel is engaged. One of the elders agrees that the Captain's behavior was "far frae beseeming—But what will ye say? . . . He keeps a high hand ower the country, and we couldna deal wi' the Hielandmen without his protection, sin' a' the keys o' the kintray hings at his belt; and he's no an ill body in the main, and maistry, ye ken, maws the meadows doun" (B, XXI, 303). Here is, then, a short definition of traditional government, the people surrendering their freedom for military protection against semi-barbarian enemies, and justifying their acquiescence by the general tolerableness of the rule.

The final judgment is given to Davie Deans, that life-long rebel against all secular authority unguided by spiritual sanctions. Throughout the novel, Scott has treated Deans's political individualism much as he had treated Covenanter fanaticism in *Old Mortality*, as admirable in its integrity but fundamentally antisocial. Now Scott sums up his own picture of Roseneath in Deans's discovery of its nature: he "began to feel from experience, that the glen of Knocktarlitie, like the rest of the world, was haunted by its own special subjects of regret and discontent" (B, XXI, 304). His response to this truth is to begin at last to compromise, to come down from his rigid idealism. He accepts Butler's subscription to the oaths of secular government, which he had bitterly opposed, as inevitable for survival in such a world. But the implication of the Roseneath episode is that the Argyles—representing native leadership and aristocratic noblesse tempered by political sophistication—must rule in their own land if it is to enjoy an enlightened government in tune with its economic and social development.

❧

Despite the marked limitations of existing government, the fruitful order of life at Roseneath would serve to confirm the value of any rule of law, even Knockdunder's. In the final phase of the novel this confirmation is made again by means of an image of utter lawlessness: the life outside society exemplified by the Whistler. In the course of this episode, the primary ethical norm of mercy is no longer placed in tension with abstract justice, but with historical legality. Mercy, which had encouraged flexibility and conciliation in religious justice, now brings about an ironic modification of the political absolute that the laws of the state must be obeyed.

The significance of Scott's creation of the Whistler cannot be minimized by referring to the melodramatic and conventional trappings in which he appears. That this concluding episode was no mere sensational filler is evinced by the fact that Scott departs from the source material on which the novel is based; as noted in his introduction and postscript to the novel, the original child's body *was* found. One of Scott's purposes in inventing a survivor must have been to provide a providential vengeance upon the sinful father, and it must be granted to critics who have protested against the coincidence of his murdering Sir George Staunton that this is one of the weakest turns of the plot, although it is rich in thematic interest. Yet this melodrama and its historical implications may be considered transitional to another ethical situation: the confrontation of Jeanie and the Whistler in the latter's cell. Here, it seems to me, we arrive at the highest emotional peak in a highly emotional novel, and reach at the same time its most profound moral revelation. By freeing the Whistler, Jeanie takes the longest step away from the absolute morality in which she began; she shows mercy, at the expense of retributive justice; she commits a personal rebellion against the civil law based on a sense of higher justice; she allows another criminal to escape the law, but not to infect the body politic—rather to seek his home in a realm of lawlessness away from Scotland.[11]

The crisis of conscience through which Jeanie passes leaves behind even her thoughts on exposing Staunton and her speech to the Queen in point of moral complexity:

"To let him be execute in this dreadful state of mind would be to destroy baith body and soul—and to let him gang I dare not—what will be done?—But he is my sister's son—my own nephew—our flesh and blood—and his hands and feet are yerked as tight as cords can be drawn.—Whistler, do the cords hurt you?" (B, XXVIII, 410)

And Jeanie begins to bargain and quibble, though her decision has been made, partly unaware of it as she is. She cuts his bonds and, when he tries to escape, is prepared to free him on some unspoken condition ("I wunna [let you out], unless you promise——" B, XXVIII, 411), when he relieves her of her difficulty by clearing out. The denouement of the Whistler's career has its own interest—the

11. The classic description of the reversion from an over-refined and repressive civilization to barbarism, with its freedoms as well as its crudities, is Ferguson's (*History of Civil Society*, p. 279):

When the fence is destroyed, the wilds are open, and the herd breaks loose. The pasture of the cultivated field is no longer preferred to that of the desert. The sufferer willingly flies where the extortions of government cannot overtake him; where even the timid and the servile may recollect they are men; where the tyrant may threaten, but where he is known to be no more than a fellow-creature; where he can take nothing but life, and even this at the hazard of his own.

noble savage wending his way to the New World and eventually joining an Indian tribe—but it is Jeanie's development which fulfills the novel: "As Jeanie kept her own secret, the share she had in his escape was not discovered. . ." (B, XXVIII, 411). The paragon of truth, law and justice has become a fallible and typical citizen, affirming an all-too-human sense of the laws which hold society together and yet must be evaded at times for the sake of persons.

The focus of the novel's ethical dialectic lies, then, in the character-changes of Jeanie Deans. But the significance of her development is no more a study of personal psychology than it is an abstract disquisition on philosophic problems. The intensity with which Scott here takes up an individual psyche and an ethical situation may seem uncharacteristic of him, and *The Heart of Midlothian* may remain a thing apart in his *œuvre*, seemingly more modern than his more overtly historical novels. Yet it must be emphasized that this, too, is a historical novel, not by virtue of its setting in time and contact with historical personages (although that is sufficient to qualify it), nor even because of its interest in antiquated customs and values, but because it traces the historical development of cultural modes into their contemporary form. The stages which we have found in the sequence of the plot beautifully crystallize the actual changes that had occurred in Scottish culture from the time of the action to the time of writing. From the predominantly Calvinist ethos of Scottish tradition to the enlightened relativism of Scott's time: this is the cultural transformation which is embodied in the career of the heroine. It is the final triumph of Scott's view of history that he is able to show a grand change of this sort without losing sight of the value of the past in upholding the progressive developments of the present. Calvinism and Enlightenment, Scottish and English elements are superimposed on each other in Jeanie's mind in the way that history adds layers of meaning to an institution like the Tolbooth. This sense of history as the mental and moral experience of living men it is reserved to the work of the great historical novelists to embody. Jeanie Deans becomes a symbol of all Scotland, for the form of the novel reveals her development as exemplifying the processes at work in Scottish history.

The final vision of the novel is of a Britain brought into the modern world. The new regime at Roseneath bears all the marks of the speculative historians' warnings of the threats of high civilization and advanced economic life. Yet if the image of a society governed by the Knockdunders and imperfectly assimilating its aristocracy (typified by the Stauntons as well as by Argyle) does not guarantee social and political progress, we are nevertheless given the image of cultural progress in the development of Jeanie Deans. Not only does she move from puritan tradition toward the more supple culture of the Enlightenment, but she demonstrates that *natural* aristocratic virtue has not died with the passing of aristocratic class-domination. Given that growth and that potentiality, Scott proposes to his countrymen that they recognize in shaping their future both the traditions of the past and the powers at work in the present.

Chapter 4 # Dickens: Visions of revolution

A widely accepted view of *Barnaby Rudge* and *A Tale of Two Cities* acknowledges their status as historical novels but minimizes their historicity by reading them as tracts for their times, thinly-veiled commentaries on the threat of revolution, particularly from the Chartist movement. Substantial evidence has been assembled by Kathleen Tillotson[1] and others to show that Chartist agitation existed at precisely the time the first novel was being written, and that the English upper classes had reason to be alarmed at the potentialities for subversion. Partly as a result of this view of the novels' political reference, they have often been found wanting as fiction; a subtler view of them as historical novels may lead to a higher estimate. The present study has postulated that historical novels are historical in some degree because they are concerned with their own time and place. But just as a historical novelist may overdo his contemporaneity, a reader's urge to discover contemporary implications may make him blind to the historicity of a

---

1. Introduction to *Barnaby Rudge* (London, New York and Toronto, n.d. [1954]), p. vii. Further political reference has been provided in the chapter on *Barnaby Rudge* in Steven Marcus's *Dickens: From Pickwick to Dombey* (London, 1965). While Marcus emphasizes the novel's relevance to Dickens's age—as revealing the psychological distortions created by the "unresolved contradictions" of Victorian society—he also discusses the persistent presence in English radical movements of a traditionalist "demand that antecedent justice be restored" (p. 181). The utopian strain in Dickens's popular tradition needs to be further developed and brought to bear on his political and historical views.

novel.[2] Criticism must be on guard against the fallacy of historical relativism which reduces every projection of the past to a commentary on the present simply because it is the view of a present perspective. A closer reading shows these novels to be not clarion-calls by a thoroughly frightened upholder of the *status quo*, but complex visions of social permanence and change, of the persistence of the past and the inevitable transition beyond it.

The meager expressions of Dickens's political sentiments at the time of writing *Barnaby Rudge* reveal a broadly radical tendency, given the implications of the term in contemporary parlance: "By Jove how radical I am getting!" he wrote to Forster on August 13, 1841; "I wax stronger and stronger in the true principles every day." This, like most of Dickens's political statements, does not amount to an unambiguous assertion of views, but it does mark a drift. There is also apparent in the letters a tendency to identify himself with the rioters: "I have just burnt into Newgate, and am going in the next number to tear the prisoners out by the hair of their heads." The customary explanation of such radicalisms relies on the Edmund Wilson-George Orwell thesis[3] that Dickens, despite (or because of) his virulent antipathy to revolution and deeply-ingrained conservatism, was at heart a rebellious hater of his society and perhaps of all social order—indeed, that the respectable-Victorian-social-climber in him repressed his intense hostility to society and allowed it to emerge only in sporadic strains of violent energy in his fiction. Despite the force of the Marxian and Freudian assumptions of this view, one cannot identify Dickens's latent anarchism with the outspokenly condemned nihilism of the rioters in *Barnaby Rudge*. He is not expressing his radical feelings on one

2. Dickens was prepared to find such readers: ". . . Barnaby Rudge has nothing to do with factories, or negroes—white, black, or parti-coloured. It is a tale of the riots of Eighty, before factories flourished as they did thirty years afterwards, and containing—or intended to contain—no allusion to cotton lords, cotton slaves, or anything that is cotton"; *The Letters of Charles Dickens* (Pilgrim Edition), eds. Madeline House and Graham Storey (Oxford, 1965 ff.), I, 507. The quotations below are from vols. II, 357 and II, 377 of this edition.

3. Cf. Wilson, "Dickens: The Two Scrooges," in *The Wound and the Bow: Seven Studies in Literature* (London, 1961 [1941]), especially pp. 17–20 on the historical novels, and pp. 25–26 for the rebellion thesis; and *The Collected Essays, Journalism and Letters of George Orwell*, ed. Sonia Orwell and Ian Angus (New York, 1968), I, 419–23 on the historical novels and I, 460 for a summary of the thesis.

level and reproving them on another, but distinguishing between an observable social urge toward the abyss and his own urge toward social health and regeneration, which may take the form of revolution as it does in *A Tale of Two Cities.*

While it takes a comprehensive view of all strata of English society, *Barnaby Rudge* is largely occupied with the class which Dickens's early fiction made its hallmark. The milieu of these novels has been vaguely described as that of the "lower" or "working" class, depending on the commentator's sociological sophistication, but it is not working class at all. The name given to the lowest portion of the city poor by Marx-inspired sociologists is *Lumpenproletariat,* the proletarians in rags: criminals, beggars, chronically unemployed, the mental, physical and moral rejects of society— what Dickens in the novel calls "the very scum and refuse of London."[4] In the *Communist Manifesto,* Marx describes this as "the 'dangerous class,' the social scum, that passively rotting mass thrown off by the lowest layers of the old society, [which] may, here and there be swept into the movement by a proletarian revolution; its conditions of life, however, prepare it far more for the part of a bribed tool of reactionary intrigue."[5] Historically, from ancient Rome to Weimar Germany, this asocial class has always been a danger to the neat arrangements of the other classes. The déclassés do not want a workers' state but a return to some symbolic earlier condition of society, or a reduction of social life to no order at all. Therefore, they are putty in the hands of nationalists, racists, and militarists of the right, and rarely follow the working class or the political left; usually, strike-breakers, secret police and militia are recruited here. It is this class that is the subject of *Barnaby Rudge*: the list of Gordon's supporters is made up of "widow's mites," "scavengers," "link boys" (torch-bearers), "anti-Popish prisoners in Newgate," "the 'Prentice Knights"–in general, the poorest and most degraded denizens of the London slums. It is true, however, that their *anomie* is easily spread to the proletariat proper: "sober

---

4. Chapter XLIX, page 374. All quotations are from the Oxford Illustrated Dickens, which follows the text of the Charles Dickens and Nonesuch editions; citations are henceforward inserted parenthetically in the text by chapter and page number.

5. In *Basic Writings on Politics and Philosophy: Karl Marx and Friedrich Engels*, ed. Lewis S. Feuer (Garden City, N. Y., 1959), p. 18.

workmen, going home from their day's labour, were seen to cast down their baskets of tools and become rioters in an instant . . ." (LIII, 403).

The first thing to be said about the Gordon Riots, the historical event on which the novel focuses, is that they were—and Dickens portrays them as—not a revolution but a pogrom. The point would probably be clearer to modern readers if the victims of the riots were Jews rather than Catholics, for the physical form and emotional content of the violence were much the same as those of recent memory. The Catholics attacked were generally wealthy, the inheritors of popular religious hostility and accusations concerning fantastic past crimes, and easy victims—given the indifference of the authorities to their plight. The dereliction of duty by the Lord Mayor which so outraged Dickens is, he makes clear, caused not so much by cowardice or incompetence as by his belief that Catholics are not necessarily protected by the laws—that is, that they are an alien body who may be flung to the mobs with impunity (LXI, 468). When the state excludes some groups from its protection, anarchy may be said to have already infected the social order.

The contemporary reference of Dickens's historical vision is unambiguously stated in his preface: the Gordon Riots "teach a good lesson. That what we falsely call a religious cry is easily raised by men who have no religion, and who in their daily practice set at nought the commonest principles of right and wrong; that it is begotten of intolerance and persecution; that it is senseless, besotted, inveterate and unmerciful; all History teaches us" (p. xxiv). Putting these clauses in other terms, we find him saying: religious demagogues are a special danger to modern societies (Dickens is among the first to represent the modern demagogue in fiction—see the dialogue of Gordon and Gashford in Chapter xxxv); the *Lumpenproletariat* is the readiest resource of the demagogue, and is motivated by "intolerance and persecution"—i.e., the intolerance and persecution of that class by society motivates it to similar treatment of religious minorities; the legal breaches that occur in the persecution of any portion of society reflect a general moral breakdown and engender a slackening of the bonds that hold society together. Dickens's preface is alive to the fact that all right-thinking readers are already aware of these truths, but his emphasis on the lesson of "History" suggests that he viewed them from a perspective wider than the topical. It is not the Chartists or other Victorian mobs that Dickens has in mind but the anarchic tendency in modern civilization at large.

It may be objected that the distinction I have drawn between the *Lumpenproletariat* and the working class is one that Dickens, because of the limitations of his time or of his own mind, could not have drawn. There is, however, one genuine worker in the novel, and Dickens's conception of him reveals both the subtlety of his powers of discrimination and the sources of his sociological notions. Gabriel Varden, for whom the novel was tentatively named, is portrayed not only as a courageous hero in his opposition to the storming of Newgate, but as a Carlylian hero of labor:

No man who hammered on at a dull monotonous duty, could have brought such cheerful notes from steel and iron; none but a chirping, healthy, honest-hearted fellow, who made the best of everything, and felt kindly towards everybody, could have done it for an instant. . . . It was a perfect embodiment of the still small voice. . . . There he stood working at his anvil, his face all radiant with exercise and gladness, his sleeves turned up, his wig pushed off his shining forehead—the easiest, freest, happiest man in all the world. (XLI, 307)

Now Varden is, of course, a special kind of worker, a self-employed skilled craftsman, still partaking of the ethos and socio-economic position of the guild master. But he belongs—and Dickens's description enforces this—to the manually *working* class; as he introduces himself to the effete aristocrat, Sir John Chester, "I am a working-man, and have been so, all my life" (LXXV, 575). He is dedicated to labor by the "still small voice" of duty and fulfills his humanity as well as earning a livelihood by it. This is Dickens's conception of the true working man, and he upholds him as a faintly comic model of social health, without committing himself on the workers' political demands in his own day.

What Dickens leaves out of account is just this working class development, and the omission may partly account for the novel's relative lack of sociological timeliness. Not too much but too little contemporaneity may have caused *Barnaby Rudge* to suffer as a historical novel. The mass of the working class consisted—even by 1780—of factory or cottage laborers who were not, like Varden, able to make a jingle or a hymn out of their monotonous motions. They were not craftsmen but adjuncts of the machine. There is one look at them in the novel, during the description of Barnaby's flight with his mother after Rudge returns:

> In a small English country town, the inhabitants of which supported themselves by the labour of their hands in plaiting and preparing straw for those who made bonnets and other articles of dress and ornament from that material,—concealed under an assumed name, and living in a quiet poverty which knew no change, no pleasures, and few cares but that of struggling on from day to day in one great toil for bread,—dwelt Barnaby and his mother. (XLV, 339)

There is no sentimentality here about the life of the mass of Englishmen, merely a recognition that it is devoid of the elements of a humane culture. It is not, however, the quality of life that by itself creates revolutions, and Dickens leaves out—although he was acutely aware of—the more outrageous and revolution-provoking aspects of factory labor. *Barnaby Rudge* is set in London and Chigwell, the metropolis and the village, not in the new towns of the industrial revolution.

Even with this chosen limitation of perspective, Dickens's portrayal of the historical significance of the Gordon Riots is broader than an explanation on sociological grounds. The *Lumpenproletariat*, he holds, is "composed for the most part of the very scum and refuse of London, whose growth was fostered by bad criminal laws, bad prison regulations, and the worst conceivable police . . ." (XLIX, 374). The riots are not, then, a revolt created by the misery of the proletariat; they are the result of a failure of government to perform its elementary function of containing the criminal elements.[6] From this standpoint—which Dickens shared with the Utilitarian reformers—the solution is obvious: repeal of the so-called "hanging laws," creation of a responsible police force, and progressive prison design to replace the horrors of Newgate. All of these were tenets of Dickens's humanitarian program, but much of it had already been accomplished by the time of his writing. Thus the well-established charge that Dickens's social criticism was often the beating of a dead horse has a special bearing on a historical novel like *Barnaby Rudge*. That many of the abuses it portrays had already been reformed makes its portrayal historical: it is a

---

6. Cf. Philip Collins, *Dickens and Crime* (London, 1962); for *Barnaby Rudge* in particular, see pp. 44–51, 220–25.

novel which celebrates the progress of the present beyond the "bad old times." To this extent it expresses an Enlightenment attitude to history that was carried on in Victorian progressivism.

Dickens's attitude to the past is among the most complicated in a century that usually expressed its anxiety about change by various forms of nostalgia. Pre-eminent reformer that Dickens was, he was not proof against the heritage of antiquarianism. The Old Curiosity Shop appears in every Dickens novel in various forms of quaintness, to which one breed of Dickensian is still devoted. But Dickens held in contempt the reactionary mystique that was often associated with it. We may put in evidence certain texts that have not been quoted as extensively as they deserve. There is "The Fine Old English Gentleman, to be said or sung at all Conservative dinners."[7] a political squib that Dickens wrote at the time he was working on *Barnaby Rudge* and that evinces his superiority to any politics of nostalgia. Then there is *A Child's History of England*, which he began planning in 1843, a few years after the novel. It maintains a thoroughgoing "crimes and follies" view of English history down to 1688, with passing comment on antiquarian political attitudes, e.g., "A number of charming stories and delightful songs arose out of the Jacobite feelings, and belong to the Jacobite times. Otherwise I think the Stuarts were a public nuisance altogether" (p. 531). Putting aside both the exaggeration involved in political satire and the oversimplifications of a children's book, what is under fire in both these pieces is the "Tory" habit of mind: a veneration of the past simply because of its patina of age. In *Barnaby*, Dickens never misses an occasion for sarcastic remarks about the rhetoric of conservatism, putting them in the mouth of Dennis after his description of the hanging of Mary Jones (XXXVII, 284), and summing up his account of the country squire who persecutes Barnaby by citing the Tory encomia that would be showered upon him for doing so (XLVII, 357).

We may refer Dickens's attitudes toward the past to a turn in the fortunes of Romanticism and the emergence of a complex Victorian spirit. He is deeply committed to certain virtues that may have flourished in the past, but he is equally convinced that history

7. The poem is given in John Forster, *The Life of Charles Dickens*, ed. A. J. Hoppé (London, 1966 [1872–74]), I, 164–65.

as a whole is a deeply flawed state of affairs. In the view of J. Hillis Miller, "the most important single change in Dickens' novels, and the true turning point of his imaginative development, is a reversal which corresponds to a fundamental transformation of attitude in his century. This change can be defined as the rejection of the past, the given, and the exterior as sources of selfhood, and a reorientation toward the future and toward the free human spirit itself as the only true sources of value."[8] We may locate the underlying change in the emergence of the speculative and liberal historians, in the acceleration of Victorian political and social reform, or in the broad march of the idea of progress. Dickens's stature as a historical novelist must be measured by his maintaining the dual perspective on past and present that Scott had established,[9] but which had been lost on his immediate followers. For Dickens, as for Scott, a mixture of antiquarianism and progressivism in contemplating the spectacle of the past permits him to make genuine historical fiction. Both impulses are at work in *Barnaby Rudge*.

℘

The novel has been sometimes read as a spontaneous overflow of Dickens's powerful feelings about the French Revolution, which is cast in the form of an English equivalent of mob violence in the years just before 1789. One implication of this view—that the fear of the mob in *Barnaby* and *A Tale of Two Cities* is a sublimation of Dickens's fear of Chartist agitation—may be found wanting, but another of its implications calls for attention. In imagining rebellion not in the alien atmosphere of France but in the relatively

8. J. Hillis Miller, *Charles Dickens: The World of His Novels* (Cambridge, Mass., 1958), p. 333. Dickens's is not, to be sure, the progressivism of the Utilitarian reformers but, as Humphry House has suggested, it does resemble that of non-Utilitarian liberal historians like Buckle; see *The Dickens World* ed. Humphry House (London, 1941), pp. 173–74. Especially relevant to *Barnaby Rudge* is Buckle's thesis that "Every great reform which has been effected has consisted, not in doing something new, but in undoing something old"—one of his main illustrations being archaic legal institutions. House develops the relation of Buckle's extreme Liberalism and of Dickens's later despair of government, and raises important questions about that anarchic tendency of the middle class known as *laissez-faire*.

9. Dickens's literary relations with Scott are developed most fully in Wilhelm Dibelius, *Charles Dickens* (Leipzig and Berlin, 1916), pp. 138–43.

recent past of England, Dickens can express not a mere phobia of revolution but a powerful sense of transition—a sense of the passing of old England that informs even his novels of contemporary life. Without stinting the crimes and follies of the past or the marks of progress in the present, Dickens evokes the pathos of historical change more vividly in *Barnaby Rudge* than his anti-antiquarianism might have been expected to allow.

The opening chapter, with its description of the Maypole Inn—which, together with the Haredale estate, the Warren, constitutes the rural contrast to the novel's London scenes—immediately raises the theme of historical change and loss:

> In the year 1775, there stood upon the borders of Epping Forest, at a distance of about twelve miles from London—measuring from the Standard in Cornhill, or rather from the spot on or near to which the Standard used to be in days of yore—a house of public entertainment called the Maypole; which fact was demonstrated to all such travellers as could neither read nor write (and at that time a vast number both of travellers and stay-at-homes were in this condition) by the emblem reared on the roadside over against the house, which, if not of those goodly proportions that Maypoles were wont to present in olden times, was a fair young ash, thirty feet in height, and straight as any arrow that ever English yeoman drew. (I, 1)

The emphasis of the passage falls equally on the virtues and on the transiency of the past, which accounts for the faintly ironic archaisms of the prose. The time of mythic grandeur, of well-proportioned Maypoles and straight-arrowed English yeomen, is already past in the eighteenth century (if it ever existed). That period in turn is seen as a time when a "vast number" of men were illiterate, and this tends to detract from its pastoral advantages over the present. The Standard—suggesting both a geographical and a moral norm—is gone, and men must trace their course from their historical memory of its position. If this condition pervades even the period of *Barnaby Rudge*, it is much more the case for Dickens's time.

There follows a typically rationalist debunking of the Maypole's legendary antiquity, jibing at the credulity of Englishmen in tales of their sovereigns' exploits, and concluding: "Whether these, and many other stories of the like nature, were true or untrue, the Maypole was really an old house, a very old house, perhaps as old as it claimed to be, and perhaps older, which will sometimes happen with houses of an uncertain, as with ladies of a certain, age" (i, 1–2). The ensuing description of the house itself is, however, not in the manner of Augustan wit but in that Romantic symbolism:

With its overhanging stories, drowsy little panes of glass, and front bulging out and projecting over the pathway, the old house looked as if it were nodding in its sleep. Indeed, it needed no very great stretch of fancy to detect in it other resemblances to humanity. The bricks of which it was built had originally been a deep dark red, but had grown yellow and discoloured like an old man's skin; the sturdy timbers had decayed like teeth; and here and there the ivy, like a warm garment to comfort it in its age, wrapt its green leaves closely round the time-worn walls. (i, 2)

The organic metaphor does more than humanize the house; it connects it with the processes of history itself, moving through cycles of growth and decay, yet retaining its continuity and values. In the subsequent vision of the glow of the setting sun upon the house and upon the perennial oaks and chestnuts of the adjacent Epping Forest, the house assumes the symbolic stature of the nation as a whole. Dickens concludes his account of the Maypole with a faith that "he" (the pronoun is significant) seemed to have "many good years of life in him yet."

At the opposite pole from this Romantic image of history (with its sceptical touches of whimsy) lies the other major focus of historical life, London:

And, now, [Gabriel Varden] approached the great city, which lay outstretched before him like a dark shadow on the ground, reddening the sluggish air with a deep dull light, that told of labyrinths of public ways and shops, and swarms of busy people. Approaching nearer and nearer yet, this halo began to fade, and the causes which produced it slowly to develop themselves. Long lines of poorly lighted streets might be faintly traced, with here and there a lighter spot, where lamps were clustered round a square or market, or round some great building; after a time these grew more distinct, and the lamps themselves were visible; slight, yellow specks, that seemed to be rapidly snuffed out, one by one, as intervening obstacles hid them from the sight. Then, sounds arose—the striking of church clocks, the distant bark of dogs, the hum of traffic in the streets; then outlines might be traced—tall steeples looming in the air, and piles of unequal roofs oppressed by chimneys; then, the noise swelled into a louder sound, and forms grew more distinct and numerous still, and London—visible in the darkness by its own faint light, and not by that of Heaven—was at hand. (iii, 26).

This historical realm is approached not mythically but phenomeno-logically, following the perspective of someone approaching the city and building up a manifold out of his discrete sensory impressions. We are introduced to London as a busily functional world of ends and means, thoroughly secular and self-generating—but niggardly—in its provision of light.

Given these two historical realms, the action of *Barnaby Rudge* is organized as a tension between them or, more precisely, as a dramatic explosion of expansive force from the metropolis which contaminates and terrorizes the countryside. In the full tide of the riots, this force engulfs the Maypole itself, in an image of de-struction more poignant than the London horrors:

> . . . the Maypole peered ruefully in through the broken window, like the bowsprit of a wrecked ship; the ground might have been the bottom of the sea, it was so strewn with precious fragments. Currents of air rushed in, as the old doors jarred and creaked upon their hinges; the candles flickered and guttered down, and made long winding-sheets. . . . John [Willet] saw this desolation, and yet saw it not. He was perfectly contented to sit there, staring at it, and felt no more indignation or discomfort in his bonds than if they had been robes of honour. So far as he was per-sonally concerned, old Time lay snoring, and the world stood still. (LV, 417)

The imagery is consistently suggestive of death: the mob has re-duced a beautiful and beneficent part of civilization to the chaos of inorganic nature. John Willet, while a fool and domestic tyrant, is bereft of his proud connection with the past, and thereby re-duced to idiocy. Joe Willet revives the Maypole at the denoue-ment, but its real continuation is in the antiquarian memory, specifically in the mock-Maypole created for his father in his cottage (Chapter the Last, pp. 632–3).

There are, then, two realms in conflict: the explosive or dynamic force that bursts from London and the traditional equilibrium of the rest of England, typified by the folkish atmosphere of Chig-well and mildly satirized in the initially comic scenes at the May-pole. Yet these realms show more similarities than their structural antithesis would suggest: the Maypole and the Warren, the neighbor-ing country-house, are shot through with crime and parental op-pression among the Rudges, Willets, and Chesters, as Steven Marcus has shown. Moreover, the present decay is an extension of de-generation in the past: the Maypole's decline had already begun in the course of changing from a Tudor mansion to an inn (x, 78). By the same token, London is not merely an emergent new society for even its revolutionary currents are laden with traditional baggage: the apprentices who participate in the riots are haunted by conservative notions of their traditional liberties under an idealized medieval guild society (VIII, 65). Even the scavengers of the *Lumpenproletariat* decorate their shanties at Green Lanes with turrets, clock towers, and rude arbors (XLIV, 334–35).

We come to see that the historicity of this historical novel proceeds less from its setting in a specific past or reference to a topical present than from its symbolic embodiment of the transitional character of English society at large. Whatever its limitations as a detailed historical description of late-eighteenth-century England, *Barnaby Rudge* exhibits an important quality of historical fiction in that it shows man's life to be historical, i.e., shaped by the real and imaginative forms that have descended to him from the past. In the course of its protean changes, England—both city and country—is seen being shaped by men in the image of their historical memory. What makes *Barnaby Rudge* a historical novel, then, is not its accurate description of the Gordon Riots, or its account of the "abuses" of the times, or even its entry into the lower ranges of the social structure in its attempt at a comprehensive picture of eighteenth-century England. It is *Barnaby Rudge*'s achievement to make historical transition itself the subject of a novel.

The dominant emotion with which the novel leaves us is neither the hopeful sense of an open future, in line with Victorian ideas of progress, nor a nostalgic resistance to change (which is here regarded as inevitable and constant), but a sense of the great weight to be moved in any transcendence of the past. If the novel is an expression of Dickens's deep-set fears of the end of social order, it also bears his sense of the sheer persistence of the past, even amid change, which makes for social permanence.

The devils who have been found to populate the prose[10] are the burden of the past, which must be called up before they are

10. James K. Gottshall, "Devils Abroad: The Unity and Significance of *Barnaby Rudge*," *Nineteenth Century Fiction*, XVI (1961), 133–46. See also Harold F. Folland, "The Doer and the Deed: Theme and Pattern in *Barnaby Rudge*," *PMLA*, LXXIV (1959), 406–17.

exorcised. In the *Walpurgisnacht* of riot, this residue is itself consumed: "the wretched victims of a senseless outcry, became themselves the dust and ashes of the flames they had kindled" (LXVIII, 526). Nothing emerges from the flames, but they have burned themselves out; there is no return to complacency at the close, only exhaustion and a willingness to start afresh. That the novel achieves this catharsis esthetically justifies the grotesquely exaggerated mob-scenes (so often praised for their realism). Yet *Barnaby Rudge* stops short of envisioning a social conflagration that can accelerate the organic growth of the age. In his second historical novel, Dickens raises history to myth and discovers a redemptive pattern in the holocaust that allows for transcendence within history, if not beyond it.

ℰ

In great measure, *A Tale of Two Cities* is a re-imagining of the vision of revolution in *Barnaby Rudge*, in the course of which Dickens discovers potential renewal in self-sacrifice and social upheaval. The structure of plot elements brings the thematic unity of the two novels into focus. In each, an evil aristocrat (Chester; Monseigneur) has committed a crime of sexual exploitation (abandoning a pregnant gipsy woman and leaving her to a life of crime and the gallows; destroying the family of Mme. Defarge in the course of seducing her sister). This primal sexual sin breeds glowering vengeance in the survivors (Hugh; Mme. Defarge), who become leaders of the mob when the proper historical moment arrives. In each case, a supplementary crime (Rudge's murder of Haredale; the imprisonment of Dr. Manette) widens the circle of guilt and implication in the subsequent rebellion (to Barnaby and his mother; to Darnay and Lucie Manette). The inheritors of the guilt are largely innocent, but cannot rid themselves of association with their ancestors' crimes. Both Barnaby and Darnay are tried and found guilty, but their innocence (or the suffering of their women-folk) leads to their redemption (Barnaby's reprieve; Darnay's escape through Carton's self-sacrifice). Other elements of the action support the central fable: the rebellion burns up the country-houses of the aristocracy (the Warren; the Evrémonde chateau) and invades the prisons of the Old Regime (Newgate; the Bastille); a good aristocrat emerges to counter the evil ones (Haredale kills Chester in a duel; Darnay renounces the feudal privileges of his line).

Apart from the similar working of their fables, both novels revolve around the legal institutions of the two nations, as they are dramatized in a series of trial scenes. Behind the trials we hear of the great crimes of the legal system in the past (the execution of Mary Jones, which is the model for that of Hugh's mother; the public torture of the would-be regicide, Damiens). We do not see the trials of the conspirators in *Barnaby Rudge*, but the *Tale's* picture of Darnay's English and French trials gives us a view of both nations' legality. At the English trial the prosecutor uses demimondaine informers to make his case, the judge is prejudiced against Darnay because of his pro-American remarks, and there is a hovering threat of a sentence to a punishment not much different from Damiens' (Book Two, II, 57). Darnay's two trials by French, revolutionary courts are even more haphazard in proceeding and precipitously willing to convict on emotionally charged evidence. Yet both systems are also capable of humane feelings and justice: Darnay is acquitted by the English jury, suspicious of the police spies who testify against him, and (at least initially) by the French court, in personal response to Dr. Manette's testimony. Both legal systems exist amid—indeed, are fed by—the lawlessness and brutality of the *Lumpenproletariat*, which fills both the English and French courtrooms and which is motivated primarily by the desire for blood.

The *Tale* not only parallels the view of England in *Barnaby Rudge* but extends it to its view of France: this is a tale of two realms of historic crime, not a simple contrast between them. It is not a complete account of either English or French society in the late eighteenth century, but it creates the consistent milieu of major historical novels. The effort to portray this milieu is unsuccessful when it sets up as a cultural history of the period, e.g., at the Monseigneur's reception in Book Two, Chapter VII; Dickens does not know enough to write *Kulturgeschichte*. But he is one of the first novelists to adopt the Romantic historians' view of a nation—in this case, as the title and structure affirm, of two nations—as a cultural unity.

Moreover, Dickens's view of the Revolution as—to use Conrad's term—a "great outburst of morality," the inevitable outgrowth of the state of society under the Old Regime,[11] is not a historically specific one as compared with, e.g., Carlyle's—much less De Tocqueville's. But it makes a similar sweeping attempt to portray the shaping of national destinies. *A Tale of Two Cities* is not, any more than is *The French Revolution*, verifiable history, but it is on a par with Carlyle's work as historical art in establishing a mythic pattern for the event which shows it transforming the lives of social groups as well as of individuals. By this myth, Dickens, like Carlyle, aimed to induce his contemporaries to take a more profound view of their own condition—not by crude warnings of revolution but by a deepening of their historical imagination.[12]

In Dickens's search for a historical equivalent of the Christian mythos, Carlyle's similar search and discovery of the redemptive resources of man in history were before his mind. Support for almost any political position or theory of history can be gathered from Carlyle's work, and the ambivalence of his attitudes toward the French Revolution makes his history of it particularly ambiguous. Perhaps the best summary is that of an unsympathetic critic of the latter, which points out the imaginative sources from which its confusion and its power derive:

Society is a self-generating organism and revolutions are legitimate forces released to crush decaying institutions. On the other hand there are reflexions which see the Revolution as a violent punishment. The Revolution can also be seen in the context of a theory of historical cycles, or it can be said that it provided scope for the action of Carlyle's heroes. The abundant contradictions baffle any attempt to reduce Carlyle's views to a system. The mob is the beast and the mob is the hero,

11. Though there is wide recognition that Dickens acknowledged the justice as well as the inevitability of the Revolution, while deploring its violence and madness, it has not been as widely noted that he goes out of his way to convince his countrymen of it, e.g., "There could have been no such Revolution, if all laws, forms, and ceremonies, had not first been so monstrously abused, that the suicidal vengeance of the Revolution was to scatter them all to the winds" (Book Three, IX, 300). Dickens's contemporary relevance is to warn not against the Chartists or other radicals but against the anti-Jacobins of his own time, who doubted the need for reform; see Book Two, XXVI, 226, for Stryver's profession of these doubts, and the author's comment.

12. The relationships of the two works are considered in Earle Davis, *The Flint and the Flame: The Artistry of Charles Dickens* (Columbia, Mo., 1963), pp. 244–50, and in G. Robert Stange, "Dickens and the Fiery Past: *A Tale of Two Cities* Reconsidered," *English Journal*, XLIV (1957), 381–90.

the mob is incited, and the mob is nature itself, genuine and morally authoritative. The Revolution is sansculottism, born with anarchy and dead with Thermidor, but it is also history incarnate, a microcosm of world change, the authentic process designed by God.[13]

These contradictions insure that *The French Revolution*'s influence on other writers will bear out their historical and personal concerns. In Dickens's case, his choice was not its expressions of classical or Eastern views of history as an unceasing flux, or as a cycle whose constant passage leaves the world much as it was, but its Biblical, prophetic vision of a regenerative process at work in history—with or without an implication of divine providence.

The Carlylian variety of historical process that animates the *Tale* is not that of endless change or even that of organic growth. Both these types figure strongly in *The French Revolution* but there is also an undercurrent of a view that dominated Carlyle's historical speculations in the 'thirties: the notion of palingenesis, taken from the Saint-Simonians (or from German romantics) and wedded to Carlyle's inherited providentialism.[14] This theory of historical periodicity—one supremacy after another falling into conflagration and giving way phoenix-like to the next—allowed a place for the warring forces of good and evil, the inheritance of historical guilt, and the cycle of rise and fall in the mighty of the earth. In sum, it provided a secular equivalent for many elements of the Biblical prophets' vision of history.

As John Holloway has described them,[15] Carlyle's narrative methods are rooted in a Romantic organicist metaphysic, among whose principles are these: that the world, both of nature and of history, is dynamic; that its natural course is destruction and renewal; and that change is usually effected in cataclysmic moments of conflict, which give way to renewed organic growth. Carlyle

13. H. Ben-Israel, "Carlyle and the French Revolution," *Historical Journal*, 1 (1958), 134.

14. For Carlyle's cyclical and regenerative theories, see Hill Shine, *Carlyle and the Saint-Simonians: The Concept of Historical Periodicity* (Baltimore, 1941). For his inveterately prophetic (or Calvinist) view of historical struggle, see René Wellek, *Confrontations: Studies in the Intellectual and Literary Relations Between Germany, England, and the United States During the Nineteenth Century* (Princeton, 1965), pp. 82–113.

15. John Holloway, *The Victorian Sage: Studies in Argument* (London, 1953), pp. 58–85.

is especially awestruck before the spectacle of mass revolution, seeing it as destructive demonism but also as creative Dionysian energy. He values it because it breaks down men's habitual state of egoism, rationalism, and selfishness, inspires the mob to be god-hungry if not god-like, and makes it willing even to destroy itself in the effort to transcend its normal condition:

> Whatsoever is cruel in the panic frenzy of Twenty-five million men, whatsoever is great in the simultaneous death-defiance of Twenty-five million men, stand here in abrupt contrast near by one another. As indeed is usual when a man, how much more when a Nation of men, is hurled suddenly beyond the limits. For Nature, as green as she looks, rests everywhere on dread foundations, were we further down; and Pan, to whose music the Nymphs dance, has a cry in him that can drive all men distracted.[16]

This is no longer Romantic organicism but a discovery of the unconscious "death-defiance" and leap "beyond the limits" that fuels historical upheavals. In descending to the irrational sources of cultural change, Carlyle anticipates the modern readings of the Pan and Dionysus myths by Nietzsche, Lawrence, and Freud.[17]

Here is also a discovery of the potentialities for renewal in individuals and nations. Carlyle's explanation of the Reign of Terror is an eschatological one: ". . . the black desperate battle of Men against their whole Condition and Environment,—a battle, alas, withal, against the Sin and Darkness that was in themselves as in others: this is the Reign of Terror. Transcendental despair was the purport of it, though not consciously so. . . . Despair, pushed far enough, completes the circle, so to speak; and becomes a kind of genuine productive hope again." The effort to overcome "Sin and Darkness" by more sin and darkness is an effort to transcend the human condition within history, and despite its "bad faith" in substituting historical for divine means of salvation, the question of its efficacy is not prejudged by Carlyle. Without determining its outcome, he describes it as "genuine productive hope."

---

16. *The French Revolution: A History* (New York [Modern Library Edition], n.d. [1837]), p. 473. Subsequent quotations are from pp. 635 and 726–27.

17. The latest study of this relationship is Albert J. LaValley, *Carlyle and the Idea of the Modern: Studies in Carlyle's Prophetic Literature and Its Relation to Blake, Nietzsche, Marx, and Others* (New Haven and London, 1968).

If it is remarkable that a politically unreliable, lapsed-Calvinist, Victorian prophet should be capable of such strikingly modern views of history and eschatology, how much more surprising is it that an unintellectual novelist should in his historical fiction approximate them! It is not certain how early Dickens read *The French Revolution*, or whether its mark is already on *Barnaby Rudge*; that history is, however, the guiding spirit of *A Tale of Two Cities*, as is clear from Dickens's prefatory adulation of the "philosophy of Mr. CARLYLE's wonderful book."

A Tale of Two Cities presents a vision of revolution as a myth of rebirth. The old society of *Barnaby Rudge* lies stagnant under the weight of the past, and its rebels are incapable of reinvigorating it. The world of the French Revolution—both France and England —while closer to death, has the potentiality of renewal. Despite a note of anguish at the spectacle of history, Dickens is more hopeful in the *Tale* than he had been in his more blithely resolved early work. In the dark novels of the 'fifties he retains faith in the power of love—resembling Christian *agape* and personified in such characters as Little Dorrit—to bring even moribund modern men like Arthur Clennam to life again, but by no means their entire society. In the *Tale*, the novel following, not only personal but also social life is seen to move through suffering, chaos, and sacrifice to rebirth. Without recourse to the divine miracle but only to the human drama of Christian redemption, Dickens sees his characters—Carton, Manette, and Darnay—in various ways dead and in a fairly uniform way reborn. It is not love alone that effects this regeneration but their willingness to die for others. Without dependence on but by imitation of an intervening savior, Dickens shows salvation at work in history, both personal and national.

After moving through a wide variety of metaphors for the French Revolution in the course of his exposition, Carlyle returned to the language of Biblical prophecy when he drew his conclusion:

"IMPOSTURE is in flames, Imposture is burnt up: one red sea of Fire, wild-bellowing, enwraps the World. . . . Desolate, as ashes, as gases, shall they wander in the wind.

. . . RESPECTABILITY, with all her collected Gigs inflamed for funeral pyre, wailing, leaves the Earth: not to return save under new Avatar. Imposture how it burns, through generations: how it is burnt up; for a time. The World is black ashes;—which, ah, when will they grow green? . . ." This Prophecy, we say, has it not been fulfilled, is it not fulfilling?

The prophecy is that which Carlyle had ascribed to the "Arch-quack" prophet Count Cagliostro in "The Diamond Necklace," and which he here quotes with only a trace of his habitual self-irony. Aside from its phoenix-imagery, the language is Biblical, not only in its sense of an impending holocaust but in its promise of passage to a promised land. The sea of fire is a Red Sea (it re-appears capitalized in the same paragraph), which consumes the unjust but allows the just to pass through. The note of conclusion is affirmative, the prophecy is fulfilling, and the redemption is organically natural, but its time is not sure: "when will they grow green?"

However muddled with other matter, this motif emerges as the dominant one in *The French Revolution*, and it is this that Dickens took as his leading motif in *A Tale of Two Cities*. The chapter after the storming of the Bastille is titled, "The Sea still Rises"; the next, the burning of the Evrémonde chateau, is called, "Fire Rises"; and the next after it begins: "In such risings of fire and risings of sea—the firm earth shaken by the rushes of an angry ocean which had now no ebb, but was always on the flow, higher and higher, to the terror and wonder of the beholders on the shore —three years of tempest were consumed" (Book Two, XXIV, 223).

Such images pervade the novel, as is well known, but it has not been seen how closely the attitude toward, as well as the image of, conflagration resembles Carlyle's. The response Dickens exhibits is neither to praise nor blame the Revolution but to stand back in awe at the divine and natural spectacle. Whatever its shortcomings as theological or historical thought, this is a contemplative and esthetic rather than an active and political view of history. Dickens particularly despairs of the conscious attempt to direct the course of the flow for good ends, as Darnay decides to do at the close of the chapter quoted above. The novel provides numerous images of the Revolution as an inevitable debacle, but it is also a fortunate fall, yielding a new life to a dead society. This grace is not given from beyond this world but seems to be an inherent power of renewal in history, like the seasonal processes in nature. Dickens joins Carlyle, then, in an immanent, vitalist view of the renewal of life in nature and in man.

So thoroughly does the pattern of death-and-rebirth animate *A Tale of Two Cities* that not only its plot but its language, the thought of its characters, even its comic interludes are carriers of the theme. The status of Dr. Manette in the Bastille is described as "buried alive"; the process by which he is rescued in Part I is named in the title (also used as a code-term), "Recalled to Life." The otherwise scarcely relevant sub-plot of the "Resurrection-Men" (as Jerry Cruncher calls body-snatchers like his father) is given point by its relation to this theme.[18] Intimately bound up with this pattern is the notion of renewal of life through a substitute death—whether conceived in pagan, Christian or natural terms. Darnay enacts the process when he initiates the final workings of the plot: he returns to France in order to save the life of Gabelle, the tax-collector. His propensity to stake his life for another is rendered unnecessary by the intervention of Dr. Manette, who exhibits his own sufferings before the revolutionary court in token of his son-in-law's expiation. But this substitution becomes unacceptable when the Doctor himself becomes the accuser, through Defarge's introduction of his prison manuscript.

The characters themselves talk in such terms, and the author shows himself to have consciously entertained them. When Manette decides to save Darnay he declares: "As my beloved child was helpful in restoring me to myself, I will be helpful now in restoring the dearest part of herself to her; by the aid of Heaven I will do it!" (Part Three, IV, 257). When he achieves Darnay's release, "He was happy in the return he had made her, he was recompensed for his suffering . . ." (Part Three, VI, 273). How precise is the substitution is suggested when Darnay is thrown into a cell and begins to pace

18. The comedy of the Resurrection-Man Jerry Cruncher, and his son of the same name, is also connected with the pattern of substitution by the innocent for the guilt of the elders. When the young Jerry spies on his father's grave-robbing and confronts him with the question, "What's a Resurrection-Man?" (getting the answer, "he's a tradesman"), he goes on: "Oh, father, I should so like to be a Resurrection-Man when I'm quite growed up!" (Part Two, XIV, 156). Fortunately, he does not inherit the guilty role but substitutes for his father at Tellson's Bank after Jarvis Lorry learns the secret trade; as the father pleads, ". . . let that there boy keep his father's place, and take care of his mother; . . . and let that father go into the line of the reg'lar diggin', and make amends for what he would have un-dug—if it wos so—by diggin' of 'em in with a will, and with conwictions respectin' the futur' keepin' of 'em safe" (Part Three, IX, 292). Whether Jerry redeems his father is no more clear than the commensurability of grave-digging as a compensation for grave-robbing; the point is that the characters seem to think so, and the novel operates in their terms.

it off in the same words used by and about Manette: " 'Five paces by four and a half, five paces by four and a half, five paces by four and a half.' The prisoner walked to and fro in his cell . . ." (Part Three, I, 244). The pattern of substitution merges with the renewal theme in the images of fathers and children that are present throughout. Carton, who feels "like one who died young. All my life might have been" (Part Two, XIII, 143), becomes the shaper, if not the progenitor, of Darnay's life when he prepares him for escape: "The prisoner was like a young child in his hands" (Part Three, XIII, 333). Carton lives again—as far as natural man is able—in the child of Lucie and Darnay who is to be named after him, and who replaces—as far as one child can—their first boy, who is to die young. When Sydney Darnay shall bring *his* son to France to tell the tale of the past—as seen in Carton's vision—the renewal of life will be complete.

Finally, the self-sacrifice of Carton for the return to life of Darnay is set to the text of the Christian promise of redemption: " 'I am the Resurrection and the Life, saith the Lord: he that believeth in me, though he were dead, yet shall he live: and whosoever liveth and believeth in me shall never die' " (Book Three, XV, 357). Carton had quoted the text earlier when recalling his own father's funeral, and his repetition of it at the climax suggests that it is the imaginative source of his—and Dickens's—vision. In choosing to give his life as blood-price for another's, he identifies himself with Christ, acting in history on the model of divine intervention.

Carton's vision at the close is of a redeemed city of men: "I see a beautiful city and a brilliant people rising from this abyss, and, in their struggles to be truly free, in their triumphs and defeats, through long long years to come, I see the evil of this time and of the previous time of which this is the natural birth, gradually making expiation for itself and wearing out." It is true, as Miller observes, that this rebirth requires a death, and that "in order to fulfill the theme of 'resurrection' (that is, descent into death and return from it to a life at last given meaning), Dickens must divide his hero into two persons"—but this is the mark of a translation of Christian redemption into a historical process. In the absence of a redeemer who dies and lives again and also brings others to life again, men in history must die that others may live. Since Dickens uses the language and dramatic form of Christianity "demythologized" of its literal historicity, he sees the community going through the process of death-and-rebirth; individuals are not resurrected here—though they may give other individuals a chance to live—but nations are.[19] Personal salvation in Christ is translated into and is designed to give authenticity to the promise of social regeneration through sacrifice. This redeemed realm figures in the title of the novel: it is not a tale only of Paris and London, but of the city of history in which men presently live and the "beautiful city" of Carton's vision.

The lack of impressive characters in the novel is therefore the defect of a virtue: the *Tale* ascribes personality to the mass, and is one of the first historical novels to characterize and dramatize social groups as major carriers of the action. Yet the strength of *A Tale of Two Cities* does not rest entirely with its group characters but also with its individuals. If it is a greater historical novel than *Barnaby Rudge*, it is so by virtue of introducing recognizably focal heroes. The innovation of their *Doppelgänger* relationship should not obscure the fact that they are fundamentally traditional figures. Charles Darnay is the classic case of the "Waverley hero,"[20] an aristocrat who breaks with his class, but not sufficiently to give his wholehearted support to the Revolution. He is the odd man out, tried by both British and French courts as a traitor, the irony of whose situation is completed by the fact that he is guilty of neither charge. His ambivalence is further complicated by his inability even to explain his political position—if he has one—as in the scene where Stryver interprets his reserve as Jacobinism.

19. A similar emphasis is found in Carlyle; Louise Young, *Thomas Carlyle and the Art of History* (Philadelphia and London, 1939), p. 86, draws a conclusion at variance with his reputation for hero-worship: "His real concern as a historian was with the fate of social groups and not of individuals. The heroes of the epic, whose actions and passions offer the historian his primary material, are really borne along on a tide of events to which they are virtually subordinate."

20. Jack Lindsay calls attention to Dickens's use of the Waverley hero: "He took over from Scott the theme of the private person snatched up, without will or intention, into a great historical movement . . . ("Barnaby Rudge," in John Gross and Gabriel Pearson, eds., *Dickens and the Twentieth Century*, London, 1962, p. 93 ff.). In this article and in his *Charles Dickens: A Biographical and Critical Study* (London, 1950, pp. 364–69), Lindsay discusses the influence of other sources, including Bulwer-Lytton's *Zanoni*, on *A Tale of Two Cities*.

Dickens sketches him as a misplaced idealist, whose ideals are doomed to political ineffectuality:

His latent uneasiness had been, that bad aims were being worked out in his own unhappy land by bad instruments, and that he who could not fail to know that he was better than they, was not there, trying to do something to stay bloodshed, and assert the claims of mercy and humanity. . . . Then, that glorious vision of doing good, which is so often the sanguine mirage of so many good minds, arose before him, and he even saw himself in the illusion with some influence to guide this raging Revolution that was running so fearfully wild. (Book Two, XXIV, 231–32)

Dickens's greater achievement in characterization is not his hero of divided loyalties and ineffectual idealism but his hero of alienation. Sydney Carton is one of the first of the modern anti-heroes to carry his personality problems over into the political realm. His condition may be described, in terms of a later organicist philosophy, as the quest for an object of loyalty, and his discovery of that object in simple virtue—expressed by his devotion to Lucie—leads to his involvement in political intrigue in order to remove Darnay from LaForce prison. But Dickens, in common with most of his contemporaries, sees political engagement as an antithesis to, not an expression of, personal fulfillment, and this stark antithesis vitiates the significance of his hero's development. Although Carton can see his self-sacrifice as "a far, far better thing . . . than I have ever done," he is most of all satisfied by his release from history and from his own *anomie*: "it is a far, far better rest that I go to than I have ever known" (Book Two, xv, 358).

The well-known afflatus of Carton's final words has led one recent critic, Robert Alter, to an indictment of the Christian element in the novel: "The symbolic conflict around which the novel is organized ultimately alludes . . . to an opposition between promised regeneration in Christ and threatened annihilation by the forces of the anti-Christ. The trouble is that while the threat of moral anarchy is as constant and close to Dickens as his own heartbeat, his imagination of resurrection, whether for individuals or for societies, is conventionally pious and little more."[21] But

21. Robert Alter, "The Demons of History in Dickens' *Tale*," *Novel*, II (1969) 141. Alter sets out much of the Christian-allegorical imagery with which the novel is filled: e.g., Evrémonde-Everyman, the Woodman Fate and the Farmer Death, the Four Horsemen of the Apocalypse, the putative substitution of the

that is to take the ritualist standpoint that the symbols do not work without the thing they symbolize; in literature and, quite possibly, in history, religious symbols can function to indicate a secular process at work. Carlyle had already made these symbols of holocaust, sacrifice and rebirth available to Dickens with some detachment from their Christian content. They provide the imaginative forms in which the drama of history is seen in the *Tale*, without suggesting that Dickens asserts a Christian view of history or even a sentimental employment of half-believed dogmas.

A Tale of Two Cities expresses neither a redemption from the sins of history through Christ, nor a natural purging of crime and suffering through a passage to the next generation, but a fusion of the two. Some images in the novel carry the former, some the latter valence. When Carton first thinks of his Christ-like role as the "Resurrection and the Life," he stands by the Seine through the night:

Then, the night, with the moon and the stars, turned pale and died, and for a little while it seemed as if Creation were delivered over to Death's dominion.

But, the glorious sun, rising, seemed to strike those words, that burden of the night, straight and warm to his heart in its long bright rays. And looking along them, with reverently shaded eyes, a bridge of light appeared to span the air between him and the sun, while the river sparkled under it. (Part Three, ix, 299)

These archetypes of natural renewal—river, sun, night, and dawn —give way to Christian images of apocalypse at the close, as Carton comforts the little seamstress on the tumbril:

"If the Republic really does good to the poor, and they come to be less hungry, and in all ways to suffer less, [my cousin] may live a long time: she may even live to be old. . . . Do you think . . . that it will seem long to me, while I wait for her in the better land where I trust both you and I will be mercifully sheltered?"

"It cannot be, my child; there is no Time there, and no trouble there." (Part Three, xv, 356–57)

---

guillotine for the Cross as "sign of the regeneration of the human race," the unholy sacrament of the broken wine-cask ("the wine, tasted by all the people, smeared on their lips and faces, becomes blood; there is, pointedly, no bread of life—no body of Christ—for the hungry in this mass, and for that very reason the blood is solely a portent of destruction, not a promise of redemption"; p. 140).

Here the promise of an earthly redemption through the Revolution, even if resulting in better and longer life, is seen as insignificant in comparison with the infinity of life and time in the Christian millenium.

That Dickens wavered between these two visions is no accident, for they are the polar alternatives of the Western utopian imagination.[22] That he was unable to rest in the hope for a political salvation, an improved life in history, is an indication of the intellectual situation of his time. But as in Carlyle and other Victorians, Dickens's return to the hope of eternal life in a realm outside time cannot divorce itself from a final vision of utopia brought down to earth.

22. Frank Kermode, following the work of recent specialists in millenarian movements, has suggested that as divine salvation became doubtful and the establishment of a heavenly utopia unpredictable, Christian thought tended to discover salvation and utopia figured in historical events: "No longer imminent, the End is immanent. So that it is not merely the remnant of time that has eschatological import; the whole of history, and the progress of the individual life, have it also. . . . History and eschatology, as Collingwood observed, are then the same thing": *The Sense of an Ending: Studies in the Theory of Fiction* (London, Oxford and New York, 1968 [1967]), p. 25. Thus Dickens's visionary treatment of the Revolution and of Carton's self-sacrifice may stand in a tradition of Christian figuralism without being a mere secular reduction of an outworn faith.

Chapter 5 Thackeray:
Beyond
Whig history

It is tempting to join Georg Lukács in accusing Thackeray of a disengaged scepticism which denies him the possibility of seeing history as in any light meaningful, for there are statements from the novelist's own hand that lend support to the charge. In an early piece of satirical reportage, "The Second Funeral of Napoleon," he writes:

It is no easy task in this world to distinguish between what is great in it, and what is mean; and many and many is the puzzle that I have had in reading History (or the works of fiction which go by that name), . . . with a vain set of dates relating to actions which are in themselves not worth a fig, or with a parcel of names of people whom it can do one no earthly good to remember.[1]

Despite his tendency to reject history out of hand, Thackeray's persistent return to historical subjects, not only in his fiction but in statements attempting to define the study itself, indicates his continued concern with its meaning.

In another journalistic piece, a satirical fantasy called "The History of the Next French Revolution," he adds an envoi which proposes five possible sources of interest in history: "It records the

1. *The Works of William Makepeace Thackeray* (London [Centenary Biographical edition], 1910–11), xx, 347–48. Subsequent references are to this edition and are inserted parenthetically in the text by volume, chapter, and page numbers, except for references to *Henry Esmond*, where book, chapter, and page numbers are given (the novel is Volume x in this edition).

actions of great and various characters; the deeds of various valour; it narrates wonderful reverses of fortune; it affords the moralist scope for his philosophy; perhaps it gives amusement to the merely idle reader" (VIII, 222).

The first interest, history as the record of great men, marks the biographical approach prevalent in the eighteenth century and is never dissociated from popular works pandering to curiosity about the splendor and foibles of the famous. Thackeray's own position on the great-man-theory-of-history is shown in his treatment of Marlborough in *Henry Esmond*. Despite a systematic campaign to discredit his politics, his honesty, and his motives, Thackeray cannot get away from the fact of his victories, and comes to see him somewhat as an inhuman force, like fate itself. There are resemblances between this position and the Hegelian and Carlylian ones in which the great man is a "world-historical individual," expressing through his personal motives and self-seeking behavior the larger forces by which he is powered and of which he may remain quite unconscious.

Even more striking is Thackeray's denigration of a more popular and less tendentious English hero, Wolfe, in *The Virginians*. Not only does he assure us, by means of invented eye-witness characters, that the famous dying utterance was never spoken, but he accounts the capture of Quebec to a stroke not of military genius but of gambler's luck. It may be seen in this typical debunking of a nationalistic myth (which is also a feature of the picture of Marlborough) that more is at stake than popular adulation of heroes; it is the question of the role of the individual, reason and fortune in history that Thackeray raises constantly in his work.

A second possibility of historical writing is to recite a narrative of events for its own sake: story-telling, as in the picaresque *Memoirs of Barry Lyndon*. Here, too, Thackeray is reserved about the possibility of coherent accounts of historical events: "It would require a greater philosopher and historian than I am to explain the causes of the famous Seven Years' War in which Europe was engaged; and, indeed, its origin has always appeared to me to be so complicated, and the books written about it so amazingly hard to understand, that I have seldom been much wiser at the end of a chapter than at the beginning . . ." (VII, iv, 69). Despite the fact that this is the rogue-hero speaking, we may be sure that his creator sympathized with him. In trying to account for the course of the American Revolutionary War, one of the brother-heroes of *The Virginians* proposes various causes to explain the surprising victory of the colonists, then throws up his hands with expressions like "marvels of coincidence" and "freaks of fortune," and finally takes solace in the Providential view—which Thackeray consistently rejected. Yet the author does not stop with his creature Barry Lyndon's anti-intellectual shrug: his fictional career is a sustained effort to discover precisely such an order of events in life at large and in history in particular.

Given Thackeray's initial tendency to scepticism, a third response to historical events is, as a throw-back, wonder. Thackeray is fond of discovering and mulling over—not very profitably—history's little ironies: that, for example, George Washington was the leader of the troop which fired the first shots between British and French forces in America—an incident which led eventually to the enlargement of hostilities in the French and Indian War and ultimately to the American Revolution—and yet this obscure young officer emerged at the head of his nation when all was done. Such bemused speculations are ever-present in Thackeray, and their danger lies in encouraging his tendency to lapse into a withdrawn sentimentalism that refuses to look further than the irony itself. Fortunately, he does not often stop there.

A fourth tendency in Thackeray is to see history as affording the moralist food for thought—the eighteenth-century "teaching-by-examples" theory of history-writing. This tendency sometimes ends in an abstention from moral commitment:

. . . when you have well studied the world, how supremely great the meanest thing in this world is, and how infinitely mean the greatest, I am mistaken if you do not make a strange and proper jumble of the sublime and the ridiculous, the lofty and the low. I have looked at the world for my part, and come to the conclusion that I know not which is which.[2]

We sense that Thackeray's usual moral vigor in judging his characters, often reducing them to types, tends toward moral relativism when he comes to consider the historical patterns of human be-

2. Quoted in Gordon N. Ray, *Thackeray: The Uses of Adversity: 1811–1846* (London, 1955), p. 218; the speaker is in *Catherine*, but he apparently represents Thackeray's view.

havior. Yet the exigencies of plot require at least an *ad hoc* scale of values, and the practicing novelist usually cannot maintain a historicist's abstention from judgment. For all the subtlety and complexity of his picture of Becky and her social conditioning we are able to judge her and others in *Vanity Fair* as they injure others or help them to flourish.

The final option among the quoted responses to history is to take it as a form of entertainment. For Thackeray, there are two ways to look at the spectacle for amusement. On the one hand, he may regard it from the esthetic distance of the artist, absorbed in life, yet surveying the composition of the broad scene, as in his use of the world-as-stage motif in *Vanity Fair*. On the other, he may share the antiquarianism of the withdrawn and somewhat jaded man-of-the-world, bemused by the variety of past follies and outdated fashions. The latter attitude often appears when Thackeray speaks in his own person, as in introducing his public lectures, *The Four Georges*:

Not about battles, about politics, about statesmen and measures of State, did I ever think to lecture you: but to sketch the manners and life of the old world; to amuse for a few hours with talk about the old society; and, with the result of many a day's and night's pleasant reading, to try and while away a few winter evenings for my hearers. (xi, 6)

The seasoned reader overcomes the impulse to lump Thackeray with his typical antiquarian persona-figure in the novels: the club-man who finds leisure in mulling over gossipy historical vignettes. Thackeray wished, of course, to maintain an almost professional historical accuracy. But there is a little too much pride in his tone when he announces that he "had chapter and verse for every action and movement of the army which I narrated"[3] in *Esmond*. When his notes for the unfinished novel, *Denis Duval*, reveal him collecting historical tidbits to season his material—when he makes a note of the fact that Marie Antoinette's saint's-day was the *Fête des Morts,* or when he reminds himself to inquire how Pearson got away from John Paul Jones—we are led to see him not as an esthetically detached artist but as an antiquarian indulging in detail for its own sake.

3. *The Letters and Private Papers of William Makepeace Thackeray*, ed. Gordon N. Ray (Cambridge, Mass., 1945–46), III, 447; 2 May 1855.

It is not, however, by these interests that the range of Thackeray's imagination can be determined. A German dissertation[4] has catalogued the elements of social life which come into the above-mentioned historical novels, and the sum is an impressive testimony to the seriousness of Thackeray's interest in the past. It is not only the manners and the costumes nor only the aristocratic names and the tricks of fortune that enter the novels, but allusions to every social class and to a wide variety of institutions—limited, indeed, more sharply at the top of the scale than at the bottom (there are scenes in the slums but none at court). This thesis proposes that Thackeray lies in a tradition that has become a time-honored one in modern historiography, the school of cultural history. We must add that he arrived at this perspective by responding to the growth of historiography in his own time and particularly to the most successful of Victorian social historians, Macaulay.

۞

It would be too much to claim, on the available evidence, that Thackeray turned to the writing of historical novels simply because of Macaulay's success in popularizing late seventeenth- and eighteenth-century history. We can be sure, however, that the working novelist knew the current sales trends that made the historian a powerful competitor. The last installment of *Vanity Fair* appeared in July, 1848; the first part of the *History of England* followed hard upon it in November of that year. The historian quickly fulfilled his desire to supersede "the last fashionable novel on the tables of young ladies." Thackeray's reaction was not immediate, but in 1852 there appeared, in sumptuous format and archaic typography, *The History of Henry Esmond, Esq. A Colonel in the Service of Her Majesty Q. Anne: Written by Himself.* The antiquarian trappings of the volume were designed to help win back for fiction the audience that Macaulay had captured by making historical truth more attractive than fiction. Their relationship touches not only on Victorian publishing practices and literary

4. Gudrun Vogel, *Thackeray als historischer Romanschriftsteller* (Leipzig, 1920).

influences but on Victorian ideas of history, historiography, and the historical novel.

The personal relations of Thackeray and Macaulay were fairly extensive but may be briefly summarized. As early as 1834, Macaulay and a Thackeray converged on eighteenth-century history, when the historian reviewed Rev. Francis Thackeray's biography of Pitt and found the novelist's uncle guilty of hero-worship. Thackeray surely learned from his uncle's chastisement. His first published comment on Macaulay is a review in 1843 of the *Essays*, showing evident relish in their wealth of anecdotal detail. Thackeray was never a Whig but he moved in Whig society—that of the enlightened peers of Holland House—and must have met Macaulay at about this time. Not all their social contact was unruffled; a surviving anecdote may best be told in Thackeray's own words:

I am afraid I disgusted Macaulay yesterday at dinner at Sir George Napiers: we were told that an American lady was coming in the evening, whose great desire in life was to meet the Author of Wanaty Fair and Author of the Lays of A. Rome, so I proposed to Macaulay to enact me, and let me take his character—but he said solemnly that he did not approve of practical jokes, & so this sport did not come to pass.[5]

The difference of temperament also shows up in Macaulay's journal, when he describes Thackeray's talk about his own career and finds it vulgar. A similar cooling took place on Thackeray's part, at least towards Macaulay's work, for he pronounced the last volumes of the *History* to be not up to the first and felt challenged to write a history himself some day. In the end, however, it was the first number of Thackeray's *Cornhill Magazine* that was found by Macaulay's death-bed, open to *Lovel the Widower*, and it was the novelist's role to pronounce *nil nisi bonum* in a memorial essay on the historian's death. In a remarkable passage of this obituary, Thackeray suggests a comparison of the dome of the British Museum and the dome of Macaulay's brain—both repositories of enormous erudition open to the enquiring public as an English birthright. He planned to carry Macaulay's unfinished history down through the reign of Queen Anne, but time, strength, cash, and patience were too short.

5. *Letters*, II, 593; 13 Sept. 1849. The subsequent quotation from the *Letters* is from III, 38; 17–19 April 1852.

Though Thackeray did not become a historian, he conceived *Henry Esmond* itself as history, on the model of Macaulay:

I wish I had 6 months more to put into the novel: now it's nearly done it's scarce more than a sketch and it might have been made a durable history: complete in it's parts and its whole. But at the end of 6 months it would want other 6: it takes as much trouble as Macaulays History almost and he has the vast advantage of remembering everything he has read, whilst everything but impressions I mean facts dates & so forth slip out of my head. . . .

Thackeray's desire to be as authentic as the historian is the counterpart of Macaulay's wish to make his work as appealing to the imagination as fiction. Both employ a mixture of styles for an age that wanted its fiction to be realistic and its histories to be filled with facts stranger than fiction.

The idea of an art as true as history came to the Victorians not from Aristotle but from the fountainhead of nineteenth-century historical interest, Scott. And, curiously enough, Scott's idea of fiction probably descended to Thackeray by way of a historian—Macaulay himself. In his widely-read essay, "History," Macaulay established Scott's art as an ideal for his own field:

The perfect historian is he in whose work the character and spirit of an age is exhibited in miniature . . . by judicious selection, rejection, and arrangement, he gives to truth those attractions which have been usurped by fiction. . . . Sir Walter Scott, in the same manner, has used those fragments of truth which historians have scornfully thrown behind them in a manner which may well excite their envy. He has constructed out of their gleanings works which, even considered as histories, are scarcely less valuable than theirs. But a truly great historian would reclaim those materials which the novelist has appropriated. The history of the government, and the history of the people, would be exhibited in that mode in which alone they can be exhibited justly, in inseparable conjunction and intermixture.[6]

For Macaulay, then, history must include an account of the private affairs of social life, as well as the public record of dynastic policy, wars and treaties. But by including vivid social detail in his *History*

6. *The Works of Lord Macaulay* (New York, London and Bombay [Edinburgh edition], 1897), v, 157–58.

of England, Macaulay comes close to the traditional domain of the novelist: man in society, with all his concrete particularity and inwardness of sensibility. His accounts of mass psychology in the Glencoe, Darien, or Londonderry episodes and his largely hypothetical picturing of the states of mind of Monmouth, William, or James succeed as imaginative literature though they may be faulted as history.

From the novelist's side, the pull toward an integration of history and fiction was equally strong. Thackeray developed a manner of writing about past times which aimed to recapture the *sentiment de l'existence* of men bounded by manners, literary and other cultural forms, and social institutions. To express how it felt to be alive at a particular time was, he maintained, possible only by using the imaginative tools of literary art. In an apostrophe to the historical muse, in the essay on Steele in *The English Humorists,* he writes:

> "O venerable daughter of Mnemosyne, I doubt every single statement you ever made since your ladyship was a Muse! . . . I take up a volume of Doctor Smollett, or a volume of the *Spectator,* and say the fiction carries a greater amount of truth in solution than the volume which purports to be all true. Out of the fictitious book I get the expression of the life of the time; of the manners, of the movement, the dress, the pleasures, the laughter, the ridicules of society—the old times live again, and I travel in the old country of England. Can the heaviest historian do more for me?" (XI, 199–200)

While Thackeray declares fiction to be a specially favored medium in presenting human life in history, Macaulay similarly conceives of history as a "history of people." Our current conception of history approximates this view: it is the endowment of nineteenth-century historical study, particularly as it grew up in Germany under the name *Kulturgeschichte.* That we take it for granted today should not blind us to the significance of Thackeray's and Macaulay's early adherence to it.[7]

Not only did Macaulay's range of material open up history to

7. Cf. Robert L. Schuyler, "Macaulay and His History—A Hundred Years After," *Political Science Quarterly,* LXIII (1948), 177–78 for a historian's assessment of his position. A thorough historical evaluation is Charles Firth, *A Commentary on Macaulay's History of England* (London, 1938).

artistic treatment, but his methods of writing were consciously esthetic:

> No picture, then, and no history, can present us with the whole truth: but those are the best pictures and the best histories which exhibit such parts of the truth as most nearly produce the effect of the whole. . . . History has its foreground and its background: and it is principally in the management of its perspective that one artist differs from another. Some events must be represented on a large scale, others diminished; the great majority will be lost in the dimness of the horizon; and a general idea of their joint effect will be given by a few slight touches.[8]

Macaulay's account of the art of historiography might stand as a fair description of Thackeray's method in his historical novels. Both are perspectivists, using foreshortening and other painterly devices that were later to be formally codified by James and his followers.[9] But there is this difference between them: the historian uses the "history of the people" as a vital background to his "history of the government"—it is still diplomatic and military history that is the foreground of the *History of England*. The novelist uses recorded incidents of political affairs to provide a background for the life of individuals, who are more-or-less representative of their time. Both writers show the two realms in "inseparable conjunction and intermixture," but their emphases are characteristically different.

Despite their affinities of intention and method, Thackeray and Macaulay differ also in imaginative response to the present, and this makes all the difference between their treatments of the past. Though they are both, at bottom, men of the eighteenth century in their social and esthetic tastes, they are very unequally at home in their nineteenth-century world. Macaulay, for all his love of the past for its own sake, is never out of his century. He views history as a member of the governing class of his time. As Walter Bagehot acutely put it: "He is still the man of [18]32. From that era he

---

8. Macaulay, *op. cit.*, v, 129–30.

9. The much-exercised question of Macaulay's style is treated in John Clive, "Macaulay's Historical Imagination," *A Review of English Literature*, I (1960), 20–28; in George Levine, *The Boundaries of Fiction: Carlyle, Macaulay, Newman* (Princeton, 1968), 79–163, especially pp. 147–48 n.; and in William A. Madden, "Macaulay's Style," *The Art of Victorian Prose*, ed. George Levine & Madden (New York, London, and Toronto, 1968), pp 127–53.

looks on the past. . . . With a view to that era everything begins: up to that moment everything ascends."[10]

Thackeray, on the other hand, was—as we know from his biography and letters—uneasily at home in his world. The brooding anxiety that hovers over his vision of the nineteenth century responds to its moral emptiness and injustice and harshness. The impulse to glorify the past at the expense of the present is widespread in the Victorian Age, as we have seen. But Thackeray is too sceptical to hanker for lost fairy-lands in the Middle Ages or lost nobility in the Stuart dynasty. The past, for him, is as defective as the present, and the prevailing tone of *Esmond*, his greatest historical novel, is one of nostalgia strongly tinged by disgust. The best picture of Thackeray's political views is that which emerges in *Pendennis*: the hero accepts change, while standing pat against revolution; he takes conservative pleasure in the "old society to which we belong," yet remains compromising and tolerant of innovation. Nevertheless, his friend Warrington calls him "self-satisfied," and it is part of his charm that Thackeray knew that such an undoctrinaire position as his own was open to the charge. "The great revolution's a coming a coming," he wrote his mother; ". . . I take a sort of pleasure in my little part in the business and in saying destructive things in a good humoured jolly way."[11]

When we turn from this fairly conventional picture of the politics of a British gentleman-intellectual of the mid-century, we are startled by the apparent extremism of some of his historical judgments. He never quite makes up his mind about the relative merits of home country and colonists in the American Revolution, but suggests in *The Virginians* that his loyalty to the mother country might have been shaken had he been on the scene. There is no shadow of a doubt in his justification of the French Revolution against royal and aristocratic decadence, and one of his deftest executions as a critic is his exposure of a self-proclaimed liberal writer as at heart a snob in his sympathies for the French nobility. On English history, *The Four Georges* should, given its date, be seen as a considerably more forceful attack on the monarchy than

10. Walter Bagehot, *Estimations in Criticism* (London, 1909), II, 70.
11. *Letters*, II, 761; 26 March 1851.

it appears today. The Hanoverians were still a subject of partisan controversy in the political thought—if not in the practical affairs —of the day, and for a popular lecturer to take up the reigning house required a delicately balanced position. On the Hanoverian Elector, Thackeray had no illusions: he was a cynical adventurer who was out for what he could get, but he was a better solution than the legitimate Stuart, who would have mortgaged the country to France and the Pope. His view of the later Georges is even more cutting, though more amusing:

> It was lucky for us that our first Georges were not more high-minded men; especially fortunate that they loved Hanover so much as to leave England to have her own way. Our chief troubles began when we got a King who gloried in the name of Briton, and, being born in the country, proposed to rule it. (XI, 37)

The implication is clear from this and much else in Thackeray's writings that that monarchy is best which governs least.

It comes as no surprise then, that *Henry Esmond* is, in contrast to the *History of England*, a study of how much of the meanness of the Victorian Age descended to it from the past. The contrast between Thackeray's and Macaulay's historical perspectives is borne out in the political bearing of their work. Macaulay is the chief exemplar of what has been called "The Whig Interpretation of History,"[12] which makes the Glorious Revolution the climactic moment of English history, the point at which the dark feudal past gave way to the harmonious development of the present industrial and commercial age. From this standpoint, his *History* becomes epic: it is the heroic tale of the triumph of William of Orange— the standard-bearer of Whig limited monarchy—over the forces of authoritarianism, superstition and reaction. But Thackeray's hero, while he loses his Tory commitments, does not welcome the ultimate supremacy of the Hanoverians. He sees, in place of the Augustan peace, only a society crumbling in an unheroic ruin about him. England is made safe for progress, but it becomes Vanity Fair in the process. *Henry Esmond* is not an epic celebra-

---

12. Herbert Butterfield, *The Whig Interpretation of History* (London, 1931). But cf. Andrew Browning, "Lord Macaulay, 1800–59," *Historical Journal*, II (1959), 155–57, to the effect that Macaulay was not as Whiggish in his historical judgments as has been supposed.

tion of a nation's fulfillment of its destiny,[13] but a critique of the eighteenth century and—by extension—of the nineteenth. Its unmasking of the crimes and follies of the past serves to debunk the historical myths of the Victorian Age, such as the Whig interpretation of history.

ᘏ

It has generally been held that the conclusion of the novel, in which Esmond declares a pox on both your houses—Stuart and Hanoverian, Tory and Whig—is an unsatisfactory one. The grounds of this criticism have never been made clear, but seem to be that the novel does not end by assimilating its hero into the social order—in short, that it is not a typically Victorian novel. These preconceptions balk at the fact that *Henry Esmond* is a novel of alienation—at least as much so as *Vanity Fair*. Both novels despair of finding the good society in the England of the eighteenth or of the nineteenth-century and Esmond takes himself off to America, the traditional haven of the European refugee and expatriate. It is no accident that the novel is written from the perspective of a comfortable Virginia planter, looking back on the broils of English war, love, and politics—with nostalgia, to be sure, but also with the wisdom gained by experience. The form of the novel as a *Bildungsroman* establishes the hero's final politics as the highest wisdom to be learned from history, for the typical hero of that tradition learns to judge, if not adjust to, his society.

---

13. The use of the term "epic" has recently been expanded into a regulative framework for *Henry Esmond* in John Loofbourow, *Thackeray and the Form of Fiction* (Princeton, N. J., 1964). Despite Loofbourow's excellent treatment of the place of the historical novel in the eighteenth- and nineteenth-century search for a substitute epic, the framework is too confining to encompass his many fine, non-epic insights into *Esmond*. Moreover, the tendency to apply classical genre to modern works seems to lead away from history toward archetypal criticism: *Esmond*'s epic metaphors "generate forms that convert historical experience into a recurrent allegory of human event" (p. 165). Given its high degree of specificity to English history, the universalization of experience in *Esmond* shows up most clearly in moving *outside* history rather than in establishing recurrent historical patterns. We shall have to keep on thinking of it as a historical novel. But the epic strain is indeed appreciable in *Vanity Fair*, where Thackeray's impulse to moral generalization is given freer rein: when all life is conceived as vanity, historical experience becomes one among a number of fields for its display.

A number of these assumptions have been questioned in recent criticism, straining to see beyond traditional interpretations. The novel has been said to be no *Bildungsroman*, for its hero does not significantly develop but remains the same throughout;[14] it has even been said to be no historical novel since the major concern is not with history but with love.[15] In both the adulation of *Esmond* as an epic and the denigration for its "unresolved" ending a common trait of these contentions is their mutual exclusiveness—if the novel is not one thing, it is another. There is a possible reading, however, that takes all these emphases into account, and shows them cooperating with each other in a coherent development.

The *Bildungsroman* pattern occurs not only in Esmond's personal life—leading him from the worldly love of Beatrix to the otherworldly love of Rachel—but equally in his political life and professional career. He begins as a politically unsophisticated, hereditary Tory and, through the experience of war and dynastic rivalry, comes to welcome the Hanoverian extension of the Revolution. The final proof of the Stuarts' ineptitude for rule is rendered in the farcical scene in which the Pretender's attempted seduction of Beatrix ends in a ballet of Cavalier postures of dueling and reconciliation. These events do not strike Esmond as a revelation of the higher truth or virtue of the Whigs, and Esmond does not acquire the Whig ideology (which was, in any case, to develop only in the later eighteenth century), nor join the Whig camp.[16]

14. The strongest statement of the *Bildungsroman* pattern of development is in G. Robert Stange's introduction to the Rinehart edition (New York, etc., 1962) of the novel. See also George J. Worth, "The Unity of *Henry Esmond,*" *Nineteenth-Century Fiction*, xv (1960–61), 345–53. For a denial of the *Bildungsroman*'s relevance, see Robert A. Donovan, *The Shaping Vision: Imagination in the English Novel from Defoe to Dickens* (Ithaca, N. Y., 1966), pp. 199–203, and Francis R. Hart, *Scott's Novels: The Plotting of Historic Survival* (Charlottesville, Va., 1966), pp. 18–23, which emphasize Esmond's and his world's consistency; and Geoffrey Tillotson, *Thackeray the Novelist* (London, 1963 [1954]), pp. 152–53 on the static nature of character in Thackeray, rejecting theories of organic growth.

15. Cf. J. Y. T. Greig, *Thackeray: A Reconsideration* (London, 1950), pp. 159–60, on the preeminence of love over historical interests in *Esmond*.

16. The closest study of the novel's treatment of historical data is Robert S. Forsythe, *A Noble Rake: The Life of Charles, Fourth Lord Mohun: Being a Study in the Historical Background of Thackeray's "Henry Esmond"* (Cambridge, Mass., 1928). Forsythe's most interesting insight into Thackeray's exaggeration of Mohun's dueling crimes comes in the account of the Hamilton murder: the duel was over an inheritance, but was trumpeted by Hamilton's

It is here that Thackeray parts company from Macaulay: his hero does not simply change parties but acquires a perspective broader than the partisan's. His experience of Whig generals like Marlborough, of Whig apologists like Addison, and of Whig machinations like those to bring in the Hanoverians, lead him to a summary judgment: "A strange series of compromises is that English History: compromise of principle, compromise of party, compromise of worship!" (Book III, ch. v, p. 410). From this perspective, it is impossible for Esmond merely to ride another current in the stream of English politics. In leading his hero out of British political life and removing him to another land, Thackeray has not reneged on his responsibility to render the hero's career thematically significant. Going off to America, Esmond leaves behind him the Whig interpretation of history, the Hanoverian peace, and even, as we shall see, history itself.

It is largely in pursuit of Beatrix that Esmond has pursued military and social advancement, and with the discovery of her worldliness and cruelty he drops the race for worldly honors. In his lust for false values, and in his belated abandonment of them, the hero inevitably suffers some diminution in our eyes—as do all the bungling heroes of the *Bildungsroman*. We are lenient with Esmond's social climbing, with his political and passional confusions, as we are warm toward all innocents in their education, and we even consider that this inveterate Tory who suddenly discovers the Whig in himself has made a step in his self-development. The hero's development from Tory to non-partisan, from public life to private life, from England to America, is confirmed and dramatically motivated by his shift of affections from Beatrix to Rachel. It is their relation to the larger scope of Esmond's development that allows us to believe in the reality and value of Esmond's love-affairs, despite their muted sexual vibration. Public and private planes of the novel reinforce each other perfectly here; the novel is historical to the degree in which it gives its characters' affections a relation to their fortunes in the world.

Tory followers as a political assassination by the Whig Mohun. Thackeray "has accepted an interpretation which the facts of history, as they appear to the student, will not bear out, but yet which is in perfect harmony with the point of view of the pretended witness of these occurrences" (p. 251). It is misleading, however, to conclude that "Esmond, as a Tory, . . . swallows completely the Tory accounts of the termination of the duel" (p. 241).

In the same way that his political change of heart is a judgment of English political life, Esmond's rejection of his family ties is a rejection of his class: he burns the patent of his aristocratic rank and chooses to become Henry Esmond, Esq. (this irony of the book's title has generally been overlooked—Esmond is by right a marquis). We should recall that Esmond carries from the outset a mixture of social origins. As the stray spawn of a rakish Cavalier, he inherits from his maternal line of Flemish weavers and from his foster parents, the Huguenot Pastoureaus, a strongly Puritanical set of values. This independence of spirit and moral enthusiasm make him from childhood a rebel against tyrants and trimmers. As a boy, he is the natural antagonist of Tom Tusher, the Blifil-figure who rises to become a Bishop and the husband of Beatrix. Tusher "was always a friend to the powers that be, as Esmond was always in opposition to them. Tom was a Whig, while Esmond was a Tory" (Book I, ch. 10, p. 114). It should be clear that they are Whig and Tory because they are time-server and rebel by nature, while those parties happen to be, respectively, in and out of power at the time their characters are formed. From then on, Esmond rebels actively against the Whig ascendency, but rebels emotionally against the Tory cant of his class. He becomes the man in the middle, caught up in historical commitments not of his own choosing, fulfilling a role that is not really his, ever more alienated from all social ties. This situation—of the kind that generates the tragic careers of Conrad's heroes—is saved from tragedy by the safety-valve of emigration to America.[17]

Even in his new home, Esmond does not lose his rebelliousness, though it is muted in old age. He is at ease in his anticipations of

---

17. It might properly be objected that emigration to America and abandonment of the given milieu hardly amount to a significant conclusion for a historical novel—that it suggests a refusal of the artist's responsibility to resolve his material in its own terms, and an easy avoidance by the ostensible hero of his social duties. It might be pleaded in defense of both Thackeray and Esmond that just as emigration was a heroic and even socially dedicated action in the eighteenth century, it was still regarded so by many of Thackeray's contemporaries. The list includes not only such obvious figures as Carlyle and his followers, Kingsley and J. A. Froude, but also John Stuart Mill; if the former saw in emigration a safety-valve for excess population and social tensions at home and a spreading of the industrious virtues of Britain abroad, the latter saw it as promulgating the higher values of British liberalism and liberty. See C. A. Bodelsen, *Studies in Mid-Victorian Imperialism* (New York, London and Toronto, 1960 [1924]).

the American Revolution, and he scorns the typically British values of tradition and aristocracy:

In England . . . you take the house you live in with all its encumbrances, its retainers, its antique discomforts, and ruins even; you patch up, but you never build up anew. Will we of the New World submit much longer, even nominally, to this antient British superstition? There are signs of the times which make me think that ere long we shall care as little about King George here, and peers temporal and peers spiritual, as we do for King Canute or the Druids. (Book III, ch. v, p. 411)

More is implied by this passage than a prediction of and a predilection for republican democracy. Esmond in America is almost beyond history: from a geographically distant perspective, temporal affairs fade into myth, and all politics are equally remote. Indeed, his prose reminds us of the Brobdingnagian king's sneer at the pettiness of all European affairs. For in the last movement of the novel, Thackeray parts company not merely from traditional British politics but from history itself.

The History of Henry Esmond, Esq. is one of the great historical novels by virtue, in part, of its movement beyond history. It leads its hero through the toils of historical life to a vision of the emptiness of all life in history and to a hint of the ideal of a life outside history. Despite a note of Victorian muckraking that creeps into his summary accounts of English society, Thackeray's critique of it is part of a broader perspective on history: "Should any clue be found to the dark intrigues at the latter end of Queen Anne's time, or any historian be inclined to follow it, 'twill be discovered, I have little doubt, that not one of the great personages about the Queen had a defined scheme of policy, independent of that private and selfish interest which each was bent on pursuing . . ." (Book III, ch. x, p. 467). This perception of the ubiquity of personal motivation in politics goes deeper than a simple rejection of all political involvement. One is not free of historical distortions of perspective, even if one disengages from politics while remaining in society. Esmond extends the perception to himself, reasoning that if Marlborough had not snubbed him, he might have become his loyal follower and biographer. Esmond continues with a variation of the historicist perspectivism that was already growing in his age: "We have but to change the point of view, and the greatest action looks mean: as we turn the perspective-glass, and a giant appears a pigmy" (Book II, ch. x, p. 269). Thackeray applies this relativism radically: to avoid historical error, we must avoid history altogether, turn our backs on it, and contemplate an unchanging reality.

Vision, once it is free to range, can see not only historical things in a different scale, but new things, or the old order of things within a larger order. From time to time, Esmond draws back from the foreground of history, not merely to see the grand design but to see that whole in a yet wider perspective. What he finds, as he views the larger continuities of life, is the relation of history to two other realities: the common life of men in their collective existence, and the personal life, lived at its best in the condition of love.

After Mohun's defeat of the Duke of Hamilton, Esmond takes a broad view of the common people in terms that capture the Macaulayan sense of the humming life of the metropolis:

The sun was shining though 'twas November: he had seen the market-carts rolling into London, the guard relieved at the palace, the labourers trudging to their work in the gardens between Kensington and the City— the wandering merchants and hawkers filling the air with their cries. The world was going to its business again, although dukes lay dead and ladies mourned for them; and kings, very likely, lost their chances. So night and day pass away, and to-morrow comes, and our place knows us not. (Book III, ch. VI, p. 428)

But in catching the subliminal pulse of human activity, Esmond fails to find a connection with the organic life of the community. His meditation enlarges on the theme of mutability and ends on a bitter note. This Epicurean tendency in Thackeray does not, however, proceed to negate earthly values and counsel *apatheia*.

Esmond grows to believe in the transcendent value of one, at least, of earthly goods:

As he had sometimes felt, gazing up from the deck at midnight into the boundless starlit depths overhead, in a rapture of devout wonder at that endless brightness and beauty—in some such a way now, the depth of this pure devotion (which was, for the first time, revealed to him) quite smote upon him, and filled his heart with thanksgiving.... What is ambition compared to that, but selfish vanity? To be rich, to be famous? What do these profit a year hence, when other names sound louder than yours, when you lie hidden away under the ground, along with idle titles engraven on your coffin? But only true love lives after you—follows your memory with secret blessing—or precedes you, and intercedes for you. *Non omnis moriar*—if dying, I yet live in a tender heart or two; nor am lost and hopeless living, if a sainted departed soul still loves and prays for me. (Book II, ch. VI, p. 234)

This is the attitude of "Love Among the Ruins" (which was written in the same year that *Esmond* was completed); "love is best" is in both works an attitude toward history. The phrasing of both the poem and the prose suggests the Ecclesiastes note, but here the denial of the historical world turns into a quest for an earthly good—a value that can confer, if not immortality, at least a meaning to earthly life. Poet and novelist name love as their way of salvation from history—though they do not erect it into a goddess or identify it with God, as Tennyson does.

In such scenes as these—and in the famous meeting of Esmond and Rachel in Winchester Cathedral—Thackeray's style reaches beyond his usual phenomenalism. He is no longer content to accept the world as given, no longer ready to accept its transitoriness and insubstantiality without insisting that some human things are real. This is not a pre-Proustian recovery of the passage of time in memory, as has been claimed,[18] nor any ideal principle beyond or permeating the evanescent temporality. For Thackeray's humanism precludes any philosophical abstraction: that is why he is so unsatisfactory to critics of an absolutist stamp. Without erecting man into an absolute, he finds love the ultimate source of value.

It is possible, therefore, not only to see Thackeray reflecting the anti-historical attitudes of his contemporaries, but to award him a high place in the tradition of historical fiction, with its inherent movement toward the universal in its conception of

18. In a provocative article, "Time and Memory in Thackeray's *Henry Esmond*" (*Review of English Studies*, n.s., XIII [1962], 147–56), Henri-A. Talon has suggested that the finished reality that Esmond contemplates in the act of writing his memoirs is the shape of his own life: ". . . it is in the nature of his *meditation* to be retrospective rather than anticipatory. He always likes to study the shape that his life has assumed rather than consider that which it might take" (p. 149). We might be more willing to credit this view if Talon had followed Esmond's career to America, but instead the critic finds a fulfillment in the hero's allegiance to the Stuart cause. Nevertheless, the article illuminates this English novel in a way that has been effectively employed by French critics on their own literature.

history. For the tendency to withdraw from historical action to a vision of the eternal—whether embodied in the constants of daily life or in the genuine sentiments of personal relations—this tendency is to be found in the great historical novels from *Michael Kohlhaas* and *The Charterhouse of Parma* through *War and Peace* to *Man's Fate*. Nicola Chiaromonte, in an essay on Malraux, has brilliantly described it as

> . . . one of the great insights of nineteenth century sensibility. It was a flash of pure wonder at the utterly paradoxical relation between an individual destiny and whatever general significance might be attached to a "historical event." . . . The myth is about man and history: the more naively, and genuinely, man experiences a historical event, the more the event disappears, and something else takes its place: the starry sky, the other man, or the utterly ironical detail. That is, the unhistorical. . . . History does not reveal its meaning, but gives way to destiny.[19]

It is possible, then, to place this thoroughly Victorian novel in a larger Continental tradition. *Esmond* approaches most closely to Stendhal's comic scorn of the historical world and his romantic devotion to an encompassing and transforming love by which the disgusted historical actor at least temporarily escapes from history.

Thackeray's hero takes a step further beyond the Scott hero than Stendhal was willing to take. Though the novel resembles a *Bildungsroman*, its hero does not begin as naive a young-man-from-the-provinces as Scott's or Stendhal's, nor does he end either as a socially-adjusted man of his times or as one distorted into absurdity by the madness of history and of love. He is portrayed throughout as a reflective consciousness conducting a painful investigation— *une recherche dégradée*, to use Lucien Goldmann's phrase—into the meaning of history, and of his own experience. Esmond is one of the first fictional heroes of thought—to be followed by Marlow, Strether, and Marcel—who attempt to piece together, in the manner of an artist, the fragments of experience which an anarchic world has tossed about them. By constructing the novel as a memoir written by Esmond in his retirement, Thackeray exhibited in its form the perceptual structure of his world: on the one side, the

---

19. Nicola Chiaromonte, "Malraux and the Demons of Action," in R. W. B. Lewis, ed., *Malraux: A Collection of Critical Essays* (Englewood Cliffs, N.J., 1964), pp. 98–99.

crimes and follies of history, as the Enlightenment mind conceived them; on the other, the synthetic imagination of the intellectual or artist, as the type has emerged in modern literature. Thackeray stands at the. midpoint of the transition between the classic and the modern historical novel, as he finely articulates the nineteenth-century myth of the world and the self, of history and consciousness.

℘

Although *Esmond* is Thackeray's only convincing historical novel—*pace The Virginians*, with all its laborious efforts to describe the American Revolution, and *Barry Lyndon*, foiled by its picaresque conventions and sarcastic tone[20]—there is also much historical authenticity in *Vanity Fair*. The Tillotsons' edition of this novel conveys how much of the life of the second and succeeding decades of the nineteenth-century the author crowded in. The more accurate description of *Vanity Fair* as a "novel of the recent past" should not blind us to its power as a historical novel. It is not simply that Thackeray fills his canvas with detail and gets most of his facts right, but that he portrays the effect on social life of the entry of major historical events. He traces the slow process by which Waterloo comes to assume a distorted but living place in the consciousness of individuals, both those who have been on the scene of battle and those who know it at second or third hand. It is the turning point in the lives of most of the characters, and becomes a memory which grandly and darkly hovers in the minds of all. Its presence serves to fix events in historical time more firmly than in any other novel of the age. Events are dated from Waterloo as though it were the turn of an era: Before Waterloo, After Waterloo. It is an epochal event that not only stands at the center of a nation's historical development, but shapes the destiny and character of all its members. The plot it-

---

20. Thackeray wrote his picaresque novel to satirize the swashbuckling stage-Irishmen of Charles Lever and Samuel Lover, whose novels were appearing regularly in the 'forties. That these works maintain a connection with historical events would not lead anyone to think them serious historical novels. See Robert A. Colby, "Barry Lyndon and the Irish Hero," *Nineteenth-Century Fiction*, XXI (1966), 109–30.

self may be said to derive from this event: "So imprisoned and tortured was this gentle little heart [Amelia's], when in the month of March, Anno Domini 1815, Napoleon landed at Cannes, and Louis XVIII. fled, and all Europe was in alarm, and the funds fell, and old John Sedley was ruined" (I, xviii, 210).

There are no battle scenes in *Vanity Fair*. The only sounds that history makes as it moves through the novel are heard from far off, as though from an English club-room. The visual account is not that of an eye-witness; the point of view is second-hand:

[The final battle] came at last: the columns of the Imperial Guard marched up the hill of Saint Jean, . . . the dark rolling column pressed on and up the hill. It seemed almost to crest the eminence, when it began to wave and falter. Then it stopped, still facing the shot. Then at last the English troops rushed from the post from which no enemy had been able to dislodge them, and the Guard turned and fled. (I, xxxii, 404)

But we know this is no account of the battle of Waterloo at all; this is nationalistic chronicle history, not the living perspective of the participants.[21] We have only to compare George Osborn's baptism of fire with that of Nikolai Rostov in *War and Peace* to see how far the actual event is hidden from Thackeray.

He was well aware of his place in the baggage train, well back from the combatants. In a revealing observation on the subject matter of all his historical novels, Thackeray says of *The Virginians* that it cannot be concerned with the "real business" of history— putting aside the exception of war—but only with the sentiments and activities of private life. Thackeray's work does not even fully exploit his "single exception of war": his only sea-novel, *Denis Duval*, builds up toward major battle-scenes but stops short, unfinished. In his novels, a sense of historical actuality is conveyed by descriptions of the impact of public on private life, rather than by accounts of public events. The latter rarely go beyond their dry-as-dust text-book sources; the former allow us to sense how history is *lived* by those not engaged in but directly

21. On Thackeray's historical sources, particularly his preference for the local-color material of Gleig over the military details of Siborne, see Geoffrey and Kathleen Tillotson, eds., *Vanity Fair* (Boston, 1963), pp. xxvii–xxxii. The editors decided against designating the work as primarily a historical novel, on grounds of its universality and its owing "nothing essential to the time of its action" (p. xv)—both questionable premises, although the conclusion is sound.

affected by it. It is the historical perspective of the innocent by-stander, history on the home-front. Consequently, these historical novels remind us of what we are apt to forget, that everyday life, too, is part of history. We feel history in *Vanity Fair* not when the point-of-view shifts to the troops (as it does only after the event), but when it breaks in upon the man-in-the-street: most intensely at the point when Jos Sedley's butler, Isidor, stops short while serving Jos as he hears the opening cannonade—*"C'est le feu!"* (I, xxxi, 384). This is the moment at which history impinges on the individual life; it is the meeting-point of external reality and subjective experience. Such moments give *Vanity Fair* the quality of a genuinely historical novel, but this historicity is not brought to bear on its Ecclesiastes-view of the unchanging nature of human experience. The historical and the universal in this great novel are equally strong, but remain distinct from each other.

Chapter 6 The late Victorian
historical novel

After the success of *Henry Esmond* and *A Tale of Two Cities* in
the 1850's, the new cultural emphasis that G. M. Young designated
"Late Victorian" marked a change in the fortunes of historical fiction. While the genre had, from Scott to Thackeray and Dickens,
combined a display of great events with the drama of the individual's response to those events, the characteristic Late Victorian
historical novel shifts the terms of this relationship. Although there
remains an interest in both public incident and the inner life, the
latter assumes an autonomy that turns historical circumstance into
a background or frame. Even stronger atmospheric effects than
Scott's are obtained from increasingly precise descriptions of cultural forms, but the external world loses much of its role in the
shaping of consciousness. Nor does consciousness ordinarily express
itself in political action—even in the politics of withdrawal represented by Sydney Carton's or Henry Esmond's final actions. The
Late Victorian hero does not, like the Waverley hero, formulate
his life-role through exposure to the extremes of political conduct
in his time; nor does he, like the Dickens-Thackeray hero, make a
grand gesture of rejecting the entire nexus of politics, either by
self-sacrifice or emigration. He is never fully in the historical world
from the outset, but is caught passing through it toward a definition
of his own identity, a religious affirmation, or a predestined vocation.

The form of the major historical novels of this period—*The
Cloister and the Hearth, Romola, John Inglesant,* and *Marius the*

Epicurean—is that of the journey in quest. The motive of their heroes' quest is, in the main, religious, and it is not accidental that their scene is, uniformly, the Italian peninsula (involving, in two cases, a movement from Northern Europe to Italy). These strains of Late Victorian imagination—religious doubt, the quest for spiritual discovery, and the rage for Italian culture—are not randomly related. This was the age of the "emigration of the talents"—not the radical or bohemian artists like those who emigrated in the Romantic period, but the more respectable yet culturally alienated group that centered around the Brownings at Florence. A number of recent studies[1] have shown the degree to which they shared a sense of standing between two worlds—not precisely Arnold's but the more concrete worlds of England and Italy. They felt fully at home in neither, yet maintained both their inveterate Englishness and their warm response to Italian life and political evolution. Curiously, it was not the expatriate historical novelists Charles Lever and G. P. R. James who brought Italian religious and political history to bear on the spiritual needs of their own age, but a number of authors who spent extended visits abroad and were moved to write novels of ancient Rome, the Renaissance, and the Risorgimento. Not being historical novelists by vocation, Reade, Eliot, Shorthouse and Pater—and, although *Vittoria* is set too close in time to be included here, Meredith—took Italy as a screen onto which they could project their responses to the problems that touched them and their contemporaries most closely.

Setting aside the innumerable pot-boilers of the hacks and the weaker productions of the masters, the important Late Victorian historical novels follow the spiritual quest pattern with remarkable consistency. It is a pattern which is sometimes difficult to distinguish from that of another Victorian type, the novel of religious history, which drew sustenance from the curiosity about the primitive church which the Oxford Movement had awakened. Kingsley's *Hypatia* (1853), Wiseman's *Fabiola* (1854), and Newman's *Callista* (1856) established the practice of setting contemporary religious problems in the past, but no one would pretend that these are primarily historical novels, given their employment of history for dogmatic exposition. Yet the historical novels with which we shall

1. See, e.g., Giuliana Artom Treves, *The Golden Ring: The Anglo-Florentines 1847–1862*, trans. Sylvia Sprigge (London, New York, and Toronto, 1956).

deal are also heavy with the burden of modern experience, and there is no clear-cut way to set them apart from the novels of religious history—indeed, most of them figure in studies of the religious novel like Margaret Maison's *The Victorian Vision*.

Perhaps the best way of getting at the nature of the group is to consider J. H. Shorthouse's term for his own work: "Philosophical Romance." He distinguishes it from the historical novel proper (which, employing the term naively, he calls "historical romance"):

> As . . . I believe that all that is wanted to constitute an historical romance of the highest interest is the recovery of the detailed incidents of every-day life, and the awakening of the individual need and striving, long since quiet in the grave; so, in books where fiction is only used to introduce philosophy, I believe that it is not to be expected that human life is to be described simply as such. The characters are, so to speak, sublimated: they are only introduced for a set purpose, and having fulfilled this purpose—were it only to speak a dozen words—they vanish from the stage.[2]

Shorthouse's description of the latter type is really a good definition of the religious–history novels mentioned above, for they take the way of "sublimated" history to introduce philosophical or religious speeches. *John Inglesant* and the other novels to be treated here combine this sublimation with the "recovery" of the past in an absorbing, if not always successful, way. The author is wrong, then, to consider his novel merely philosophical; it is also historical—and it is the presence of a relatively disinterested view of the past that sets it and its group apart from the novels of religious history.

Moreover, Shorthouse's definition calls attention to the "individual need and striving" that take place in historical novels, i.e., to the exploratory form in which one alternative idea or role and then another is considered by the hero, dramatized in the action, or discussed directly by the author. To describe these mixed philosophical and historical novels we may use the term *meditative* historical fiction. They are not meditations on history itself but meditations taking place in a historical environment which gives them their provocation but does not limit their universality. If we seek to capture the distinguishing tone of these works, we will find them (with

2. *John Inglesant: A Romance* (London and New York, 1881 [1880]), "Preface to the New Edition." Subsequent references will be parenthetical in the text, and will follow the pagination of the one-volume edition of 1883.

the partial exception of *The Cloister and the Hearth*) elegiac. They are novels of loss—loss of enthusiasm as well as of intellectual commitments—with very little to show by way of vital renewal, despite their movement toward religious or moral truths. As such, the meditative historical novel is an especially sensitive indicator of the dominant movements of mind in the period which saw it emerge.

☙

The powers and limitations of the Late Victorian historical novel are nowhere better illustrated than in the first and best-known of the group, *The Cloister and the Hearth* (1861; serialized in 1859). To the taste of critics like Arthur Quiller-Couch and Walter Besant, Reade's was the greatest of English historical novels, but its picaresque ramblings, boys'-book adventures, and disturbed sadism have not allowed it to maintain its reputation—however much they contributed to its original popularity. It is all too easy to belabor the book's esthetic failings, but more rewarding to consider its unquestionably powerful evocation of history. Reade has decisive faults as a novelist, but his vividness of historical portrayal allows him in a measure to transcend them. And while his novel exhibits many of the features typical of the age—the quest-journey to Italy, religious meditation, disengagement from commitment, authorial reference to the present—it is nevertheless a unique and problematic work.

As set out in a study of "the making of *The Cloister and the Hearth*," Reade prepared himself to write about fifteenth-century Western Europe by reading most of the available historical works on the subject, including a fair sampling of the contemporary sources. His assiduousness arose neither from amateur antiquarianism nor from a historicist ideal of scholarship, but from a Baconian or Utilitarian conviction of the primacy of factual knowledge in the artistic treatment of any subject, and particularly of history. The root of this conviction lies in Reade's revolt against the prevailing Carlylian historical attitude, against what he held to be its medievalist sentimentalism, veneration of great men, and romantic afflatus.[3] He programatically set out to tell of the unsung heroes of

3. On Reade's scholarship, see Albert M. Turner, *The Making of The Cloister and the Hearth* (Chicago, 1938). On his anti-Carlylism, see Wayne Burns, *Charles Reade: A Study in Victorian Authorship* (New York, 1961), pp. 53–57.

common life and to debunk the myth of the Middle Ages in the cool light of fact. There can be no doubt that *The Cloister and the Hearth* provides an intense realization of the daily life of the late-medieval or early-Renaissance period, a wealth of vitality and concreteness which makes possible its survival as something more than a school text. Why, then, does it fail to convince as historical fiction?

Reade presents his anti-Carlylian theory of the hero—and, incidentally, of the historical novel—in the opening paragraphs of *The Cloister and the Hearth*:

> Not a day passes over the earth, but men and women of no note do great deeds, speak great words, and suffer noble sorrows. Of these obscure heroes, philosophers, and martyrs, the greater part will never be known . . .; but of others the world's knowledge may be said to sleep: their lives and characters lie hidden from nations in the annals that record them. The general reader cannot feel them, they are presented so curtly and coldly . . . .
>
> Thus records of prime truths remain a dead letter to plain folk: the writers have left so much to the imagination, and imagination is so rare a gift. Here, then, the writer of fiction may be of use to the public—as an interpreter.[4]

This variation of the "country churchyard" theme distinguishes a class of minor historical figures from the totally unhistorical ones; it celebrates the unsung great not the unachieved great. The historical novelist's role is described along the lines of the view maintained in the present study: he fills in interstices in the data where there is legitimate room for speculation on inner motives; he does this by exercising the esthetic faculty of imagination; imagination acts as an "interpreter" of historical fact.

Reade's ideas of history extend, however, well beyond his interest in unsung heroes. *The Cloister and the Hearth* puts forward a critical judgment of the Middle Ages and Renaissance, and in doing so reflects a progressivist theory of history more baldly than any other Victorian historical novel. At first the *Gemütlichkeit* of Dutch village life at Tergou seems almost to compensate for its obvious deficiencies in justice and civility, and Reade's general view of the Middle Ages is inclined to be sympathetic: "Gunpowder has spoiled war. War was always detrimental to the solid interests of mankind. But in old times it was good for something: it painted

---

4. I quote the Everyman edition (London and New York, 1906 ff.), ch. 1, p. 3; hereinafter cited parenthetically in the text.

well, sang divinely, furnished Iliads. But invisible butchery, under a pall of smoke a furlong thick, was it any the better for that? . . . They managed better in the Middle Ages" (XLII, 294). Gradually the scales of judgment shift in favor of the Renaissance, as when the medical prowess of Margaret Eliassoen, the heroine, is proscribed by a conservative burgomeister, egged on by the guildsmen whom the advance of knowledge is rendering obsolete. The shift becomes a tide when Gerard, the artist- (and illuminator-)hero, reports on the cultural advances of German and Italian cities as he visits them in his exile, e.g., "Sir Printing Press—sore foe to poor Gerard, but to other humans beneficial—plieth by night and day, and casteth goodly words like sower afield; while I, poor fool, can but sow them as I saw women in France sow rye, dribbling it in the furrow grain by grain" (LIII, 389–90). When Gerard reaches the flesh-pots of Italy, the defects of the Renaissance are, to be sure, shown in a satiric light, e.g., "A zealot in art, the friar was a sceptic in religion. . . . Being a lump of simplicity, his scepticism was as naive as his enthusiasm" (LIX, 439). But the shortcomings of Renaissance enlightenment are to the restraints of medieval orthodoxy as the licentiousness of Italian life is to the barbarism encountered on the way through northern Europe. When Gerard returns home and develops his bitterly frustrating Cloister-and-Hearth relationship with his wife, a pox is declared on both houses and he is made a fit father for the iconoclast Erasmus. The evils of traditional religion especially evoke condemnation: "Celibacy of the clergy," declares a summary footnote to the final chapter, "an invention truly fiendish." For all Reade's research, and despite his strong desire to project himself back into the past by the power of imagination, he is shackled by his Protestant, Whiggish perspective.

Reade is learned in the Middle Ages and Renaissance, but he is not of them. The historical sources on which he most closely models himself are often of literary as well as historical merit as expressions of their time, but he selects those most antipathetic to their contemporaries, e.g., Erasmus's *Colloquies* (especially pungent on religious narrow-mindedness), and Montaigne's *Diary of a Journey to Italy* (especially useful on traveling conditions and ritual panoply). The shortcomings of Reade's sense of the past, even when grounded in documents and consonant with past observers' views, may be estimated by recalling the works of these authors for which he can find no use.

In the portrait of his unsung hero, the father of Erasmus, Reade paints a stereotype of the Victorian virtues, common both to Reade's creed and to his arch-enemy Carlyle's. The honest, brave, reverential, mildly sadistic, sex-obsessed but self-repressive Gerard may have existed in the fifteenth century but he is a hero of the nineteenth. By setting him up to contrast with his age and to draw our sympathy towards him, Reade turns the historical setting it-self into the hero's antagonist. The novel becomes the story of the hero *against* his age. Gerard's quest, vocation, and rebellion are drawn not as responses to the special qualities of the medieval-Renaissance transition but as the inevitable chafings of a free man against the bit of society. Not only does such a structure imply a return to the Carlylian heroics against which Reade rebelled: it is a fundamentally unhistorical attitude which sees cultural forms exclusively as a set of impediments to the individual's free expression. Reade is not only a Whig but a liberal: society is merely an epiphenomenon, and only the individual has reality and worth. Unlike Thackeray's hero, Reade's does not have to move through the varieties of historical experience to discover their vanity; from Tergou to Rome, history is empty of meaning. For all its vividness, the historical world conceived in *The Cloister and the Hearth* is never taken to have independent existence and value.

❧

Long before the great debate of modern historians on the Renais-sance—centering on its degree of continuity with the Middle Ages and the significance of its rediscovery of antiquity—George Eliot was aware of its dual strain. The structure of *Romola* (1862–63) is such as to dramatize this duality: the marriage and conflict of Tito Melema and Romola de'Bardi are the marriage and conflict of Renaissance naturalism and individualism with its inherited tradi-tion of piety and asceticism. Not that the protagonists are mere allegories of these complex cultural tendencies; although they have a symbolic relation to Eliot's intellectual system, Tito is portrayed with greater imaginative sympathy than villains ordinarily earn, and Romola is shown in process of growth toward a type of being that transcends the Renaissance. Yet *Romola* is, like other Eliot novels, written according to a concept of historical development as well as a moral-psychological theory of persons. It is the artistic expression of a Comtian view of history as the progress from the theological domination of mankind to its liberation in a religion of humanity.[5]

While Comte's is the controlling historical outlook, there is reason to believe that other historians helped shape her picture of the period. It cannot be established that Eliot, during her scholarly preparation for writing, read the seminal works of Georg Voigt and Jacob Burckhardt, which appeared in the very same years;[6] but it seems unlikely that one of the few English intellectuals with a working knowledge of German language and thought would have been unaware of the tenor of discussion in German historical circles. Along with the passionate classicism (and personal deficiencies) of the Humanists, represented by Romola's father, the novel depicts the emergence of a this-worldly, esthetically self-conscious style of life among the Florentine artists and their patrons which comes close to Burckhardt's famous formulation. Not only in Tito's machiavellianism but in the fierce pride and demonic humor of his circle, Eliot parallels Burckhardt's picture of the life-style of Renaissance man.

Eliot was, however, not so dazzled by the enlightened spirit of Renaissance Humanism as to forget the depth of its traditional Christianity, and doubtless chose the period of Savonarola's brief revivalist movement as one that expressed the conflict of its underlying attitudes. Recent scholars with a sensitivity to the ascetic strain of medieval-Renaissance religion have seen it not as a life-denying obstacle to human progress but as a challenge to the higher moral sentiments and a call for a universal rather than provincial viewpoint.[7] Anticipating them, Eliot emphasized the communal religious experience of Florence under the impress of Savonarola's preaching, and portrayed it in the colors of heroic grandeur. But

---

5. "I have just been reading the survey of the Middle Ages contained in the 5th volume of the Philosophie Positive, and to my apprehension few chapters can be fuller of luminous ideas"; *The Letters of George Eliot*, ed. Gordon S. Haight (New Haven and London, 1954–55), III, 438; 12 July 1861.

6. Georg Voigt, *Die Wiederbelebung des classischen Alterthums* . . . (Berlin, 1859), Jacob Burckhardt, *Die Cultur der Renaissance in Italien: Ein Versuch* (Basel, 1860). A copy of the second edition of the latter, with Eliot's marginalia, is in the Lewes Collection at Dr. Williams's Library (London), but as the date of this edition is 1869, it cannot have been used for *Romola*.

7. E.g., Jacques Maritain, Etienne Gilson, and other Catholic philosophers; for these and other views of the period, see Wallace Ferguson, *The Renaissance in Historical Thought* (Cambridge, Mass., 1948).

the obscurantist and self-destructive elements in the ascetic creed are also pointed up; it cannot provide the heroine of this novel— as Thomas a Kempis could not provide the heroine of *The Mill on the Floss*—with a viable mode of conduct or attitude toward the self. In a denouement that seems arbitrary in its lack of dramatic realism but sound in its philosophical bases, Romola finds the meaning of her life in social action, in the role of a sister of mercy to a village suffering from the plague. Her ascetic self-abnegation is here put to the service of the larger community, and she becomes a devotee of the Feuerbachian collective ideal of humanity which Eliot's fiction is designed to foster.

While the grafting of a philosophic message onto a historical novel presupposes an interpretation of history, it need not involve a loss of historical authenticity. With the exception of a school of historians who maintain the Renaissance's near-identity with the Middle Ages, most historians are agreed that a new spirit was generated which in one way or another—the debate is now on the precise way—initiated our secular, innovative modern culture. Although Eliot's enthusiasm does not equal Burckhardt's in greeting the Renaissance as a triumph in the history of intellectual liberation, she assigns it a place—roughly corresponding to its position in Comte's system—in the record of man's dethronement of false idols and realization of his capacities for self-determination. Romola's struggle, not only with the asceticism descending from the Middle Ages and revived with Savonarola, but with the vicious strains within the Renaissance as embodied in her husband, becomes more than a personal story. As with all Eliot's heroines, the growth of the individual mind and heart is symbolic of the growth, potential and partly achieved, of mankind generally.

"I want something different from the abstract treatment which belongs to grave history from a doctrinal point of view, and something different from the schemed picturesqueness of ordinary historical fiction. I want brief, severely conscientious reproductions, in their concrete incidents, of pregnant movements in the past."[8]

---

8. "Leaves from a Notebook, " *Essays of George Eliot*, ed. Thomas Pinney (London, 1963), pp. 446–47. On Eliot's historical views, and particularly on her Renaissance studies, see Gennaro A. Santangelo, "The Background of George Eliot's *Romola*," unpublished dissertation (North Carolina, 1962). Another attempt to see Eliot's views of the Renaissance expressing themselves in the treatment of plot and character is: Lawrence Poston III, "Setting and Theme in *Romola*," *Nineteenth-Century Fiction*, xx (1965), 355–66.

So George Eliot stated her intentions in historical fiction, somewhat after the fact, in a notebook entry titled, "Historic Imagination." She goes on to define the genre in terms that identify the achievement of the classic historical novels but emphasize certain concerns that make her own work distinctive:

> The exercise of a veracious imagination in historical picturing seems to be capable of a development that might help the judgment greatly with regard to present and future events. By veracious imagination, I mean the working out in detail of the various steps by which a political or social change was reached, using all extant evidence and supplying deficiencies by careful analogical creation. How triumphant opinions originally spread—how institutions arose—what were the conditions of great inventions, discoveries, or theoretic conceptions—what circumstances affecting individual lots are attendant on the decay of long-established systems, —all these grand elements of history require the illumination of special imaginative treatment. But effective truth in this application of art requires freedom from the vulgar coercion of conventional plot. . . .

Here are expressed the historical novelist's characteristic notions of the temporal process by which ideas and sentiments are formed, of the relation of the individual to the total culture, of the possibility of filling in gaps in knowledge by imaginative hypothesis. But there is also evident a synthetic habit of mind that comes in conflict with the urge toward "brief reproductions" of "concrete incidents," and with the "vulgar coercion" of plot. For Eliot, historical imagination was the capacity to move from the part to the whole, from the isolated historical fact to its place in the larger web of reality.

The frequent charge that Romola is too researched, too decorated with cultural data, therefore misses Eliot's point: the social medium of the characters is the substance of their lives, out of which they draw their ideas, values, and options. Her concept of fictional realism is the esthetic equivalent of that strain of historicism which views individual action in the context of the social organism. The society of the barber-shop, so tiresome in the reading, thus emerges as the embodiment of the social substance of Florence, its ideas, values, jokes, personalities, rivalries, etc. This is the medium in which individuals swim and sink. The re-creation of milieu by historical imagination is then, an application of Comte's inductive method, the Positivist ideal of applying scientific thinking to social problems.

Of this approach, *Romola* is the embodiment; we are never allowed to forget that the carefully individualized persons and situations are instinct with general principles that characterize and sometimes transcend the age. The esthetic problem that arises is not simply one of allegorical thinness; Eliot is too great an artist to descend to the construction of figureheads and straw-men. But the tendency toward generalization from particulars may leave the historical data behind as a husk from which the philosophic truth has been extracted. While we ought not to require of the novelist the same resistance to generalization often demanded of the professional historian, our discovery of the principles with which his historical vision is informed may be as disturbing as a sign of scholarly prejudice.

The measure of Eliot's achievement in *Romola*—its limits as well as its success—lies in the application of her conception of realism to the historical novel. In a letter to Frederic Harrison she describes her effort "to make art a sufficiently real back-ground, for the desired picture, to get breathing, individual forms, and group them in the needful relations, so that the presentation will lay hold on the emotions as human experience—will, as you say, 'flash' conviction on the world by means of aroused sympathy."[9] We may assent to the motive but not to its fulfillment in this novel: the "background" is concrete and expressive enough, the characters are individuated and interesting enough, but the presentation does not generate the required suspension of disbelief. What is missing is the "needful relations" of the characters not to each other but to the "back-ground." In *Romola* itself, Eliot conceives of the relations of individuals to their environment as an organic one: ". . . as in the tree that bears a myriad of blossoms, each single bud with its fruit is dependent on the primary circulation of the sap, so the fortunes of Tito and Romola were dependent on certain grand political and social conditions which made an epoch in the history of Italy."[10] It is just this we are not given to see. There

9. *The George Eliot Letters*, IV, 300–301; 15 Aug. 1866. See also the letter to R. H. Hutton (IV, 96–97) of 8 Aug. 1863, describing her effort to create historical milieu with the same realism as in her novels of contemporary life: "It is the habit of my imagination to strive after as full a vision of the medium in which a character moves as of the character itself."

10. *The Works of George Eliot* (Boston [Illustrated Cabinet edition], n.d.), Bk. II, ch. i [in editions numbered consecutively; ch. xxi], p. 1. Subsequent references will be made parenthetically in the text, and will follow this sequence of identification.

is nothing in the main movement of the plot—the gathering crimes of Tito, in consequence of his moral deficiencies—that could not be situated in another time and place. Nor does the plot make a significant comment on the nature of Renaissance man: Tito's filial defects, bigamy, and marital tyranny are hardly to be set down to the account of the Renaissance.

There is, to be sure, one major point of dramatic interaction between the characters and their historical situation. Eliot's motive in setting the action in Florence in the 1490's was that Savonarola preached at that time and place and could therefore exert a powerful influence on a young woman in quest of a moral order for her life. For all Eliot's scepticism as to his complete sincerity at the delivery of his great Duomo sermon—"He felt in that moment the rapture and glory of martyrdom without its agony" (ii, iv [for xxiv], 37)—she does not stint the power of his creed. Of the Burning of Vanities she concludes: "a religious enthusiasm like Savonarola's which ultimately blesses mankind by giving the soul a strong propulsion towards sympathy with pain, indignation against wrong, and the subjugation of sensual desire, must always incur the reproach of a great negation" (iii, iv [or xlix], 34–35). Transcendence of egoism and dedication to human welfare are parts of Eliot's humanistic creed for which Savonarola serves as a religious carrier, but genuine doubt is introduced by his lack of humanity. "The subjugation of sensual desire" for Savonarola turns out in practice to prohibit separation from one's husband, even when the husband is revealed to be immoral and criminal, as well as tyrannical. Savonarola's championing of the absoluteness of the marriage bond represents not merely a Catholic (or a Victorian) sentiment but an extreme of self-abnegation; even if her husband were a malefactor, he tells Romola, "your place would be in the prison beside him" (ii, xx [for xl], 226). While we may reject his absolutism in this situation, there is an underlying social principle invoked here that must be reckoned with, as Eliot reckoned with it. For Savonarola's thinking is along Eliot's lines: "My daughter, your life is not as a grain of sand, to be blown by the winds; it is a thing of flesh and blood, that dies if it be sundered." The irony of Romola's situation is that she affirms the ties to the social community, of which the marriage-bond is a prime representative, while her personal sense of value cannot accept their application as an absolute moral principle.

Ultimately Romola does leave Tito, but only when she makes a sweeping rejection of the larger community, Florence, and of its ideal spokesman, Savonarola. She leaves after the execution of her godfather, Bernardo del Nero, when she is disillusioned by Savonarola's refusal altruistically to intercede for one of his Medicean enemies. Her flight is, then, a flight from the world: not merely a withdrawal from the political complexities and moral shortcomings of Florence, but a cloistral abstention from all worldliness. "Justice is like the Kingdom of God," Eliot concludes the account of Tito's death; "it is not without us as a fact, it is within us as a great yearning" (III, xxii [for lxvii], 212). Given this radical despair of historical justice as enacted in the workings of the social community, Eliot can envision justice only in the mind of the individual. This inner life has its outward manifestation, to be sure, for Romola's flight becomes an intensely social activity at a plague-stricken village and not a hermit-like isolation. But she fails to become attached to this simple community—except insofar as she allows herself to be venerated as the Virgin. She does not establish a new historical relationship but addresses herself to the eternal sorrows of the human condition:

In Florence the simpler relations of the human being to his fellow-men had been complicated for her with all the special ties of marriage, the State, and religious discipleship; and when these had disappointed her trust, the shock seemed to have shaken her aloof from life and stunned her sympathy. But now she said, "It was mere baseness in me to desire death. If everything else is doubtful, this suffering that I can help is certain; if the glory of the cross is an illusion, the sorrow is only the truer."
(III, xxiv [for lxix]), 227–28)

This "new baptism," as it is called in the same passage, is not only an awakening from egoistic illusion but a rejection of history, of the complications of "all the special ties of marriage, the State, and religious discipleship," i.e., of the system of social limitations that constitutes historical experience.

It is, preeminently, a leap at religious clarity and moral certainty, free of "the sense of a confusion in human things which made all effort a mere dragging at tangled threads" (III, xvi [for lxi], 145). For the mind that desires clarity in an age of cultural transition —whether Renaissance or Victorian—not only religious but political ideals must seem indelibly tainted by the partisanship and selfishness of their human embodiments. This is the lesson Romola learns from her contact with Savonarola, when she replies to his claim that "the cause of my party *is* the cause of God's kingdom," with the cry, "God's kingdom is something wider,—else, let me stand outside it with the beings that I love" (III, xiv [for lix], 134). It is also the lesson the narrator enforces in her portrayal of Florentine political affairs. Tito's is only the extreme case of a condition that affects all politicians, including Savonarola at his Trial by Fire: "the doubleness which is the pressing temptation in every public career, whether of priest, orator, or statesman" (III, xx [for lxv], 189).

Unlike the earlier rejection of the given political structures by Scott's or Thackeray's heroes, Romola's rejection is not based on a thorough engagement in and knowledge of the vagaries of parties and personalities. She is, to be sure, personally touched by the internecine warfare of Florence, but her entire career is conducted on the lofty plane of a quest for a spiritual purity, untainted by political life. In a way peculiar to the Late Victorian historical novel, a period of history is described in learned and incisive detail, and then rejected in behalf of a non-historical "higher life."[11] Like Reade's liberalism, Eliot's humanism acts ultimately as a critical standard by which to assess all historical experience and find it wanting.

Eliot was fully aware of her heroine's—and her own—tendencies toward withdrawal from worldly commitment. Romola becomes stricken not only by homesickness but by guilt: "What if the life of Florence was a web of inconsistencies? Was she, then, something higher, that she should shake the dust from off her feet, and say, 'This world is not good enough for me'? If she had been really higher, she would not so easily have lost all her trust" (III, xxiv [for lxix], 229–30). She does, of course, return to her organic ties but is mercifully relieved by Tito's death from continued self-effacement and passivity before his evil. Instead, she finds the Victorian woman's role in domesticity, as the doyenne of Tito's other menage, Tessa and her children, although this doing of

11. I am glad to find myself in agreement on this point with the most incisive of Eliot critics: W. J. Harvey, *The Art of George Eliot* (London, 1961), p. 183; see also Harvey's discussion of time in *Romola*, p. 114. George Levine's attempt to explain the novel's failures by ascribing them to its generic design as a romance or "fable" begs most of the questions about its historical realism; but see his outstanding discussion of the novel's ring (and related) imagery, in Barbara Hardy, ed., *Critical Essays on George Eliot* (New York, 1970), pp. 86–88.

"the duty which lies nearest thee" is meant to represent the ties that connect the individual with humanity as a whole.[12] It is left for her, in the Epilogue, only to repeat to Tito's son the moral imperatives that Eliot maintains from novel to novel—the necessity of unegoistic endurance and wide sympathy. But the lesson is based not on the individual's connection with his historical community but on an implicit vision of the ideal human community, of which Florence and other concrete instances are pale shadows.

In the end, Eliot's historical imagination failed organically to unite her "sufficiently real back-ground" and her "breathing, individual forms"—or even to sustain the "working out in detail of the various steps by which a political or social change was reached." Her most impressive achievement in *Romola* is to avoid the "schemed picturesqueness of ordinary historical fiction," and to create a severely conscientious portrait of a total society. But she left the novel, as she said, an "old woman," not because she had worked so hard on it, but because she had failed to find a historical community for her heroine—as she had failed to find one for herself at this point in her career.

ଡ

One of the most remarkable of Late Victorian historical novels is the work of a literary amateur, a businessman with religious preoccupations—and one so receptive to culture that his work is not proof against the charge of plagiarism. Despite his lack of expertise, Shorthouse wrote *John Inglesant* (1880) according to a theory at once religious, literary, political, and historical:

. . . this formula I will not call Revelation *v.* Humour, because what I want is the *synthesis* of Revelation (on the divine principle) with Humour, *not* their *opposition.*

12. U. C. Knoepflmacher has noted that the picture of Romola at the close resembles an emblem on the banner of the Comtean Positivists: a woman holding a child and preaching a gospel of love; *Religious Humanism and the Victorian Novel* (Princeton, 1965), pp. 40–41 n. Knoepflmacher's suggestions as to the relation of *Romola* and *Marius* to their creators' religious crises are made a matter of direct influence between them in David J. DeLaura, "*Romola* and the Origin of the Paterian View of Life," *Nineteenth-Century Fiction*, XXI (1966), 225–33; such influence has been denied in Donald J. Hill, "Pater's Debt to *Romola*," *Nineteenth-Century Fiction*, XXII (1968), 361–77.

All history is nothing but the relation of this great effort [Revelation] —the struggle of the divine principle to enter into human life. The effort of this principle, represented in us, in this age, by our love of the person of Christ, and in the enthusiasm of our sacramental hours, is at work in every one of us, constantly endeavoring to permeate our daily life; but the contrast between this divine love and these sacramental hours and the everyday life of ourselves and others is so appalling. . . .

[Humour] is the cultivation in the hearts of men, which are never sterile to such cultivation, of a feeling which I should call the enthusiasm of humanity. . . . This is an interest and attraction in man *as studied in the circumstances of his existence,* and indeed *because* of such circumstances, by which the various fortunes, sorrows, failings, and littlenesses of mankind constitute an infinitely varied drama of absorbing interest. This enthusiasm is excited, not by what man *might be* but by what he *is,* and is therefore essentially different from that feeling which Seeley attributes to Christ and to some other great reformers, for the student of human life is . . . far from wishing to *alter* its circumstances. . . .[13]

Many of the characteristic elements of Late Victorian imagination are present here: a busily secular age's groping for a meaning in mundane existence, the post-aristocratic urge to find value in the commonplace as well as in the heroic life, the sacramental vision that invests not only the present but the past, history as well as nature, with spiritual significance, the complacent standpoint of the spectator who can understand and forgive all—the ethical equivalent of art for art's sake.[14]

Some of these features resemble Arnoldian or Paterian "culture" closely enough to have led Shorthouse to employ that term: "In one sense it is the object of [*John Inglesant*] to show 'nothing done.' Perhaps the chief object is to promote culture at the expense of fanaticism, including the *fanaticism of work*; to exalt the unpopular doctrine that the end of existence is not the good of one's neighbour, but one's own culture." This tells us much about the motives of a Birmingham manufacturer in writing a romance

13. *John Henry Shorthouse: Life and Letters,* ed. [Mrs.] S. Shorthouse (New York and London, 1905), I, 84–85 (from a letter to Matthew Arnold, urging him to lend his approval to Shorthouse's ideas; Arnold's reply is, predictably, politely cool). The quotations immediately following unless accompanied by a parenthetical reference, are from pp. 124–25 of this work.

14. These ideas are elaborated in Shorthouse's essays, "The Humorous In Literature" and "Religio Historici," *Literary Remains* [*Life and Letters,* vol. II], (New York and London, 1905), pp. 248–80, 168–83.

about a dashing Cavalier, but the literary implications of the impulse are even more specific than the personal:

> The leading idea I had in my mind when I first conceived the idea of the book was, that ordinary life in past ages was itself so full of interest that nothing is needful but to recover the minutiae to make history as interesting as romance. Human life has never presented itself to me as divided into well-defined and elaborate plots and "unities," but as jogging along in haphazard fashion, making an acquaintance and a friend here, an enemy there, forgetting them, losing sight of them, and very often finding nothing come of the most promising events.

Given these premises about life and history, Shorthouse can combine "historical" with "philosophical" romance—can recover past experience as Humour, valuable in its own right, as well as being the carrier of Revelation or general significance. How well does this "synthesis" of the past for its own sake and for higher meaning succeed?

Shorthouse does acknowledge a "chain of circumstance" that unifies his novel: Humour is not entirely free and indulged. The hero is educated by his Jesuit teacher in "perfect toleration of and indifference to all creeds and opinions," and he is led to experience them one after the other in the manner of a *Bildungsroman*. These varieties of religious experience are not chosen to constitute a thorough picture of Inglesant's cultural milieu, but arrange themselves in a religious dialectic. The novel's considerable popularity in its time must be accounted, then, to qualities that lie outside the scope of traditional historical fiction. *John Inglesant* does not quite fulfill its author's intention to convey "that exquisite age-spirit" of the seventeenth century by collecting fragments of political, military, and religious experience. Its main preoccupation is with the spiritual growth of the hero, and his involvement in worldly affairs acts only as the catalyst for internal events that remain mysterious.

Shorthouse puts this best when he explains, "Altogether I should say that Inglesant's life was one gallant struggle for freedom. The struggle of a being handicapped in every way,—by constitutional heredity, by circumstance, by accident of training, by course of events,—but a struggle triumphant to the end, and bringing satisfaction to himself." If we are to summarize his ultimate freedom from family, circumstance, education, and the course of events, it must be seen as freedom from history. It is realized fully only with his final retirement from political service, but his impulse throughout the novel is an inward turning, which involves turning away from almost all the commitments of his career. Neither the failure of his political efforts in support of Charles i, nor the loss of his spiritual lady-love, Mary Collet, seems greatly to move him. Only the murder of his brother, mistaken for himself, provides him with the impetus to do so much as pursue a series of cloak-and-dagger adventures in Italy. Even when established as a lord-of-the-manor in Northern Italy, he discovers no profound involvement with his wife and child (these are, in fact, the most unconvincing pages in an often highly improbable book). Inglesant is, like his author, a devotee of mystical detachment and contemplation, a man-of-the-world who is never fully of the world. The most attractive quality of the novel for its Late Victorian audience must have been its aura of non-involvement, of cool indifference to life.

The Quaker strain in Shorthouse's background was evidently that brand of quietism which does not return the mystic to the world, armed for the struggle, but provides him with a mask of calm disconcertingly resembling a death-mask. Following Fox's view, Shorthouse can look on history as vanity, or as he puts it, as a "long and dismal night of apostasy and darkness." The advantages of this sweeping rejection are, however, too easily gained: Shorthouse made light of the historian S. R. Gardiner's criticism of his historical accuracy as "little to do with a criticism of my book." If the author had not committed himself to an imaginative recovery of "humorous" concrete phenomena, he would have been on firmer ground in disavowing the relevance of historical facts. His method depends, as we have seen, on the assembling of the "minutiae" of experience in order to contemplate the holiness of mundane phenomena. When these are discovered to be unrewarding, and when no general theory arises to give coherence to the historical pattern, the reader is left only with the inner activity of the individual. *John Inglesant* becomes the drama of Inglesant's soul in his muted response to and withdrawal from a dimly apprehended historical world.

Another of Shorthouse's frequent confessions of his motives in writing the novel is set down in the Preface: ". . . it is an attempt, and an honest one, to blend together these three in one philosophy

—the memory of the dead—the life of thought—the life of each one of us alone" (p. x). The most remarkable feature in the creation of Inglesant is to make him a man of thought, though neither a philosopher like Marius the Epicurean nor a scholar like Romola, but a courtier, soldier, and diplomat. This man of action need not grow contemplative but is so from the first. Indeed, his contemplative tendency is something of an embarrassment, not only in worldly but in moral terms: "Surely it behoved him to look well to his steps, lest he should be found at last absolutely and unequivocally fighting against his conscience and his God; if, indeed, this looking well to their steps on such occasions, and not boldly choosing their side, had not been for many years the prevailing vice of his family, and to some extent the cause of his own spiritual failure" (xxvi, 304). Inglesant's speculative bent and tendency to "look well to his steps" is to be distinguished from his family's tradition of trimming but infects his career as well. He is a Church-and-King man, and despite his sympathy for Catholic principles and persons he never hedges his loyalty. Yet the value of his object of loyalty comes to be questionable when he is imprisoned for his part in Charles's plan to bring Irish Catholic troops into England to revive his sagging fortunes. While never a Waverley hero, caught between opposite sympathies or loyalties, Inglesant is subject to much the same alienation when he chooses to sacrifice himself to defend his King, while the King's self-protective silence brings his courtier to the verge of the scaffold.

It is not his unflinching obedience in politics that is Inglesant's most spectacular trait—although it is much acclaimed and also subtly decried at various points in the narrative—but his curiosity in religious matters. The hero's career resembles neither a quest for experience nor a "gallant struggle for freedom" so much as it does a course in comparative religion, as successive tutors and sages pass in review. His first teacher, an Anglican divine, uses religious precepts to inculcate the ethics of "my station and its duties": ". . . I have never told you to act freely in this world; you are not placed here to reason (as the sectaries and precisians do), but to obey" (ii, 24). His increasing involvement with Catholic priests leads him to the mystical doctrines of the "Divine Light"— the initial stimulus being *The Flaming Heart*, furthered by a meeting with Crashaw. When he is deeply moved by his visit to

Nicholas Ferrar's semi-monastic community at Little Gidding, Ferrar counsels him to pursue his researches further before indulging his tendencies toward Rome. Hobbes himself offers him a taste of Hobbesian pragmatism—"Truth is that which we have been taught, that which the civil government under which we live instructs us in and directs us to believe" (v, 67)—but its effect is to confirm him in his budding career as a courtier without bringing intellectual conviction. Later colloquies with the Cambridge Platonist Henry More have less of an impact on him than a direct experience of the supernatural in an astrologer's crystal ball (in which he sees a vision of his brother's impending death). Pursuing the daemon of his revenge, Inglesant, at the death-bed of Mary Collet, has one of a number of his mystical experiences (which, in this description, are difficult to distinguish from epileptic seizures, from which Shorthouse himself suffered). At about the same time, he is converted to Catholicism, although this remains but a vague precondition for his adventures in the service of the Jesuits.

After this fairly thorough exposure to seventeenth-century English culture, the Italian portion of *John Inglesant* settles into a simpler confrontation between the worldly and other-worldly tendencies of the hero. The first stimulus to withdrawal comes from a Benedictine, the English convert Serenus de Cressy, who urges him to repress his intellectual pursuits and find rest in humility and simple service. But Inglesant cannot give up either his curiosity or his impulse to avenge his brother's death. In Italy, his Jesuit master's introductions bring him into the highest aristocratic and Papal circles, and a succession of Browningesque speakers encourage his predilections to esthetic refinement. His absorption into the Italian Renaissance is, however, a progressive alienation from his own nature, and as his identity becomes confused we feel we know the hero less and less. Only in this light can we accept—if we do at all—the grotesque plotting of the latter half of the novel. When Inglesant's personal intrigues have come to some resolution, his final return to himself takes the form of a struggle on behalf of the quietistic Molinist Order against the Jesuits. From the Vicar-General of the Jesuits, who argues for absolutism in much the same terms as Dostoyevsky's Grand Inquisitor, Inglesant demands "spiritual freedom—the freedom of silence" (xxxvii, 420), and is allowed to beat a retreat to England. There he returns to the Anglican fold, accepting its contradictions in the absence of revealed truth, and expressing his world-weariness in the melancholy notes of his violin.

Whatever the deficiencies of *John Inglesant*—its discontinuous and confused plot, its crudely ingested philosophical passages and derivative echoing of *Henry Esmond* (and *I Promessi Sposi?*), its unreflective condemnation of the Commonwealth (in contrast to its subtle view of Charles)—it remains a major contribution to the tradition of the historical novel. By relaxing the dialectical structure of the Waverley type of novel, by leading its hero a wandering course through the politics, personalities, and religious currents of the seventeenth century, by maintaining the hero's intellectual stature throughout his variety of involvements so that he never becomes a mere passive reflector of the historical world, Shorthouse achieved a high refinement of the genre's possibilities. Yet the "Revelation" of the denouement comes dangerously close to cancelling its interest as a historical novel: if all Inglesant's explorations of his milieu ultimately constitute a series of false starts and then take their places in a spectrum of pre-arranged alternatives, much of the spontaneity of the hero's life in history is lost. From an esthetic standpoint, the most effective way of writing *John Inglesant* would have been to apply Shorthouse's idea of "Humour" to the religious as well as to the other cultural phenomena of history. If these had been taken up with historical curiosity about their psychological functions and social relationships, *John Inglesant* might have ranked with the finest evocations of personal experience in the past. But as Shorthouse himself was too much identified with his hero's quest to adopt this esthetic distance, the novel's absorption in history is subordinated to its ahistorical religious preoccupations.

༄

The religious quest continues in *Marius the Epicurean: His Sensations and Ideas* (1885), yet it does not lead to a dismissal of history. Marius is, even more consistently than Inglesant, a seeker after religious experience, but his career becomes a model of the historical process itself. This formal balancing of the patterns of personal and historical development is not, however, without its price for historical fiction.

It has been widely agreed (with occasional dissent) that Pater's scepticism precluded his finding intellectual satisfaction in any of the "religions" brought to the dock in *Marius,* so that there is no progressive unfolding of religious truth in the novel.[15] Pater's only distinguishing criterion for them is their viability—their ability to satisfy Marius's emotional and esthetic needs rather than to solve ethical or transcendental problems—and this viability Marius finds in Christianity, ironically, on his death-bed. The religion into which Marius is born, "the religion of Numa" or Roman paganism, is well-remembered for its "usages and sentiment"—its ritual organization of life and its rich encrustation of tradition. The second of Marius's "religions," the philosophical hedonism (of which his Epicureanism is one variant) that he acquires in the Rome of Marcus Aurelius, is of intellectual and psychological value, but only in stimulating the sensibility and disciplining the feelings, not in arriving at conviction. A stage further is reached with the teachings of the Stoic Cornelius Fronto, which suggest an over-arching cosmic and moral order in which individual experience can find lasting significance. But this "Humanity—. . . a universal commonwealth of mind" lacks a visible community of which Marius can feel himself part. Finally, the Christianity by which Marius is tantalized in the charismatic figure of the angelic Knight Cornelius, exerts a powerful attraction, but the voluntarist assent it evokes is unable to end the splendid isolation of Marius's reflective ego.

Were these samplings arranged in a kind of religious smorgasbord, we would find in *Marius* merely an application of Pater's doctrine of experience for its own sake to the realm of sacred things. What saves this novel from becoming a journal of personal experience is Pater's employment of a system of thought that organizes the hero's quest in a historical pattern. The novel's well-known allusive leaps from second-century Rome to medieval, Renaissance, and modern analogies represent not mere anachronism but a conscious attitude which sees all Western history as a repetitive form.

15. There have been numerous listings of Marius's religions, none of which quite agrees with the others on their progressive sequence. David J. DeLaura, *Hebrew and Hellene in Victorian England: Newman, Arnold, and Pater* (Austin, Texas and London, 1969), p. 265, interprets the fact that all these religious impulses are already present in Marius's childhood religion to mean that the novel is not about historical progress but about Pater's own development. I would take this evidence to mean that the stages are not only structural in any personal experience but repeat themselves in historical cycles.

Anthony Ward has recently emphasized the importance of Pater's Oxford Hegelian milieu for his conception of history.[16] For Pater, Hegel was not the source of an organic social theory—as he was for the contemporary Oxford neo-Hegelian T. H. Green and his followers—nor was Pater content to call upon Hegel for confirmation of his Heraclitean sense of universal flux (although he did so in *Plato and Platonism*). Pater shared with his evolution-minded age a predilection for the now-discredited notion that "ontogeny recapitulates phylogeny"—that the life of the species can be seen reflected in the life of the individual, and that the latter can serve as an inductive model for evolutionary speculation. Whether drawing on Hegel or on more popular notions, Pater could trace in the career of a single mind the course of intellectual development in Western civilization.

Marius is, like Pater's Renaissance studies, never confined to the realm of the particular but hovers on the borderline of historical generalization. It puts forward the Hegelian dictum that "truth indeed, resides, as has been said, 'in the whole,' "[17] and elaborates the stages of "ardent pre-occupation" with it. In the Hegelian treatment of the stages of human growth—especially in *The Phenomenology of Mind*, where the historical unfolding of philosophical progress and the dialectical growth of personal thought function as illustrations of each other—Pater had a model for treating Western intellectual history as the drama of an individual mind. His reduction of intellectual history to basic types of mind is expressed in the following terms (II, xvi, 20–21):

Perhaps all theories of practice tend, as they rise to their best, as understood by their worthiest representatives, to identification with each other. For the variety of men's possible reflections on their experience, as of that experience itself, is not really so great as it seems; and as the highest and most disinterested ethical *formulae*, filtering down into men's everyday existence, reach the same poor level of vulgar egotism, so, we may fairly suppose that all the highest spirits, from whatever contrasted points they have started, would yet be found to entertain, in the moral consciousness realised by themselves, much the same kind of mental company. . . .

16. Anthony Ward, *Walter Pater: The Idea in Nature* (London, 1966), pp. 44–55 *et seq*. For previous commentators on Pater's Hegelianism, see R. T. Lenaghan, "Pattern in Walter Pater's Fiction," *Studies in Philology*, LVIII (1961), 69 n.

17. I quote the Macmillan Library edition of Pater's collected works (London, 1910): *Marius the Epicurean*, vol. II, ch. xvi, p. 19. Subsequent quotations to this and other volumes of this edition are cited parenthetically in the text.

The stages of development are not, therefore, the sequence of philosophic schools in history but the formulation of "disinterested ethical *formulae*" by one or another of the "higher spirits," followed by a "filtering down" into the "vulgar egotism" of everyday life. This is not only a record of Western philosophy, but an eternal process.

The difficulties of reading *Marius* as a historical novel are, beyond this theory of historical and individual types, accountable to the peculiarities of Pater's habits of mind. Where two ideas were equally attractive yet contradictory, he saw no necessity to divest himself of precious baggage in order to reach a logical goal. As Ward shows, the progressive and cyclical views of history are both present in Pater's thought—not, as in most philosophies of history, the one qualifying the other, but in cavalier alternation, sometimes within the same page or argument. When affirming the "historic sense" (which he finds lacking in Pico della Mirandola and the Renaissance generally)—the sense which "estimates every intellectual creation in its connexion with the age from which it proceeded"— Pater is able to see the uniqueness of the past, the "differences of ages" (*The Renaissance*, p. 34). But in the preceding paragraph he takes the ontogenetic or cyclical view that the world's religions tend toward reconciliation, following the pattern of "the fancies of childhood and the thoughts of old age [which] meet and are laid to rest, in the experience of the individual." These religions are reduced to "successive stages in a regular development of the religious sense," having a historical evolution predetermined by a universal pattern of growth.[18] Both these views are fruitful for fiction; both the unique character of an age and the pattern of Western culture may be symbolized in the fictional biography of a single intellectual—but not both at the same time. It is between these two stools, similar to the twin directions of Shorthouse's "historical fiction" and "philosophical romance," that *Marius the Epicurean* falls.

The historical progression traced in Marius's life is from the ritualized folk religion of childhood, through the hyper-intellectual ethical philosophies of youth, to the resigned religion of the self's and the world's maturity. The pagan gods of the elemental processes, worshipped in a close family group and providing

18. See also *Plato and Platonism* for this historical view: "It is humanity itself now—abstract humanity—that figures as the transmigrating soul, accumulating into its 'colossal manhood' the experience of ages; making use of, and casting aside in its march, the souls of countless individuals . . ." (III, 72–73).

scope for imaginative reverie, are perfect for the child, and were appropriate for mankind in its earliest stages. The youthful flowering of Western civilization is marked by the development of philosophical systems, answering to the enlarged demands of the individual's and the race's mind:

> . . . Cyrenaicism is ever the characteristic philosophy of youth, ardent, but narrow in its survey—sincere, but apt to become one-sided, or even fanatical. It is one of those subjective and partial ideals, based on vivid, because limited, apprehension of the truth of one aspect of experience (in this case, of the beauty of the world and the brevity of man's life there) which it may be said to be the special vocation of the young to express. In the school of Cyrene, in that comparatively fresh Greek world, we see this philosophy where it is least *blasé*, as we say; in its most pleasant, its blithest and yet perhaps its wisest form, youthfully bright in the youth of European thought. But it grows young again for a while in almost every youthful soul. (II, xvi, 15)

This applies also to the naturalistic Epicurean doctrines, which correspond in this sequence not to decadence but to spring tide. Yet their very strength is seen as a limitation, stamped, as they are shown to be, by sophisticated indifference to cruelty, unwilling to identify themselves with suffering mankind (chapter XIV —"Manly Amusement"), yet with their *apatheia* grossly inadequate to the fact of death (chapter XVIII—" 'The Ceremony of the Dart.' ").

Marius's accession to Christianity is an instance of the Western world's tendency toward a religion which will comfort man's approach to death by the promise of immortality. In the weariness of advancing age, both the individual and the race are willing to ignore their inability to comprehend the enduring mysteries, and make an act of faith that amounts to a surrender of reason. Christianity, for all its tenderness of the young, is described in the autumn tones of resignation, and Marius's attraction toward it is a movement toward death: "Actually, as circumstances had determined, all its movement had been inward; movement of observation only, or even of pure meditation; in part, perhaps, because throughout it had been something of a *meditatio mortis*, ever facing towards the act of final detachment" (II, xxviii, 208–09).

However much credence we may give to Marius's—or Pater's— personal accession to Christianity, the institution in historical perspective is seen as the religion of cultural maturity, leading the individual and the West out of their late-classical miasma, whatever intellectual bogs it may entail en route. But in the case of the individual and—as Nietzsche was to state even more resoundingly—of the West, this maturity is also a step toward death and a denial of vital freedom. The second-century "Minor Peace of the Church" is a time of humanistic synthesis, in Pater's view, but he is ever mindful of the asceticism and life-denial into which it is ultimately to fall: "He had lighted, by one of the peculiar intellectual good-fortunes of his life, upon a period when, even more than in the days of austere *ascêsis* which had preceded and were to follow it, the church was true for a moment, truer perhaps than she would ever be again, to that element of profound serenity in the soul of her Founder, which reflected the eternal goodwill of God to man . . ." (II, xxii, 177). Pater closes his account of Christianity however, with a stress on its power of regeneration, both personal and historical. Just as Marius finds himself at his death connected with the Christian community and (at least passively) receiving their communion—thus emulating the common men who live on in their descendants, in the most "natural" form of immortality—so Christianity is to bring the Roman Empire at least temporary survival in the "greater 'peace' of Constantine." This is seen as another in the string of renaissances paramount in Pater's vision of history: "It was the old way of true *Renaissance*—being indeed the way of nature with her roses, the divine way with the body of man, perhaps with his soul—conceiving the new organism by no sudden and abrupt creation, but rather by the action of a new principle upon elements, all of which had in truth already lived and died many times" (II, xxi, 95–96).

This historical scheme is coherent, at least as much so as Eliot's Comtean paradigm, and certainly more so than Reade's or Shorthouse's interpretive notions of the past. But *Marius*'s power as symbolic history is vitiated by Pater's failures of "historic sense." He reminds us that "That age and our own have much in common—many difficulties and hopes. Let the reader pardon me if here and there I seem to be passing from Marius to his modern representatives—from Rome, to Paris or London" (II, xvi, 14). The intellectual crisis of the two ages may differ in content, but it is the constant philosophic cruxes in the development of individual minds that interested Pater most. Despite Pater's substitution of dialectical and directed cycles for the pagan vision of meaningless and undirected repetition in Marcus Aurelius's oration, Pater is as inclined as the Emperor to reject all past ages as fragmentary and ephemeral. It is possible to see Marius as an instance both of the intellectual situation at the close of the classical era *and* of the Victorian struggle to find spiritual assuagement. But these concrete roles are in turn made stages of man's development over the ages—Marius is universalized to become "man thinking." This accession to universality, otherwise admirable in historical fiction, comes at the expense of historical concreteness and accounts for the over-intellectualization that many readers have found in the novel.

Pater's imagination was not, in the end, historical but mythic. His consistent method in his prose sketches is to put historical personages to the service of illustrating an archetypal pattern of human life. As has recently been shown,[19] the fundamental myth in these "portraits," as well as in his critical studies of painters and poets, is that of the Dionysian dying god who brings about the regeneration of a community. Just as the Renaissance represents for Pater a heightened instance of the process of cultural renewal, Marius's death to the ancient world and awakening to the spirit of the Christian era is an exemplum—not of Christianity in particular but of the eternal return in the life of the race. As Monsman puts it: "But while the Renaissance, the 'enchanted' balance, lasted only momentarily, the reality of a great cultural flowering can be renewed repeatedly. . . . Moreover, this rebirth belongs not merely to national awakenings: it occurs continuously on a more limited scale—in villages, in families, and in individuals— whenever the opposite ends of experience are momentarily fused."

The mythic view has dominated in much of the literature that was to follow Pater, and it is one of the fountainheads of the literary imagination in every age. But it entails a cyclical view of history, and this has its dangers for the novelist's portrayal of individual men in their historical situations. The cyclical view is

19. Gerald C. Monsman, *Pater's Portraits: Mythic Pattern in the Fiction of Walter Pater* (Baltimore, 1967). The flaw in Monsman's reading of *Marius* is, it seems to me, to take Pater's absorption in Christianity as his solution to the intellectual problems he had expressed in mythic forms and theories, rather than as another instance of those problems and of Pater's mythic problem-solving process. The quotation below is from p. 15.

surely a legitimate historical theory, but its expression in fiction
leads almost inevitably to the loss of that temporal specificity and
local complexity which is the hallmark of the novel. *Marius the
Epicurean* draws away from the historical novel toward the status
of a Platonic myth, a parable of a grand historical pattern both
in the individual and the race: the spiritual quest, crisis, and
renewal that persist from age to age.[20]

In each of the cases we have been considering, a historical
novel has drawn sustenance from a theory of human affairs and
of history in particular. Reade's liberalism, Eliot's Positivism,
Shorthouse's version of Christianity, Pater's Hegelian-mythic system—all are potent sources for the novel of ideas. Indeed, this
group of Late Victorian novels brings general ideas to dramatic
expression more strenuously than had been done in any previous
period of English fiction. But the common trait of these philosophies is to compromise the representation of historical particulars.
The present study has maintained that historical fiction performs
the movement of all art toward the universal—particularly in view-
ing responses to history in terms which define man as a historical
being. It has also been stressed here that there is an inevitable
interaction in historical novels between the present and the past,
and that this interaction—far from necessarily disqualifying the

20. What can happen when the impulse to employ a past age as an
example of a degenerative rather than regenerative pattern in history may be
seen in George Gissing's unfinished and posthumously published historical
novel, *Veranilda* (London, 1905). As elsewhere in Gissing's work, e.g., *The
Private Papers of Henry Ryecroft*, the most prominent personality is that of
the narrator, in this case Maximus, an old Roman patrician dying at Sorrento
and reading Boethius for consolation. The gloom of the aged man (the persona
of the dying Gissing) is mingled with the general despair of the declining
Empire, expressed with something of the tone of an intellectual of the British
empire: ". . . in our time, what can we do, we who are born Romans, yet
have never learnt to lead an army or to govern a state?" (p. 149). The setting
of the tale is one in which the sinking man and nation try to overcome their
pessimism: Rome is hankering after the lost golden age of Theodoric, and is
stirred by hopes of his last descendant, the princess Veranilda, and by the
latest invader of Rome, the Goth Totila, who takes her under his protection. The story ends at this point, but historically it cannot have come to a
promising conclusion; Jacob Korg has suggested that the conclusion might
have come at the moment of Totila's brief conquest of Rome, but Gissing's
working title, "A Vanquished Roman," seems to cast doubt on a happy ending. See *George Gissing: A Critical Biography* (Seattle, 1963), p. 256; Korg also
gives an account of Gissing's research.

novelist on historicist grounds—may be one of the sources of an informing vision of the past. But in Late Victorian historical fiction, the concrete loses its intrinsic interest soon after it is made the symbol of a universal or of a generalization about history.

There hovers over these novels a suspicion of the *roman à thèse*, of the use of fiction to illustrate an intellectual position arrived at independently of the dramatic action. Scott, Dickens, and Thackeray had been governed by general ideas of human nature, but it was perhaps their relative innocence of theories of history that was their making as historical novelists. The historical patterns that develop in their novels may suggest a relation to be drawn between past and present, or a balanced attitude toward historical change, or a rejection of history altogether—but they do not lead to principles that can be formulated apart from the actions in the novels. On the analogy of the relation of ideas to history, ideas in art are not to be understood out of context but are expressions of the whole, and the theories of history generated by historical fiction must be seen evolving in a dramatic process, not as pre-existent forms to be fulfilled.

❧

The doctrinal drift of Late Victorian historical novels can be seen in their political as well as in their religious subjects. The many portrayals of the French Revolution and its aftermath, the Napoleonic period, make it possible to see clearly the controlling ideas at work. One of Anthony Trollope's first attempts to gain a reputation was *La Vendée* (1850), but it is disfigured by a crude hostility to the Revolution—probably the result of trying too hard to appeal to the prejudices of the British reading public. Its political lines are expressed in the simplest dramatic terms, the Loyalists playing the role of Cooper's frontiersmen and the Revolutionary forces that of Injuns. Elizabeth Gaskell, on the other hand, tried to win sympathy for the working class by realistically portraying, in *Sylvia's Lovers* (1863), a popular riot against the pressgangs at Whitby during the Napoleonic Wars. The implication for her readers was undoubtedly that industrial strikes in the present age were similar demands for elementary justice, though misguided in their violence. Where partisanship does not prevail, sentimentalism does, e.g., in the depiction of the French Revolutionary period in Henry Kingsley's *Mademoiselle Mathilde* (1868), whose heroine—so striking a personality as to gain the admiration of Marat—takes her sister's place at the guillotine à la Sydney Carton.

By far the best of the Revolutionary and Napoleonic novels before Conrad is Arthur Conan Doyle's *Uncle Bernac: A Memory of the Empire* (1896).[21] Doyle, like H. Rider Haggard and George Alfred Henty, was an inveterate writer of historical romances that can best be classified as adult juveniles, but *Uncle Bernac* is a genuine novel, with a Waverley hero, complicated villain, and close portrait of Napoleon, all deftly arranged in a tight but engaging plot. The hero's exposure to political intrigue and his fluctuations of thought gain intensity from the first-person narration, and the historical portraiture is based on the author's high amateur standing as a Napoleonic antiquarian. There is no besetting political prejudice, beyond a sense of the Emperor's mixture of awesomeness and pettiness; the point-of-view is that of an *émigré* who returns to France and finds himself overwhelmed by Napoleon's charisma. The narrative voice concludes that it is impossible to decide whether Napoleon was good or bad but only that he was very great—and that, in any case, the story was written neither to praise nor blame, "but only to tell the impression which he made upon me." We enter here the modern phase of English historical fiction.

21. In *The Historical Novels of Arthur Conan Doyle* (London, n.d.). Doyle wrote three other novels on the Napoleonic period, of which two—*The Exploits of Brigadier Gerard* and *Adventures of Gerard*—distinctly anticipate Conrad's Napoleonic novels in their familiar, yet entranced, portrayal of the "spirit of the epoch."

Chapter 7

Hardy:
The avoidance
of historical
fiction

Despite the variety of genres in which Thomas Hardy worked—
novel, story, romance, epic, drama, lyric—he has never been accused of writing a historical novel. In the one case that might
have convicted him, *The Trumpet-Major*, critics are usually careful to point out that it is not really a historical novel, in which the
drama hinges on historical events, but a tale set in the past, in
which the public actions—peripheral to the main-stream of history, at that—are mere background to personal relations. Yet
Hardy's interest in history is demonstrably greater than that of any
English novelist after Scott, and it led him to create what is
probably the greatest historical poem in the language. We can
even speak of the Wessex novels collectively as a history of an
English rural county in the nineteenth-century, as some commentators have done.[1] There is an even more marked historicity about
two novels at the beginning and end of the sequence, in point of
temporal setting. *The Trumpet-Major* (1880) and *Tess of the
d'Urbervilles* (1891) represent two new types of historical fiction
—we may call them the comic and the symbolic—which were to
become the dominant forms of the genre in the present century.

That Hardy was led to devise these original treatments of the
historical novel suggests a dissatisfaction with previous work in the
genre, if not with the genre itself. With typical iconoclasm, he

1. E.g., Carl J. Weber, *Hardy of Wessex: His Life and Literary Career* (New
York and London, 1965 [1940]).

regretted that Scott had turned to fiction, himself preferring Scott's poetry.[2] And yet, as Hardy's foremost biographer has maintained,[3] his absorption in the historical novels of Scott, Bulwer, Ainsworth, and G. P. R. James (along with Continental examples) not only occupied his boyhood reading but penetrated his mature writing, in the use of certain conventional plot devices and occasionally in prose style. It is no accident that Hardy should have bought a set of the Waverley novels while preparing *The Trumpet-Major,* just as it is no accident that he should have avoided the type of historical novel practiced by his contemporaries towards the end of the nineteenth century. The peculiar combination of tradition and innovation that marks Hardy's fiction generally is nowhere more apparent than in his efforts to bring history into his work.

Yet Hardy's originality in historical fiction is not only a matter of stylistic experiment or temperamental iconoclasm; it has to do with his attitude toward history, which takes the form of a systematic rejection of both Romanticism and Historicism. In 1884, four years after the publication of *The Trumpet-Major* and during the period when the plan of *The Dynasts* began to take shape, Hardy wrote in his notebook: "Query: Is not the present quasi-scientific system of writing history mere charlatanism? Events and tendencies are traced as if they were rivers of voluntary activity, and courses reasoned out from the circumstances in which natures, religions, or what-not, have found themselves. But are they not in the main the outcome of *passivity*—acted upon by unconscious propensity?" (*Life,* p. 168). This is not traditional Romantic distrust of the historian's rationalism as 'applied to the vital complexity of human action, but an expression of Hardy's brand of determinism, emphasizing the impotence of any historical explanation which focuses on the individual, and ascribing historical causality to a stream of tendency in the order of the universe and its components, which he here calls "unconscious propensity" and ultimately names the "Immanent Will."

In the following year, Hardy's experiences of high society and his reflections on the "roar on London"—with its myriad lives pur-

---

2. Florence Emily Hardy, *The Life of Thomas Hardy: 1840–1928* . . . (New York, London, etc., 1962), p. 49. This official biography, mainly written by Hardy himself, will hereafter be referred to parenthetically in the text.

3. Weber, pp. 11–12, 90–91, 115–16.

suing their individual ends while "playing their parts in the tragedy just the same" (*Life*, p. 171)—led him to generalize about history again, this time explicitly rejecting a favorite Romantic metaphor of historical process, as well as the Historicist assumption of an intelligible relationship among historical data:

History is rather a stream than a tree. There is nothing organic in its shape, nothing systematic in its development. It flows on like a thunderstorm-rill by a road side; now a straw turns it this way, now a tiny barrier of sand that. The offhand decision of some commonplace mind high in office at a critical moment influences the course of events for a hundred years. Consider the evenings at Lord Carnarvon's, and the intensely average conversation on politics held there by average men who two or three weeks later were members of the Cabinet. A row of shopkeepers in Oxford Street taken just as they came would conduct the affairs of the nation as ably as these.

Thus, judging by bulk of effect, it becomes impossible to estimate the intrinsic value of ideas, acts, material things: we are forced to appraise them by the curves of their career. There were more beautiful women in Greece than Helen; but what of them? (*Life*, p. 172)

The burden of this passage goes beyond a rejection of Romantic "great-men" explanations of events; it questions the value which the Romantics placed on the unique, individual phenomenon in history. Not all historical entities are in Hardy's view valuable, but only those that have had consequences—and only to the degree of their consequences. History makes a mockery of intrinsic value: the most beautiful women of Greece launch no ships at all, and "intensely average" men make historic decisions. It remains to the artist to trace the esthetic "curves of their career."

We are close here to one of the essential antinomies of Hardy's sensibility, the disjunction between fact and value that he is never tired of irritably posing to himself, e.g., "After infinite trying to reconcile a scientific view of life with the emotional and spiritual, so that they may not be inter-destructive I come to the following: . . . The emotions have no place in a world of defect, and it is a cruel injustice that they should have developed in it" (*Life*, pp. 148–49). But in the same way that Hardy's vital portrayal of the characters in his novels ignores his awareness of their puppet-like status in the grand scheme of things, his portrayal of historical phenomena ignores his low estimate of their status in the movement of historical forces.

Because of his distrust of anthropocentrism in historical thinking, Hardy was inclined to reject the going philosophies of history:

May [1886]. Reading in the British Museum. Have been thinking over the
dictum of Hegel—that the real is the rational and the rational the real—
that real pain is compatible with a formal pleasure—that the idea is all,
etc., but it doesn't help much. These venerable philosophers seem to start
wrong; they cannot get away from a prepossession that the world must
somehow have been made to be a comfortable place for man. If I remember, it was Comte who said that metaphysics was a mere sorry attempt to
reconcile theology and physics. (*Life*, p. 179)

One of the consequences of this scepticism of historical theory was
to doubt the prevailing notions of progress. Hardy noted on a visit
to Italy in the following year: "Everybody is thinking, even amid
these art examples from various ages, that this present age is the
ultimate climax and upshot of the previous ages, and not a link in
a chain of them" (*Life*, p. 191). The final step in Hardy's neutralization of history, in accord with his neutralization of nature, is to
deny the value of historical artifacts on their one incontrovertible
distinction, their antiquity. On a visit to Tintern Abbey, Hardy
remarked: "But compare the age of the building with that of the
marble hills from which it was drawn!" He went on to reflect
(speaking in the person of his "biographer"-wife); ". . . this short-
coming of the most ancient architecture by comparison with geology
was a consideration that frequently troubled Hardy's mind when
measuring and drawing old Norman and other early buildings . . ."
(*Life*, pp. 93–94).

If Hardy had succeeded in reducing his attitude toward history
to his "scientific," and eliminated his "emotional and spiritual," responses to it, he would not have been as enamored of the past as
he was. The same absorption he felt in Wessex as a region he felt
in Wessex's Napoleonic past as a period. An entire volume of his
short stories, *A Group of Noble Dames*—written in the intervals of
preparing *Tess* for serial publication—is given over to romantic-
ironic tales of great ladies of the past, and conveys the history of
the aristocracy as one long record of feminine chicanery and
masculine sadism. Two of the *Wessex Tales*—"A Tradition of
Eighteen Hundred and Four" and "The Melancholy Hussar of the
German Legion"—are cast in the form of old-timers' recollections

of the Napoleonic period (the former putatively involving the Emperor himself).[4] A group of poems, including "The Alarm," "Leipzig," "San Sebastian," "Valenciennes," and best of all, "The Peasant's Confession," follow the same anecdotal pattern of relating Napoleonic history. Another story, "A Tryst at an Ancient Earthwork," is a descriptive sketch of an Ancient-British fortress, of the pedantic obsession of an antiquarian excavator, and of the powerful impression created on the narrator by the "enormous many-limbed organism of an antedeluvian time" and the "airborne vibrations of conversations uttered at least fifteen hundred years ago" that linger about it. Finally, in one of the best stories Hardy wrote, "A Committee-Man of 'The Terror,'" history itself is the protagonist, making impossible the love of a former member of the Committee of Public Safety and the woman whose fiancé, father, brother, and uncle he has condemned.

The source of Hardy's persistent absorption in the feelings of the men of the past is in his response to the intensely individual. Rejecting Matthew Arnold's exhortations against English provincialism, Hardy noted: "A certain provincialism of feeling is invaluable. It is of the essence of individuality, and is largely made up of that crude enthusiasm without which no great thoughts are thought, no great deeds done" (*Life*, p. 147). This perception leads, a few days later, to a softening of his anti-romanticism: "Romanticism will exist in human nature as long as human nature itself exists. The point is (in imaginative literature) to adopt that form of romanticism which is the mood of the age." Hardy's particular brand of romanticism is tied up with his imaginative involvement with his own ancestry, as recounted in the early pages of the *Life*. As shall be seen, the artist's attitudes toward his own "old family of spent social energies" (*Life*, p. 5) are the attitudes that structure *Tess of the d'Urbervilles*. Even in Hardy's architectural career, his sense of the past rose (though not immediately) to challenge his work in church restoration: "Much beautiful ancient Gothic, as well as Jacobean and Georgian work, he was passively instrumental in destroying or in altering

4. *The Short Stories of Thomas Hardy* (London, 1928), p. 46; the quoted phrases that follow are from pages 865 and 869 of this edition.

beyond identification; a matter for his deep regret in later years"
(*Life*, p. 31).[5]

We are led, then, to refer the fundamental antinomy of fact
and value in Hardy to his vision of history: past events and objects
are insignificant in themselves and acquire significance only as
parts of a causal stream—which, however, moves towards no particular end and is subject to apparently meaningless diversion by
the most trivial of influences; past events and objects are also valuable in themselves, merely because they have happened to people,
have mixed themselves with personal fortunes, have been per-
meated by human emotions, and have been remembered and retold down to the present. From the last of these associations,
historical phenomena derive their peculiar importance for the
artist: just as the events of personal life—as Hardy suggests in so
much of his love-poetry—stand in danger of annihilation if not
remembered and retold by the poet, so the events of Wessex
history would be lost if not remembered and retold by the novelist
and story-writer. The artist fulfills, in this view, one of his primitive functions: he is the chronicler—not to say *bard*—of the historical life of his people.

Yet the peculiar disjunction in Hardy's perspective makes it
impossible for him to take provincial or national history as complete in itself, a subject-matter that can be set out in a history or
in a historical novel. Wessex in Napoleonic times is, after all, only
a ripple in the stream of cosmic history. From another standpoint,
this fragment is too large for the telling: it is not the course of
Wessex's (or any other community's) history but the lives and feelings of a number of individuals that have reality—often incom-
mensurate with the collective situation in which they are thrown.
When the first of these perspectives is maintained, Hardy is
driven to transform history into epic, when the latter, into comedy.
When the two orders of phenomena—the cosmic stream and the
personal value—are given equal weight, Hardy finds (despite pre-

5. This regret is explained in Hardy's address, "Memories of Church Restoration," in *Thomas Hardy's Personal Writings: Prefaces, Literary Opinions,
Reminiscences,* ed. Harold Orel (Lawrence, Kan., 1966), pp. 203–17, which ends
with the maxim, "To do nothing, where to act on little knowledge is a dangerous
thing, is to do most and best." The reasons for caution go beyond this
caveat: not only can reproduction never be exact, but the "human associations" of the actual stones of the past are always lost in replacement.

cedents to the contrary) that the historical novel can no longer
be handled in its traditional form; if it is to persist at all, it must
be treated symbolically. These three alternatives Hardy explored
in *The Dynasts, The Trumpet-Major,* and *Tess of the d'Urbervilles* respectively.

⁂

Criticism of *The Trumpet-Major* must begin with the fact that
Hardy placed it among his "Romances and Fantasies" rather than
among his "Novels of Character and Environment." Given that a
historical novel is inherently a novel of environment, does a
romance—there is no possibility of using the word "fantasy" about
The Trumpet-Major—automatically void its claim for consideration as social history? Hardy chose to write here a characteristic
plot, the story of a girl's process of choice among three or more
suitors, so similar to those of *Far From the Madding Crowd, The
Hand of Ethelberta,* and *A Pair of Blue Eyes*[6]—but why did he
set it in the Napoleonic period and bring the invasion-scare to
bear upon the characters and their relationships? Their lives are
not shaped by the grand forces of history, nature, or economics
as those of Hardy's tragic figures are, nor do they have the depth
and contradictions of character that complicate the workings of
environment. But it makes a difference to the work that they exist at
a particular historical time and place—at least, that is what makes
The Trumpet-Major what it is, and not merely one more reworking
of the basic plot. There are indications that Hardy cared less for
the story than he did for the circumstances of its unfolding: the
manuscript of the text shows changes in the rather banal names
of the characters, but almost all the place-names are literally
geographic, are left unaltered in the manuscript, and probably
were changed to their disguised form only in proof-sheets.[7] One
way—though not, of course, the only way—of interpreting such a
procedure is to find Hardy's sensibility absorbed in the sense of

6. For the diagrammatic similarity of these plots, see Henry C. Duffin, *Thomas
Hardy: A Study of the Wessex Novels, the Poems, and The Dynasts* (Man-
chester, 1937 [1916]), pp. 99–100.
7. W. G. Bebbington, *The Original Manuscript of Thomas Hardy's "The
Trumpet-Major"* (Windsor, n.d. [1948]), p. 20.

place at a particular moment in historical time, and to see the plot and characters as mere occasions for writing about Wessex: 1804–1808.

Despite the verisimilitude of the personal narrative, events in this work convey a sense of having happened long ago. The circumstantial quality of the personal story is perfectly in harmony with the legendary aura which surrounds the historical events. We are intended to feel about the love story the same mixture of conviction and sceptical indulgence that the nineteenth-century Englishman would customarily feel for anecdotes of the great war. Just as the historical events have passed out of history into legend (without losing the verifiable evidence that earlier myths have lost), the narrative gains an air of legend from the purported fact that it is the story of historical persons who were engaged in those events. These qualities are subtle and difficult to demonstrate by brief quotations from the text, but they make *The Trumpet-Major* something more than an idyllic romance, if not a full-fledged historical novel, and something special in the Hardy canon: a comic vision of reality, accepting the past in both its factual and its fictitious trappings.

If the action of *The Trumpet-Major* is shaped by history neither in the way of a historical novel nor in the way of a Hardy "novel of character and environment," it is distinctly the action of a particular moment in history. We are given enough detail of the life of all classes in a rural English county, in peace and in expectation of war, to approximate the kind of historiography known as *Kulturgeschichte*. The setting down of these copious details is no mere costumery; if it is not functional in the story, it may be said to be more important than the story itself. There is a reflection here of the contradictions in Hardy's attitude toward history: the patterns of human relationship, especially in love, are repeated from age to age, and the retelling of such tales is a permanent feature of the nature of man, yet the specific manifestation of these patterns is significant in itself, and when it occurs in a period in which the artist has a personal stake, it can become denser with value and interest than its individuality alone would allow.

With the dramatic force that the guns of Waterloo resonate when they break in upon complacent high society in *Vanity Fair*, history enters the practically timeless world of Wessex and cuts across the perennial round of agricultural village life. It is, however, a muted drama, not a grand entry of armies on the march but a close observation of personal responses:

> The girl glanced at the down and the sheep for no particular reason; the steep margin of turf and daisies rising above the roofs, chimneys, apple-trees, and church tower of the hamlet around her, bounded the view from her position, and it was necessary to look somewhere when she raised her head. While thus engaged in working and stopping her attention was attracted by the sudden rising and running away of the sheep squatted on the down; and there succeeded sounds of a heavy tramping over the hard sod which the sheep had quitted, the tramp being accompanied by a metallic jingle. Turning her eyes further she beheld two cavalry soldiers on bulky grey chargers, armed and accoutred throughout, ascending the down at a point to the left where the incline was comparatively easy. The burnished chains, buckles, and plates of their trappings shone like little looking-glasses, and the blue, red, and white about them was unsubdued by weather or wear.[8]

This is how the Napoleonic era came to Wessex, as seen by one caught in the act of entering into history.

It is the naive viewpoint of the heroine, Anne Garland, that we are to share for much of the novel, and her responses to historical experience are as untrustworthy as her understanding of her love affairs. In the little lives of the characters of the novel, the historical actors are like gods: "Anne now felt herself close to and looking into the stream of recorded history, within whose banks the littlest things are great, and outside which she and the general bulk of the human race were content to live on as an unreckoned, unheeded superfluity" (XIII, 108–9). She is wrong, of course— the qualification in the word "recorded" assures us that the naive spectator and the simple folk of Wessex and of England are in the stream of history but are "content to live" unconsciously, "unreckoned, unheeded." Yet it is her standpoint, with all its comic limitations, that we are asked not only to share but to value.

Not only does Hardy engage in a campaign to build up the historical value of personal life and folk society; he also exercises

---

8. I quote the Macmillan Pocket edition (London, New York, and Toronto, 1924 ff.), I, 4–5. All subsequent quotations from Hardy's works will be to this, the most widely issued, edition, which will be cited parenthetically in the text.

the complementary tendency to belittle the images of historical individuals. Much of the fun of *The Trumpet-Major* derives from the mediocre figure of the King, grotesquely juxtaposed against the rituals of official veneration. The best-known of these occasions is the bathing-machine scene:

> All that was to be heard for a few minutes were the slow pulsations of the sea; and then a deafening noise burst from the interior of the second machine with power enough to split the boards asunder; it was the condensed mass of musicians inside, striking up the strains of 'God save the King,' as his Majesty's head rose from the water. (XXXIII, 291–92)

Less well-known are equally funny contrasts of the great and small: "I see little figures of men moving about. What are they doing?"—"Cutting out a huge picture of the king on horseback in the earth of the hill. The king's head is to be as big as our millpond and his body as big as this garden; he and the horse will cover more than an acre" (XXXVII, 335). It is not only the reader who is conscious of the frail humanity of the mighty of the earth; although Mrs. Garland exclaims, "Thank God, I have seen my King!," the royal procession arouses little enthusiasm: "Nobody else expressed any thankfulness, for most of them had expected a more pompous procession than the bucolic tastes of the King cared to indulge in; and one old man said grimly that that sight of dusty old leather coaches was not worth waiting for" (XI, 100).

The most striking disparity between the world-historical figure in imagination and the same figure in reality emerges in Anne's petition to the King. The aura of majesty is reduced to an element of wish-fulfillment (a reduction made the more poignant by its reminiscence of Jeanie Deans's similar petition in behalf of a loved one):

> She had been borne up in this hasty spurt at the end of a weary day by visions of Bob promoted to the rank of admiral, or something equally wonderful, by the King's special command, the chief result of the promotion being, in her arrangement of the piece, that he would stay at home and go to sea no more. But she was not a girl who indulged in extravagant fancies long, and before she reached home she thought that the King had probably forgotten her by that time, and her troubles, and her lover's name. (XXXIV, 311)

Given the human frailty both of the dynasts and of the common people, Hardy's attitude is not as sanguine as the usual account of the novel maintains:

[The downs] still spread their grassy surface to the sun . . . but the King and his fifteen thousand armed men, the horses, the bands of music, the princesses, the cream-coloured teams—the gorgeous centrepiece, in short, to which the downs were but the mere mount or margin—how entirely have they all passed and gone!—lying scattered about the world as military and other dust, . . . some in home churchyards; and a few small handfuls in royal vaults. (XII, 106)

This is the emotion that presides over the conclusion of the novel, as the titular hero goes off to the wars, leaving the simpler natures of his brother and Anne to carry life onward, while he joins the debris of the remorseless machine of mass destruction that is, in Hardy's cosmic view, history. Yet even this *memento mori* has its compensating vitality in his holistic view of the cosmos; the very implements of war and mock-war—the pikes used by the Wessex farmers in their absurd drills—find their way into the stream of memory which is the other, human aspect of history:

And there they remained, year after year, in the corner of the [church] aisle, till they were removed and placed under the gallery stairs, and thence ultimately to the belfry, where they grew black, rusty, and worm-eaten, and were gradually stolen and carried off by sextons, parish clerks, whitewashers, window-menders, and other church servants for use at home as rake-stems, benefit-club staves and pick-handles, in which degraded situations they may still occasionally be found. (XXIII, 203)

۶

It is not in a tale set in past time that Hardy most closely approaches the role of historical novelist, but in a novel of contemporary life designed to epitomize the fate of individuals. *The Trumpet-Major* is, for all its brooding reminders of history on the march, a comic view of the hardihood of the common people —of their ability not only to survive in all historical weathers but to remain what they are even in proximity to grand actors and events. *Tess of the d'Urbervilles* addresses itself to the destruction of a woman of the people, under the slow historical shifting of class supremacies. Yet more: it creates a symbolic model of the pattern of British historical experience, and points a way out of the modern social debacle by turning its gaze on the sources of value buried in pre-history. So thoroughly is the novel organized around its images of history, and so imposing is the historical burden of the personal tragedy it recounts, that it may be read as a symbolic historical novel—the first in a mode which became in the twentieth century the chief alternative to the conventional "realism" of popular historical fiction.

It is by now well known that *Tess*'s social theme is the destruction of the old yeoman class of small-holders and peasants, and that it confronted a process going on vigorously at the time and place of its composition, the agricultural depression of 1870–1902.[9] If there remains any doubt of this, it is readily dispelled by Hardy's essay, "The Dorsetshire Labourer," written in the same decade in which he began to compose the novel.[10] Hardy builds up a picture of the agricultural laborer's individual dignity, modifies the outsider's impression that his dirty appearance betokens acute misery, but emphasizes that his total insecurity on the periodic hiring days is the bane of his existence. Basic economic forces create the fatal social trend, depopulation: "This process, which is designated by statisticians as 'the tendency of the rural population towards the large towns,' is really the tendency of water to flow uphill when forced." (In modified form, this sentence reappears in *Tess*, LI, 395.) Hardy concludes by sounding a warning of revolutionary agitation if the problem is not relieved, and defends the labor "agitators" for their moderation and for bringing about some wage-rises.

Besides his sociological concerns, he began with an antiquarian interest in the relics of his county, which was aroused when he overheard a drunkard claim to have relatives in a gentry family vault. This, of course, provided the germ of plot and central historical irony of the novel. Hardy went on to do research on the Turberville line at the British Museum, and appropriated the contemporary incident of novelist R. D. Blackmore's brother, who took the Turberville name in much the way the Stokes do in the

9. See Arnold Kettle, *An Introduction to the English Novel* (New York, 1961 [1951]), II, 49 ff.; Douglas Brown, *Thomas Hardy* (London, 1954); *et al.*

10. In *Personal Writings*, pp. 168–89; the quotation that follows is from p. 188.

novel.[11] Even more urgent in the novelist than his sociological and antiquarian interests, however, is his absorption in his own family history and his consciousness of being the last of a line:

Hardy often thought he would like to restore the "le" to his name, and call himself "Thomas le Hardy"; but he never did so. . . . They all had the characteristics of an old family of spent social energies, that were revealed even in the Thomas Hardy of this memoir (as in his father and grandfather), who never cared to take advantage of the many worldly opportunities that his popularity and esteem as an author afforded him. . . . at the birth of the subject of this biography the family had declined, so far as its Dorset representatives were concerned, from whatever importance it once might have been able to claim there. . . . (*Life*, p. 5)

It is not far from this to Tess herself. Personal identification inspires the enormous tenderness with which Hardy treats his heroine—a feeling exposed on the title-page, not only in the pugnacious defense of Tess as a "pure woman," but in what follows:

> Faithfully presented by
> Thomas Hardy
>
> ". . . Poor wounded name! My bosom as a bed
> Shall lodge thee."—W. Shakespeare

Whatever the degree of self-pity in Hardy's self-projection, it is clear that he saw in the decline of the d'Urbervilles the same processes that were at work in his own family: not only the decline of the peasantry and their exploitation or rape by the nouveau-riche, but the exhaustion of the old gentry families by the wearing-away of their economic power, their "social energies," and everything but their potentially tragic self-awareness. If we take these concerns together—the fortunes of the peasantry, of the gentry, and of the new bourgeoisie—we may see in *Tess of the d'Urbervilles* an epitome of recent social change in England, but this is not enough to make it a historical novel. As the images of these processes expand in the novel to cover a period larger than the close of the nineteenth century, *Tess* becomes a symbolic history of modern (that is, post-medieval) England, with an added excursion into the prehistoric past at its close.

11. Cf. Weber, pp. 170–71.

The historical process is not recorded temporally, as it would be in a more straightforward historical novel, but spatially, as is required for an arrangement of symbols. The landscape of *Tess* is displayed as a series of tradition-charged centers of significance, so that it becomes possible to speak of it as a symbolic landscape. The structure of topographical symbolism follows the social structure of modern England. At the center is the village of Marlott in the Vale of Blakemore (or Blackmoor), sheltered by the surrounding hills not only in climate but in culture—it is "for the most part untrodden as yet by tourist or landscape-painter, though within a four hours' journey from London" (II, 18). The Vale enshrines a medieval heritage of *noblesse oblige*: associated with it is the legend of the White Hart, in which Henry III fines a gentleman for killing a beautiful deer that he had spared. Here is an obvious prefiguration of Tess's career as hunted prey (as well as a set of associations with a *topos* of Christ in medieval iconography); but the Middle Ages was a time of justice—at least, for the legend—and the good king rebukes the persecutor of the innocent. Not only has the post-medieval ruling class lost the inner or outer restraints shown in the legend, but the modern peasantry is dead to its heritage: the May Day dance with which the plot opens is dying out and is not potent enough in its debased modern form to fulfill its essential social function as a stimulus to procreation. Angel is attracted by it, and by Tess, but not sufficiently to join the dance, and it thereby contributes its mite to her undoing, by failing to ritualize her mating at an early and natural stage.

In sharp contrast with Marlott is Trantridge Cross, on the hill above which is situated the Stoke-d'Urberville seat, The Slopes:

It was of recent erection—indeed almost new—and of the same rich red colour that formed such a contrast with the evergreens of the lodge. Far behind the corner of the house—which rose like a geranium bloom against the subdued colours around—stretched the soft azure landscape of The Chase—a truly venerable tract of forest-land, one of the few remaining woodlands in England of undoubted primeval date, wherein Druidical mistletoe was still found on aged oaks, and where enormous yew-trees, not planted by the hand of man, grew as they had grown when they were pollarded for bows. All this sylvan antiquity, however, though visible from The Slopes, was outside the immediate boundaries of the estate. (v, 47–48)

The awe in Hardy's description of The Chase proposes it as a still viable alternative to the rape of the country by the nouveau-riche Stokes. Thereafter he narrows his vision of the landscape until it comes to focus on the figure of Tess tending the d'Urberville chickens in the peasant cottage which has been given over to them. The old order changeth, and the new is dominated by the guilt-ridden hedonists of the bourgeoisie like Alec, who shape the novel's action.

Yet not everything of the past has been lost. Tess's refuge at Talbothays farm, which has been generally regarded as a repository of natural values, is no less a repository of history: "The shovelfuls of loam, black as jet, brought there by the river when it was as wide as the whole valley, were an essence of soils, pounded champaigns of the past, steeped, refined, and subtilized to extraordinary richness, out of which came all the fertility of the mead, and of the cattle grazing there" (XXXI, 222). It is not only the land which bears the mark of time, but the people who live on the bounty of its economic fecundity. The folkish tale of the drunken prankster who kept a bull at bay by playing tunes on his fiddle is capped by the joke of his getting away when the bull knelt for the Nativity Hymn—*and it wasn't even Christmas Eve!* Angel Clare gets the historical point: "It's a curious story; it carries us back to mediaeval times, when faith was a living thing!" (XVII, 132). But the strength of the folk values in dairyman Crick and his organic community cannot resist the hard facts of their isolation in the modern world: when the harvesting is done, Crick has to let Tess go, since he cannot employ her permanently. She is thus given over to the economic forces of the present: not only to the back-breaking toil of traditional field-labor at Flintcomb-Ash farm, but to the greater dehumanization of working alongside agricultural machinery. (Hardy points out in "The Dorsetshire Labourer" that the peasants hated the threshing machines, but not the turnip-stump hacking in which Tess is first engaged.)

The loss of the past and the rigors of the present are thus presented as features of a number of localities in which the action of the novel is centered. The possibilities of prehistoric as well as historic residues in the landscape of the novel begin to emerge at this stage. The most arresting instance of the ambiguity of historical incrustations in the land is Cross-in-Hand, the landmark which Tess passes on her walk to the Clare parsonage, and which she passes again later with the reborn Alec. At first it is described ambiguously as a stone pillar which "stands desolate and silent, to mark the site of a miracle, or murder, or both" (XLIV, 335), but on the return journey its ambiguity is given wider scope:

The place took its name from a stone pillar which stood there, a strange, rude monolith, from a stratum unknown in any local quarry, on which was roughly carved a human hand. Differing accounts were given of its history and purport. Some authorities stated that a devotional cross had once formed the complete erection thereon, of which the present relic was but the stump; others that the stone as it stood was entire, and that it had been fixed there to mark a boundary or place of meeting. Anyhow, whatever the origin of the relic, there was and is something sinister, or solemn, according to mood, in the scene amid which it stands; something tending to impress the most phlegmatic passer-by. (XLV, 349–50)

Despite the agnosticism proclaimed, the passage indicates fairly clearly that the Christian interpretation is a travesty, and that the pagan rude-stone is a socially functional phallic symbol (as may be confirmed from the photograph of the original stone in Pinion's *Hardy Companion*). Hardy's point is not to find sex on the rural scene, but to note the persistence of prehistoric cultural strata in the present civilization of England. Alec tries to palm it off as a Holy Cross, but the shepherd whom they meet leaves no illusions on that score: "Cross—no; 'twer not a cross! 'Tis a thing of ill omen, Miss. It was put up in wuld times by the relations of a malefactor who was tortured there by nailing his hand to a post and afterwards hung. The bones lie underneath. They say he sold his soul to the devil, and that he walks at times" (XLV, 351). The crimes and follies of history that hover over the land are associated in the peasant imagination with these repositories of primitive experience. As long as the archetypal structures remain, there will be awe-struck responses and attempts at historical interpretation, even in the "most phlegmatic passer-by."

We are thus prepared for what is probably the most profoundly imaginative scene in this or any other English novel, the capture and liberation of Tess at Stonehenge. The details of the description are too well known to require extended quotation: we need recall only the humming of the wind, in which the stones act as a "gigantic one-stringed harp"—like the wind-harp of Romantic poetry, expressing the rhythm of the universe; the sacrificial stone, still warm from the preceding day's sun, on which the scapegoat lies down; her wish to "bide here," feeling that "now I am at home"; Angel's explanation of the sacrifices made there, not to God but to the sun; the appearance of the police, walking "as if trained," and waiting for Tess's waking "as still as the pillars around"; her wakening by the sun and awareness that her hour has come; her final expressions of joy and readiness. Two passages from the manuscript which Hardy omitted from the published version strengthen the ritual meaning, although it does not depend on them: " 'I like very much to be here,' she murmured. 'I like the old worships where youth and love had a part' "; " 'Who [did they sacrifice] to?' 'Among other things, to beauty like Tess's.' "[12] Having recorded throughout the novel the passing of the aristocracy, of medieval culture, and of Christianity, Hardy points—we can see from his omissions how hesitantly—at a primal value implicit in the prehistoric culture that still dwells within the English landscape. This is a naturalistic culture of vitality, sexuality, and beauty—it is civilization without repression. There is no danger of confusing Hardy with Nietzsche or Lawrence, for this set of values is not presented as a historical fact or even as an ideology for belief; it is there simply as an imaginative possibility available to the historical-minded modern observer.

The final image of history in *Tess of the d'Urbervilles* is presented in the final scene at Wintoncester (or Winchester). The architectural ensemble, from the elevated and distant perspective of the withdrawing Angel and Liza-Lu, comprises a summary of the whole of English history: the Norman cathedral tower, the Gothic buildings around it, the grotesque ugliness of the prison in a modern, utilitarian style, which forms a "blot" on the history-laden city-scape. The bitterness of the final chapter does not, however, imply that modern times are simply a blot on the unmitigated virtue of the past; the crimes of the d'Urbervilles to which the narrative has repeatedly alluded are sufficient to dispel any medievalist nostalgia. The past is dead; the present is death-dealing—especially to an anachronistic survivor of the past like a peasant

12. Manuscript in the British Museum (Add. MS. 38182), p. 519 ff.

girl who has the strength of personality of an aristocratic heroine.

The dichotomy between Hardy's care for historical persons and his remote, trans-historical perspective is nowhere more ironic than in his tracing of Tess's career. In effect, the author's attitude toward the experience he has "faithfully presented" defines itself by a process of allowing the actors to express their own responses to it. He begins by distinguishing himself from Clare's sentimentalism, which he exposes at the heart of the modern intellectual's scepticism: "There is something very sad in the extinction of a family of renown, even if it was fierce, domineering, feudal renown" (xxx, 214). Hardy's sadness is not at all for the family, only for the descendant: it is not historical institutions in themselves that are valued, only the truly great individuals among them.

On the other hand, the author sees more widely than his heroine's limited perspective: "what's the use of learning that I am one of a long row only—finding out that there is set down in some old book somebody just like me, and to know that I shall only act her part; making me sad, that's all. The best is not to remember that your nature and your past doings have been just like thousands' and thousands' " (xix, 149). For the victim of history, consciousness is consciousness of impotence, of determination by external forces, and of the repetitive pattern of all human careers. Hardy has something of Tess's weariness of history, but it does not preclude the discovery of meaning within it:

> Thus the Durbeyfields, once d'Urbervilles, saw descending upon them the destiny which, no doubt, when they were among the Olympians of the county, they had caused to descend many a time, and severely enough, upon the heads of such landless ones as they themselves were now. So do flux and reflux—the rhythm of change—alternate and persist in everything under the sky. (L, 394)

This historical wisdom is Greek, not Biblical; it is a non-theistic restoration of the balance of nature, not retributive justice. Flux and reflux are not mere random change but have something to do with moral events; great crimes incur some sort of Nemesis not because they are evil but because they are great, i.e., extreme. In Hardian phrase, " 'Justice' was done," but it is the justice of the whole and not of the part. Though disdaining Hegel's teleology, Hardy was close to his faith that "Die Weltgeschichte ist das

Weltgericht": there is an economy and balance in the sum of events, though there be none for the individual.

Our pleasure in *Tess* is a tragic pleasure: it does not subsist entirely on our pity for the heroine, but also on our fear that the order of events in her life—accident, evil, and folly, all—is "as it should be." It is she who offers herself as a sacrifice, identifying herself—as the tragic hero does—with her fate. If we ask to what she makes sacrifice, the answer can be only: to the course of history itself. The individual suffers all the absurdity of existence, but the grand economy of the universe is maintained: the d'Urbervilles have raped and they are raped, they were masters of the land and are now cast off the land, they sleep in the rich vault at Kingsbere and they are left homeless in the shadow of the church. It is a sobering and painful perception, and Hardy does not hold to it so sternly as to mitigate his love for the beautiful human individual or his sense of outrage at her unmerited suffering. But in *Tess of the d'Urbervilles*, the tragic sense of life becomes a historical attitude.

ॐ

Neither a work of comic romance nor an archetypal tragedy can, however, claim to be commensurate with history unless it directly confronts a specific historical situation, and Hardy made one further esthetic approach to the subject in *The Dynasts*. This great poem—which has received far better critical attention than its limited reputation would suggest[13]—has not been thoroughly examined as an approach to history and the artistic transmutation of it. The poem has, since its publication in 1904–1908, had numerous interpreters of its determinist doctrines—who remain oblivious to Hardy's anti-metaphysical disclaimers—and a few acute readers

13. A detailed analysis of Hardy's historical sources and his use of them is: Walter F. Wright, *The Shaping of The Dynasts: A Study in Thomas Hardy* (Lincoln, Neb., 1967)—which supersedes William R. Rutland, *Thomas Hardy: A Study of his Writings and their Background* (Oxford, 1938), pp. 291–317. The best commentary on the dramatic interplay within the poem, especially on the relation of the spirits to the action (treated as two concurrent dramas), is still Lascelles Abercrombie, *Thomas Hardy: A Critical Study* (London, 1912), pp. 184–225. Other literary studies are listed in the following notes; I omit the plethora of philosophical source-studies.

of its formal principles,[14] but it has also to be read as one would read a historical novel, even though Hardy's decision not to make it a historical novel is of some importance in appreciating it for what it is.

The literary analogues of this "epic-drama" have been exhaustively discussed—not least by Hardy himself, in a series of statements over the years and in his Preface.[15] They range from classical tragedy and epic to Victorian historical plays and narrative poems,[16] and there can be no doubt that this highly self-conscious artist was concerned both to relate himself to tradition and to discover an individual form to express his unique historical imagination. The most telling comparisons are, however, those to be made with the major Continental historical novels which treat the Napoleonic Wars. From Stendhal's *Charterhouse of Parma* to Tolstoy's *War and Peace*, novelists have tried to expose the soft underbelly of historical pretensions about the glory of the first general European war. Hardy matches Tolstoy's wide vision by including, at one extreme, the dregs of humanity caught in the hellish experience and, at the other, the mighty of the earth in all their pettiness and impotence. But Hardy, like Tolstoy, goes beyond the historical novelist's vision of a society's reaction to war. His is not merely a social world but a physical one, which includes all objects and processes. The

14. The most interesting perception on the formal principle at work is in Samuel Hynes, *The Pattern of Hardy's Poetry* (Chapel Hill, N. C. and London, 1961), p. 160 ff., to the effect that the antinomy of the human response (illusion) and the gross facts (reality) is the same as that of Hardy's novels and lyrics. Another structuring principle is developed in J. Hillis Miller, *Thomas Hardy: Distance and Desire* (Cambridge, Mass., 1970), p. xiv: "The tracings of the Will in history or in nature are themselves a kind of writing. . . . [Hardy's] writing, however, is also a repetition or representation of history, the copy of a copy, writing about another writing. . . ."

15. A systematic account of the work's literary relationships is: Harold Orel, *Thomas Hardy's Epic-Drama: A Study of "The Dynasts"* (Lawrence, Kan., 1963), which has chapters on epic tradition (especially Homer and Milton) and on the esthetics of sublimity (Burke), as well as a record of Hardy's developing thoughts on his enterprise.

16. Among the Victorian contenders for influence are Robert Buchanan's *The Drama of Kings* (see Hoxie N. Fairchild, "The Immediate Source of *The Dynasts*," *PMLA*, LXVII [1952], 43–64); the Spasmodics' long poems (see Rutland, *op. cit.*); Browning's, Tennyson's, and Swinburne's dramas on English history (which remain to be studied in themselves); and Meredith's *Odes in Contribution to the Song of French History*, which may well have been an immediate competitor, if not a stimulus.

sum of these is called the Immanent Will or It, but could also be called Being or the Whole or the Way Things Are. It was Hardy's intention to transcend the boundaries of the historical novel and include all the things that go to make up a historical epoch: not only Stendhal's satiric reduction of grand events and petty rulers and Tolstoy's swift movements among all classes of a nation, but also the congeries of the events themselves, human responses, documents, proceedings of government, private activities of the participants, geographical distribution of the action, and the myriad other parts of the whole.

The form which Hardy devised, called "epic-drama" but clearly neither epic nor drama, has been described as cinematographic.[17] It does, to be sure, call for shifts of perspective that are imaginative equivalents of cutting, zooming, panning, fading in and out, and it is as careful as a shooting-script about lighting, focus, angle of vision, color, atmosphere, sound-effects, and props—it even includes animated diagrams, like that of the cosmic brain, It. These techniques are already to be found in most of Hardy's novels and, indeed, in many another novelist's, though less consistently. If Hardy is the most cinematic of novelists, it is also true that his most cinematic work is a poetic extension of his technique as a novelist. *The Dynasts* can be considered an attempt to stretch the historical novel so as to include all the things that the novel—even a novel of the size and scope of *War and Peace*—must leave out.

An insight into the way Hardy worked is to be gathered from a textual scholar's observation that many of the facts mentioned casually in *The Dynasts* had already been used in *The Trumpet-Major*, but are there considered from personal perspectives and become part of the story.[18] The coherence of a novel demands that facts become dramatic, that they affect individuals, that they lose their isolation and enter into the movement of life, that they become part of a causal nexus which in fiction is called *plot*. History, on the other hand, has no plot; in Hardy's view, the world is only

17. The first to develop the point seems to be A. J. A. Waldock in *Thomas Hardy and "The Dynasts"* (Sydney, 1933), pp. 14–20. A recent restatement is in John Wain's introduction to the Macmillan-St. Martin's paperback edition (New York, London, etc., 1965).

18. Emma Clifford, "The 'Trumpet-Major Notebook' and *The Dynasts*," *Review of English Studies*, n.s. VIII (1957), 158 (one of a number of careful source-studies by this scholar).

meaningful as a whole and only to a (probably non-existent) mind that could take in the whole. Yet the facts cannot be allowed to be listed as isolated phenomena, a succession of unrelated events, for we are aware of causality even without being able to specify causes. Every fact is ultimately related to every other fact; if they cannot be fitted into a coherent novel they can be more loosely related in some new form—"epic-drama." The novelist who wants to be true to his cosmic vision of history here turns to poetry.

Hardy's struggles with the problem are patent in his preface:

> It may hardly be necessary to inform readers that in devising this chronicle-piece no attempt has been made to create that completely organic structure of action, and closely-webbed development of character and motive, which are demanded in a drama strictly self-contained. A panoramic show like the present is a series of historical "ordinates" (to use a term in geometry): the subject is familiar to all; and foreknowledge is assumed to fill in the junctions required to combine the scenes into an artistic unity. (p. ix)

Hardy rejects the principle of organic unity proper to a "self-contained" drama (or novel), as his object is to make his work something not self-contained but as extensive as its subject-matter. To do this he thinks of himself as placing the facts in a grid, without specifying the relations of each to the others; they become "ordinates" in a number of dimensions, of which space and time are presumably only the first four. Hardy closes his historical *ars poetica* with a little joke: the reader is assumed to have "foreknowledge"—which must mean knowledge not only of the general outcome of the Napoleonic Wars but of all the outcomes of the forces at work in those years. With such omniscience we could readily relate all the ordinates to each other and "combine the scenes into an artistic unity." Failing that, we may perceive as much unity as Hardy—with his well-nigh lifelong study and fifteen years' writing of *The Dynasts*—was himself able to discover in his non-significant grid. As we fail to make sense of our knowledge, we only repeat the experience of the artist, the historian, and all finite beings and we express our frustration in the various ways enacted by the spirit-voices.

It is neither a verse drama, nor a historical novel, nor a poetic history that Hardy offers us, then, for he does not claim to be able to interpret the facts and find meaning, order, or value in them.

The Dynasts is simply the facts (reality), with the addition of a number of interpretations of them (illusion) by the Spirits and, less selfconsciously, by the author. It is no more possible for Hardy than for any other mind to see reality objectively, and all his efforts to do so are accompanied by a more or less complacent sense of futility. What he indisputably succeeded in doing was to invent, if not a new genre, at least a new formal principle: *inorganic form*, the esthetic expression of a holistic yet sceptical orientation toward the universe. The truth (in Hegelian phrase) is the whole, and any statement can be only a provisional arrangement of data, building up to some enormous sum which no individual can perceive. That sum—It—is the subject of *The Dynasts*, although limited to a ten-year stretch of Its existence in one of Its corners, Europe. The poem attempts, then, a historical perspective on It. *The Dynasts* could not have been conceived as a historical novel because it envisions not the history of men or of man but of It.

The authorial interventions into the passive grid of history may be summarized under four heads: personal, national, ethical, and metaphysical. It is remarkable, however, that there is no intrusion on the ideological or economic fronts. Hardy's view of the Napoleonic conflict with the European monarchial system is perfectly indifferent: he is neither for nor against Napoleon (whatever he may have thought of Liberty, Equality, and Fraternity, and Napoleon's relation to them). Of Napoleon, the Spirit of the Years predicts, dispassionately and amorally:

> *The rawest Dynast of the group concerned*
> *Will, for the good or ill of mute mankind,*
> *Down-topple to the dust like soldier Saul,*
> *And Europe's mouldy-minded oligarchs*
> *Be propped anew. . . .*
> (Part Second, Act VI, scene vii, p. 320)

On economic matters, Hardy offers no speculations about the course of capitalism, industrialism, or imperialism, and—beyond setting down the facts of Napoleon's Continental System—seems to have no notion that national economic competition was involved in the struggle. In his aversion to generalization about historical causes, Hardy is as up-to-date as a present-day professional historian, and *The Dynasts* is a literary work well suited to an age that disdains philosophies of history.

Hardy's personal intervention is, however, palpable and even self-confessed: the Preface speaks of the "accidents of locality" that made the subject peculiarly accessible to the author, and these are psychological as well as intellectual influences. One of the accidents listed—"the same countryside happened to include the village which was the birthplace of Nelson's flag-captain at Trafalgar" (p. vii)—is meaningless unless the additional fact is included, that he was an ancestor of the author's. It is not simply a Wessex view of the Napoleonic Wars that Hardy offers in the First Part, but a Hardian view:

> NELSON (suddenly)
> What are you thinking, that you speak no word?
>   HARDY (waking from a short reverie)
> Thoughts all confused, my lord:—their needs on deck,
> Your own sad state, and your unrivalled past;
> Mixed up with flashes of old things afar—
> Old childish things at home, down Wessex way,
> In the snug village under Blackdon Hill
> Where I was born. The tumbling stream, the garden,
> The placid look of the grey dial there,
> Marking unconsciously this bloody hour,
> And the red apples on my father's trees,
> Just now full ripe.
>   NELSON
>   Ay, thus do little things
> Steal into my mind, too. But ah, my heart
> Knows not your calm philosophy! . . .
>   (Part First, v, iv, 97)

The impression grows as we read that it is not his ancestor's prominence in Nelson's final hours that Hardy is celebrating but his own capacity to be an empathic witness of historical events. From a strictly objective standpoint, all history is of equal interest to the observer; without claiming that any given event—even one as momentous as Trafalgar—is of crucial importance in the larger scheme of things, Hardy insists that some events matter more to some observers than to others. This is not so much a confession of self-interest as a relativist's credo; nor is it offered as a generalization about historical knowledge but as a truth about man's all-too-human heart. In case his dispassionate and imposing cosmic grid might give us reason to suspect him of aiming at an It-like impassivity, it is made clear that Hardy cares!

Closely allied to his personal intervention is Hardy's assumption of a national perspective. Again, this is a conscious and controlled departure from his formal and philosophic principles. In the Preface he declares: ". . . the slight regard paid to English influence and action throughout the struggle by so many Continental writers who had dealt with Napoléon's career, seemed always to leave room for a new handling of the theme which should re-embody the features of this influence in their true proportion . . ." (pp. vii-viii). It is not merely to add to the factual grid, however, that Hardy goes on to glorify English arms, English "great men" like Nelson, and English politicians like Pitt. The conclusion of · Part First, Pitt's death-bed scene, with its lament at the news of defeat at Austerlitz—"My country! How I leave my country! . . ."—comes closer to bathos than anything else in *The Dynasts*, while his evident satisfaction in Pitt's famous words on Trafalgar ("England has saved herself, by her exertions: /She will, I trust, save Europe by her example!") approaches jingoism. In a universe of immense complexity, constant flux, and impersonal teleology, national pretentions ring hollow, but Hardy no more excludes national grandeur than he does the occasional appearance of personal heroism. These, too, are facts which claim a place on the grid.

If Hardy's personal and national sentiments are usually inserted into his cosmic vision with some subtlety and with appropriate qualifications, there is no such reserve about his ethical interventions. The primary facts of the Napoleonic Wars presented in *The Dynasts* are the facts of death and suffering; the primary response to them is outrage, which takes the ethical form of pacifism. It is no accident that the work dates from a time of increasingly widespread public awareness of the impending global catastrophe, a time of the beginnings of an international, organized movement for the abrogation of war. Hardy's attitude is part of the temper of his times, and he makes no bones about the strength and urgency of his beliefs. As Harold Orel has shown, in tracing Hardy's anti-war sentiments, he first—in common with a large number of British intellectuals—thought war unthinkable, given the modern potentialities of destructiveness; was subsequently amazed that the World War was worse than the Napoleonic Wars—which are rendered in *The Dynasts* as the extreme of human horror; and then fell into despair of men's ability to renounce war.[19] Speaking of himself in the third person, he wrote: ". . . had he written *The Dynasts* after the Treaty of Versailles he could not have closed it upon a note of hope." It is possible to probe the basis of Hardy's pacificism, to discover that it rested on an anti-heroic assumption ("the need-lessness of war as a means of testing man's valor," as Orel puts it), or that it is belied by the gusto with which Hardy follows the cam-paigns. But the gross effect of *The Dynasts* is one that transcends the sentiments of the Spirit of the Pities and the distancing of the Spirit of the Years: it is the spectacle of pity and terror, which makes the work tragic in spite of all its formal divergences from traditional tragic drama. Not only is Hardy personally involved, in the ways indicated; he is involved in mankind. For all its super-human cosmic dimensions, this is a work about the human condi-tion.

The final intervention of Hardy's authorship into the impersonal grid of historical fact is his much-discussed "philosophy." Despite all his efforts to disarm philosophic criticism by claiming artistic irresponsibility, his doctrine has called more attention to itself than any other aspect of *The Dynasts*. As a professional philosophic critic of the work has shown,[20] it is Hardy's pugnacity in having the Spirit of the Years a busy corrector of other points of view that causes most trouble. If it be granted that all events are determined, is it necessary to adopt a fatalistic view of man's actions, which seem to be the only activities denied causal power? If the Spirit choruses are an artistic device to express human responses to his-tory, how can they (and even, at times, the Spirit of the Years) hope to influence men's determined minds or intervene directly in material events—for all the world like the sprites of a superstitious world-view? Finally, if the individual is as powerless as this philoso-phy insists, why does the work generate as much interest as it does in the outstanding individuals of the Napoleonic age?

The Dynasts provides something more interesting than the bare philosophic problem. It offers a hero who is one of the most self-conscious historical actors imaginable (whether or not the historical Napoleon was really as philosophical as he is portrayed as being).

19. *Op. cit.*, p. 86 ff.; the quotation that follows is from p. 89.
20. John Laird, *Philosophical Incursions into English Literature* (Cambridge, 1946), pp. 187–204.

Napoleon here is a typical Hardian hero, full of grandiose projects, blinded by egoism and sexual passion, limited by circumstance, brought to a partial recognition of his true situation—a tragic hero, in form. His peculiar interest lies in his fatalism: as with the men of certain great, dynamic movements—Calvinism and Marxism, for example—his belief in predestination or determinism serves not as a damper but as a spur to action. (If one really believes that history is on one's side, one acts with alacrity to fulfill the historical process.)

On Napoleon, the Spirit of the Years comments, *"He's of the few in Europe who discern/The working of the Will"* (Part Second, I, viii, 179). But we can see that he is manipulating it for his own advantage—his constant plea that he is following his destiny being the crudest egoism. Hardy's Napoleon is a perfect example of Hegel's "world-historical individual," who identifies his own desires with the trends of history. For a while he is right, because the Europe displayed in the Second Part of *The Dynasts* is a ludicrous collection of petty egoists—from the Czar, arguing with his mother about whether they were right to refuse Napoleon his daughter's hand, after the Austrian Emperor has succumbed to the temptation; to the Prince Regent, mad for women; to his father, who is merely mad. Yet Napoleon is the mightiest egoist of them all, and just as vulnerable to events and to his own weakness. When the forces of history prove too much for him, his fatalism shows itself to be a patch-work philosophy better suited to victory than to defeat. Nothing changes the processes of history, not even the acknowledgement that nothing changes them, and the man who can put himself in harmony with the Immanent Will often finds that it is not in harmony with him. Something like an honest acceptance of his own smallness occurs to Napoleon only at the start of the Russian campaign:

> That which has worked will work!—Since Lodi Bridge
> The force I then felt move me moves me on
> Whether I will or no: and oftentimes
> Against my better mind. . . . Why am I here?
> —By laws imposed on me inexorably!
> History makes use of me to weave her web
> To her long while aforetime-figured mesh
> And contemplated charactery; no more.
>
> (Part Third, I, i, 330)

The fatalist who finds his fate to be failure loses stature when he rejects this role; as in classical tragedy, true heroism lies in willing what the universe wills, not one's private will. It is not simply that Napoleon is shown, for the most part, to be a fair-weather fatalist, but that he is not up to the impersonal dignity that Hardy would like to—but finds, on the record, he cannot—assign him.

With Wellington, Hardy's success is complete: the triumphant hero is simply the quintessence of the blood-and-guts soldier and stiff-upper-lip British gentleman. A stage-direction shows him on a par with the armies at Waterloo: "The web connecting all the apparently separate shapes includes WELLINGTON in its tissue with the rest, and shows him, like them, as acting while discovering his intention to act" (Part Third, VII, vii, 505). There is dignity in the portrait—"WELLINGTON's manner is deliberate, judicial, almost indifferent" (Part Third, VI, v, 471)—but at times it verges on absurdity:

> UXBRIDGE (starting)
> I have lost my leg, by God!
> WELLINGTON
> By God, and have you! Ay—the wind o' the shot
> Blew past the withers of my Copenhagen
> Like the foul sweeping of a witch's broom.—
> Aha—they are giving way!
>
> (Part Third, VII, viii, 513–14)

The world-historical hero is indistinguishable from the stupid and unfeeling drudge who looks only to his immediate task and thinks simply in terms of force battering force. Wellington has put himself in the hands of It most thoroughly because it involves for him less sacrifice of personality than for other men: he has no desires but to do his job, to win the battle of the moment, to play his role in something larger than himself. The heroic ideal is reduced to the level of the faithful workman of bourgeois morality. On this score, and on others—as Hardy said—"*The Dynasts* proves nothing" (*Life*, p. 454).

Thus *The Dynasts*, having applied the cosmic viewpoint of *Tess of the d'Urbervilles* to the materials of *The Trumpet-Major*, closes without answering questions—neither the grand questions of history nor even the question of its form. The ironies of the historical novel are such that one of the least theoretical of novelists produced a vivid fictional treatment of the Waterloo period in

Vanity Fair—without even venturing directly on the battlefield, as it were—while the most historical-minded of English novelists disdained to give historical significance to his portrayal of the same period. Indeed, Hardy produced no historical novel but only a series of approximations of one.

The explanation of such twists may well lie in an observation of J. H. Raleigh's: "In Hardy and in James, then, simple historical time, built along the idea of progress, is breaking down and cosmic and existential time are becoming the province of the novelist, who is, simultaneously, developing an historical sense and an immortal desire for an immersion in the past."[21] With the passing of the sense not only of progress but even of comprehensible relationships among historical events, the historical novelist is all but put out of business. His fictional plots show themselves to be rather artificial when no historical plot or order can be assumed behind them. It is for such reasons that Hardy throughout his career avoided writing a genuine historical novel, and it is for similar reasons that novelists of the twentieth-century have been led to extraordinary lengths in their efforts to revitalize the form.

21. John Henry Raleigh, *Time, Place, and Idea: Essays on the Novel* (Carbondale, Ill., etc., 1968), p. 52. In the quoted essay, "The English Novel and the Three Kinds of Time," and in the essay on Dickens, are further suggestions on the role of time in historical fiction.

Chapter 8 Experiment
and renewal

The historical novel at the turn of the century may be seen
taking a turn in its tradition by falling into the hands of a number
of writers influenced by French naturalism and impressionism:
Ford Madox Ford, George Moore, and Maurice Hewlett. They
bring a new subjectivity to the portrayal of the past and pave
the way for the distinctively modern historical novels of Conrad
and Woolf—the one moving from impressionism toward perspectival narration, the other in the direction of archetypal symbolism.
The most powerful evocations of social history by these writers
occur not in historical fiction but in novels of contemporary life, e.g.,
Parade's End and _Esther Waters_. But the impressionists' and
naturalists' psychological curiosity also brings about a change in
the treatment of historical characters, and this contribution to the
fortunes of historical fiction can be seen in works that are at least
marginally of the genre, like Moore's _Héloïse_ and _Abélard_ (1921)
and Hewlett's _The Forest Lovers_ (1898).

The theme which these novelists hold in common is that of lovely
womanhood cruelly broken by the force of historical movements
and men. This theme echoes widely in the literature of the period—
witness only Hardy's Tess, Galsworthy's Irene, Shaw's Joan (not
so lovely, but lovable), Yeats's Maude Gonne, Moore's Héloïse, and
Conrad's Emilia Gould. A small number of historical women who
express the theme are exploited with alarming frequency during
the Late Victorian and early modern decades. There is, in particular,

a compulsive turning to the Tudor and Stuart queens for instances of suffering womanhood.

After Swinburne's trilogy of plays (1865–81) on Mary Queen of Scots (themselves members of a line that extends through *La Princesse de Clèves, Maria Stuart,* and *The Abbot*), it seems remarkable that a modern writer would pick her up again, as Maurice Hewlett did in *The Queen's Quair* (1904). Hewlett's motives are made explicit in the later chapters of the novel: he means to defend the "poor wounded name" from the historian's severity, to re-tell a tale that will discover the living feeling within the cold facts, and to psychologize history so that the movements of social forces recede into the background behind a drama of individuals. There is at work here not merely a sentimental period taste or a predilection for fictional romance, but an attitude toward history that derives from an attitude toward man—or at least toward woman:

... from this day onwards to the end of her throned life the tragedy is pure pity: she drifts, she suffers, but she scarcely acts—unless the struggles of birds in nets can be called acts. . . . She was like to become a mere tortured beast.

Love she must; and if she loved amiss it was that she loved too well. . . . She was a well of sweet profit—the Honeypot; and they swarmed about her for their meat like houseflies. . . .[1]

History is seen here as mechanical, greed-directed, and masculine; human values are feminine.

It is no great step from this conception to Ford's picture of Katherine Howard in his trilogy, *The Fifth Queen* (1906), *Privy Seal* (1907), and *The Fifth Queen Crowned* (1908). The writing is free of the sentimental bitterness of Hewlett and Moore, but the portrait of the historical individual is similar. The heroine is a mystery, distinctly motivated only in her need for love but not in her choices. She is quarry, run down by the grasping men-of-the-world around her: Henry VIII, Lord Privy Seal Thomas Cromwell, her uncle the Duke of Norfolk, and her lover Thomas Culpepper. Public affairs are more evident and more rationally conducted here than in Hewlett, and Henry is given the credit of his classical

---

1. Maurice Hewlett, *The Queen's Quair: or, The Six Years' Tragedy* (London and New York, 1904), pp. 474, 482.

learning, political acumen, and psychic complexity. But the pattern of raising sympathy for the weak, beset heroine is the same, and provides the occasion for a concluding set-piece, her defiant speech to the King: "You are as God made you, setting you for His own purposes a weak man in very evil and turbulent times. . . . I die a Queen, but I would rather have died the wife of my cousin Culpepper or of any other simple lout that loved me as he did, without regard, without thought, and without falter."[2] The use of feminine sentiments to deny meaning or value to historical forces could not be clearer.

Yet the Edwardian period's sentimentality is not sufficiently dominant to submerge the strong individuality which marks the major artist. Ford's development from his youthful estheticism and romanticism may be described as a process of modernization, and we can see in his historical trilogy the makings of his great tetralogy of contemporary history, *Parade's End*. In the former as well as the latter, character is—despite the period style in characterization—rooted in milieu, and particularly in politics. It is not only the King and Court who are politic in using the heroine as a tool of power politics; she, too, has political motives, which do not mitigate or cheapen her intense personal affections. As a Catholic, Katherine is her uncle's instrument to revive his and his party's flagging fortunes; she is also hostage to Cromwell and his policy of Protestant alliances. When his successor can use her past relationship with Culpepper to turn the King against her, it is not only she but her religion whose fate in England is sealed. These machinations are relieved of conventional Machiavellianism by the rich evocation of England in transition from medieval to Renaissance culture: both the comic notes of the roguish humanist Nicholas Udal and the tragic echoes of the yeomanry dispossessed by enclosures sound repeatedly through the novels. Not only is Henry's lechery shown up as a myth disguising his pragmatic, national motives for changing his queens, but even the villainous Cromwell is granted his rational

2. *The Fifth Queen Crowned*, in *The Bodley Head Ford Madox Ford* (London, 1962), vol. II, p. 591; the quotation below is from *Privy Seal*, *op. cit.*, p. 349. The only extended critical discussion of the trilogy is John A. Meixner, *Ford Madox Ford's Novels: A Critical Study* (Minneapolis, 1962), pp. 44–62, summarized in Charles G. Hoffmann, *Ford Madox Ford* (New York, 1967), pp. 36–43.

and fervent belief in the supremacy of state over church, i.e., in the principle of Renaissance absolutism.

These brute realities of the sixteenth century are set against the fertile Renaissance myth of the return to or resumption of a golden age. Not only is Katherine animated by a humanist belief that "God made this world to be bettered," but the urbane king is moved by the beauty (if not the practical applicability) of his vision of a classical utopia, the "Islands of the Blest." Ford's imagination is poised upon the dichotomy of historical corruption and civilized retirement, and his escapism avoids a personal tone by being expressed in the language and myths of the men of the past. By identifying his own escapism with that of the Renaissance, Ford achieves genuine historical sympathy with another world-weary age. *The Fifth Queen* represents a limit of the possibilities of traditional historical fiction, before the methods of Conrad and Woolf brought the genre into the realm of modern art. Conrad wrote of it to Galsworthy, when the trilogy was complete: ". . . a noble conception—the swan song of Historical Romance."[3] Refusing to take such a conclusive view, Ford went on to write four historical romances before finding his true métier in the contemporaneity of *The Good Soldier*.

3. G. Jean-Aubry, ed., *Joseph Conrad: Life and Letters* (London, 1927), II, 67; letter of 20 Feb. 1908.

I. CONRAD

Conrad, the novelist of the sea who has come to be highly regarded as a novelist of politics, combined both his preoccupations in his last three novels, all of them historical: *The Arrow of Gold, The Rover,* and *Suspense* (omitting *The Rescue,* an early novel which was completed in this period). It is not surprising that Conrad took to the historical novel at last, since throughout his career he had written short stories on historical themes and had, in *Nostromo,* created a major novel of contemporary history. In all, Conrad wrote more historical fiction than any other major novelist after Scott. Yet the imagination which shaped history in his fiction was of a quirky, inconsistent kind that makes it difficult to generalize about his historical sense or even to estimate the success of his historical novels.

As early as in his first collaborative venture with Ford Madox Ford, *The Inheritors* (1901)—a satirical fantasy on the decline of the tradition of English statesmanship in modern politics—Conrad indicated one of his chief historical attitudes. When the hero discovers that his political idol—modelled on Randolph Churchill—has compromised his principles, he can no longer collaborate with him on a historical study of Oliver Cromwell: "Our Cromwell! There was no Cromwell; he had lived, had worked for the future—and now he had ceased to exist. His future—our past, had come to an end. . . . I found myself curiously unable to understand what purpose remained to keep [things] in motion."[4] This apocalyptic note is often heard in Conrad's political novels. He is committed to the idea that history is the shaping power in modern experience, yet he considers recent developments to have made so sharp a break with the political values of the past that history may be said to have ended and an era of anarchy to have been ushered in. From this standpoint, as Morton Dauwen Zabel observed, "Conrad's general view of history, past or present, hinges on a persistent and incurable doubt—an inveterate suspicion of the passions that animate it; a fear of the selfish, irrational, or predatory forces it unleashes to prey on the pride and honor of men and societies; a repugnant sense of its hostility to the truth and decency in the conscience of the hero or man of honor."[5]

4. *The Inheritors: An Extravagant Story* (London, 1914 [1901]), p. 194.
5. M. D. Zabel, Introduction to Joseph Conrad, *Tales of Heroes and History* (Garden City, N. Y., 1960), p. xli.

But that is not the only role which history plays in Conrad's imagination. There is also this note: "Is it possible that you youngsters should have no more sense than that! Some of you had better wipe the milk off your upper lip before you start to pass judgment on the few poor stragglers of a generation which has done and suffered not a little in its time."[6] This is one of his old-campaigner narrators speaking, to be sure, but there is no denying that they reflect an aspect of the author's sense of the past. Much of this attitude is to be accounted to his sense of being the last survivor of a glorious family—both on its Korzeniowski and on its Bobrowski sides, as I have elsewhere maintained[7]—but its increasing prevalence in his later years indicates its power over his imagination. It is an antiquarian tendency: the urge to recollect the things of the past because they are slipping away, because they are not appreciated by the young, because they give pleasure to that faculty of late-blooming romanticism—the memory. The stories and novels that derive from this impulse—particularly "Prince Roman," on the Polish Revolution of 1831, and *The Arrow of Gold* (1919), on the Second Carlist War—evoke the past in order to convey its jewelled aura from the standpoint of the present—in the memory— not the past as it must have felt at the time. These narratives sometimes fall into the bathos of anecdote, rather than conveying the immediate press of circumstance and openness of the future. Their world is known to be ended before their stories have even begun, and they are recalled in order to be enshrined.

The distinction between these tales and "a serious and even earnest attempt at a bit of historical fiction" is implied in Conrad's words on his Napoleonic novella, "The Duel":

What I care to remember best is the testimony of some French readers who volunteered the opinion that in those hundred pages or so I had

6. *Tales of Hearsay* (London, 1946 [1925]), p. 1. This and all subsequent quotations from Conrad's works are from the Dent Collected Edition (apparently uniform with other Dent and Doubleday editions), henceforward cited parenthetically in the text, by chapter and page number.

7. Avrom Fleishman, *Conrad's Politics: Community and Anarchy in the Fiction of Joseph Conrad* (Baltimore, 1967), pp. 5–10; see also Robert R. Hodges, *The Dual Heritage of Joseph Conrad* (The Hague, 1967), whose evidence I had neglected but some of whose conclusions I would dispute. For a more detailed examination of Conrad's historical tales than I can give here, see the relevant chapters of my book.

managed to render "wonderfully" the spirit of the whole epoch. . . . In truth that is exactly what I was trying to capture in my small net: the Spirit of the Epoch—never purely militarist in the long clash of arms, youthful, almost childlike in its exaltation of sentiment—naively heroic in its faith. (*A Set of Six*, p. ix)

Conrad displayed a life-long fascination with the Napoleonic era and his temperamental affinity for it can be sensed in the qualities he singled out in his summary of its Spirit. In this novella (and in "The Warrior's Soul"), Conrad was interested not so much in the military features of the Napoleonic campaigns as in the cultural norms governing their participants' behavior. The conflict between the aristocratic and egalitarian codes of honor in the protagonists of "The Duel," which expresses itself in a protracted, serio-comic series of duels, presents a sharply focused image of the varied social impulses that made up the conquering French army—of which Napoleon was merely the summary type. Similarly, the complementary sacrifices made by the defeated Frenchman and the victorious Russian in "The Warrior's Soul"—the one, of his life, the other, of his reputation (by shooting the prisoner at his own request)—expresses poignantly the common trial of inherited values in the first of the great holocausts of modern European history.

It is only in his last two novels that Conrad returned to the standard of historical imagination maintained in his Napoleonic stories. We have the word of Mrs. Conrad that their trip to Corsica in 1921 was the fulfillment of a long-cherished dream: "The visit had become an obsession of his since his early childhood. He always declared that he was no admirer of Napoleon, but the fact remains that this tragic personality exercised a spell over the author. . . ."[8] How complicated were his feelings and ideas on Napoleon and the Revolution which he carried on and diverted can be seen in Conrad's most extended statement on politics and history, "Autocracy and War." Although he treats the French Revolution ironically— a "great outburst of morality," he calls it in *A Personal Record*— he acknowledges the justness of its cause, given the failure of the ruling classes to adapt themselves to change. Perhaps the most striking notion put forward is that the aristocracy is not inherently in opposition to revolution, and that it is possible and desirable for

8. Jessie Conrad, *Joseph Conrad and His Circle* (London, 1935), p. 219.

a monarch to put himself at the head of a popular movement. It is here that the figure of Napoleon looms up. While Conrad describes him simply as a "vulture," particularly for his shabby treatment of his Polish supporters, he is the foremost example of a monarch (although a self-crowned one) playing the role of tribune of the people. He is the leader of a grand enterprise, uniting his own nation and encouraging the rise of national movements throughout Europe. It is these impulses—the French toward unity and the Italian toward national liberation—that are the subjects of the Napoleonic novels.

☙

In *The Rover* (1923), the French Revolution and Napoleon's regime are seen from the perspective of an ex-pirate, coming home to die in his native Provence, who tends to reduce them to his narrow though intense nautical experience and to stay aloof from political involvement. The essential fable of the novel is the necessity of engagement, if not to abstract political ideals, at least to the moral beings around him—some of whom hold such ideals or have been deeply affected by them. Peyrol begins by answering the question, "Are you a patriot?" by saying, "I am a Frenchman" (ii, 22); he looks on the Revolution as "mutiny and throwing officers overboard. . . . As to this upset, he took no side" (iii, 25). But his affection for Lieutenant Réal, the coldly rationalistic but romantically attractive Napoleonic officer, and for Arlette, the daughter of *çi-devant* parents butchered before her eyes in the Terror at Toulon, leads him to take Réal's place in a suicide-mission designed to break the British blockade. In bringing an apolitical old man of the sea into a profound though only partly conscious commitment to the national cause, Conrad created a historical novel along the lines of the Waverley pattern, but gave it a distinctly modern turn by leading not a naive but an experienced hero to commitment.

The Rover is concerned with vision—with the perceptual processes by which history is seen. Its formal structure as a historical novel is devised in accordance with Conrad's tendency to subjectivize traditional fictional forms. The focus is on an individual's experience of history: not only its impact on his destiny but the more elementary ways in which it enters his consciousness. In closely describing Peyrol's consciousness of the world, the novel dramatizes a view of the subjective nature of man's historical experience.

The title itself may be taken to refer to the acute vision of the protagonist as well as to his checkered maritime career: ". . . his eyes roved here and there and his ears were open for the slightest sound" (VI, 77–78). For Jean Peyrol is a man distinguished by his powers of observation, both on distant perspectives like the sea-board vistas with which the novel is filled, and on the smaller scale of the feelings of young lovers who hardly know themselves. His extraordinary power of seeing—which is apparently indistinguishable from knowing—is bound up with a tendency to withdraw into a detached spectatorial attitude, a tendency which appealed to Conrad throughout his career as an alternative to political action and moral indignation. Although this esthetic distancing is given a resounding affirmation in the often-quoted Preface to *The Nigger of the "Narcissus,"* in which Conrad emphasized his task as being above all "to make you *see*," much of Conrad's fiction shows the consequences in inner atrophy and outer disaster which visual detachment entails. After the doctrine of "Look on—make no sound" was given its definitive critique in *Victory*, there was no possibility of a return to the purely spectatorial attitude. *The Rover* develops the advanced position that the best spectator is he who can both see clearly from a distant perspective *and* engage in historical activity—all the more effectively because of his comprehensive view.

"J'en ai vu bien d'autres" (III, 24): such is Peyrol's stock response to life in his experienced old age. Much is heard of his varied adventures, yet it is not only their exoticism that is emphasized but their sufficiency as a body of evidence on which one may form working generalizations to interpret fresh experiences. Peyrol chooses his lofty room at the Escampobar farm because its outlook resembles that of a lighthouse (III, 30), and from this position and the neighboring cliffs he spends much of the novel observing the course of the British ship *Amelia*, "the actual eyes of Lord Nelson's fleet" (V, 58). So sound is his experience that his vision can provide knowledge: he can enter the mind of Captain Vincent and anticipate his decisions—even create an "ideal conception" of what the Captain "ought to look like" (XVI, 264). This perceptual faculty provides the donnée on which the closing action of the tale is predicated: Peyrol can maneuver not only his own ship but the *Amelia* into a course that convinces the British that he is trying to carry (false) dispatches through the blockade. Peyrol's distant perspective enables him, then, to engage in effective action, and, ironically, the effectiveness of the action lies in obscuring the vision of the opposing party. As he puts it, his design is to place the Englishman where he will be "ready to have his eye put out" (xv, 238).

Peyrol's heroism does not rest on his educated vision alone, but also on his energetic imagination—not only on outward but on inward sight. He possesses the faculty of conjuring up whole scenes from his past, and even of constructing full-scale pictures of situations he has never seen but hypothetically posits: his "thoughts were far away with the English ship. His mental eye contemplated her black image against the white beach of the Salins describing a sparkling curve under the moon . . ." (xii, 180). Peyrol is, moreover, given to philosophic generalization from his mental pictures, and this habit helps to determine his fate: "The feeling which was in his breast and had been known to more articulate men than himself, was that life was a dream less substantial than the vision of Ceylon lying like a cloud on the sea. Dream left astern. Dream straight ahead. This disenchanted philosophy took the shape of fierce swearing" (xv, 233).

As a direct consequence of this disenchanted view of life as a dream—a view which had strong attractions for Conrad throughout his career—Peyrol is moved to surrender his life for those who have a stronger or less ambiguous desire to live. In his closing hours, Peyrol arrives at an almost metaphysical formula for the inadequacy of life in time because of its inherent transiency, especially in the mind: "It is no use to attach any importance to things. What is this life? Phew! Nobody can remember one-tenth of it" (xv, 235). In the moment of death, however, Peyrol experiences a totality of vision which seems a fulfillment of his historical life: "He beheld in a flash the days of his manhood, of strength and adventure. Suddenly an enormous voice like the roar of an angry sea-lion seemed to fill the whole of the empty sky in a mighty and commanding shout: 'Steady!' . . . And with the sound of that familiar English word ringing in his ears Peyrol smiled to his visions and died" (xvi, 269).

Peyrol is not the only character whose historical life is governed by his visions, optical and mental. Arlette's vision, too, expresses not only a private view of the world but also a relation to history. Her traumatic neurosis is occasioned by the sights she has seen during the Toulon massacres: "The clatter of the clogs made her raise her black, clear eyes that had been smitten on the very verge of womanhood by such sights of bloodshed and terror, as to leave in her a fear of looking steadily in any direction for long, lest she should see coming through the empty air some mutilated vision of the dead. Peyrol called it trying not to see something that was not there. . ." (IV, 48–49). She is evasive not only in visual but in social life as well: ". . . for years after her return, people that were out of her sight were out of her mind also" (XI, 161). But she greets Peyrol's advent with an intense gaze, and this initiates the process of bringing her back to life. Ultimately, her vitality is manifested first of all in her eyes (XI, 175), and so great is her confidence in them that when placed in a frightening situation during Scevola's tracking of Réal, "It never occurred to her to doubt her own eyes . . ." (XI, 164). Her hallucinations become adjusted to and predictive of reality, when she translates Réal's potential danger aboard the tartane into the images of her past: "She had seen Réal set upon by a mob of men and women, all dripping with blood, in a livid cold light, in front of a stretch of mere shells of houses with cracked walls and broken windows, and going down in the midst of a forest of raised arms brandishing sabres, clubs, knives, axes" (XV, 245–46). We might conclude, then, that the subplot of *The Rover* consists of the return to normalcy of a mad girl who awakens to love, but a more accurate picture of Arlette's mental development would be framed in terms of the changes in her powers of seeing. Her passion and her vision are directly tied to each other when she expresses her love in prayer: "I entreated the merciful God to keep the heart of the man I love always true to me or else to let me die before I set my eyes on him again" (X, 158). Arlette goes beyond her vision of historical horror by the power of love to purify her sight.

The greatest strength of *The Rover* as an evocation of the "Spirit of the Epoch" lies in its descriptions of the Terror, as it was felt in Toulon. If Conrad's portrait of Nelson pales by comparison with Hardy's, his picture of revolution is even grislier than Dickens's. Moreover, it seems to have been founded on careful research into the specific situation at Toulon, down to the individuals involved.

The most destructive of the revolutionary leaders was a certain Louis-Stanislas Fréron, who gave the order to raze the city and put its inhabitants to the sword.[9] The gory details suggest that Fréron was the inspiration for Scevola Bron, the arch-terrorist and villain of the novel. Scevola emerges as more than a caricature of the "blood-drinker" because of Conrad's depth of insight into the anarchic mentality which speaks in him: " 'There was a time when civic virtue flourished, but now it has got to hide its head. And I will tell you why: there has not been enough killing. It seems as if there could never be enough of it. It's discouraging. Look what we have come to.' His voice died in his throat as though he had suddenly lost confidence in himself" (III, 27). Conrad had portrayed this mentality in the modern world of *The Secret Agent*; by setting it back in the French Revolution he suggests its permanent place in human nature and, by implication, in history.

Most difficult to estimate in assessing *The Rover*'s historicity is its image of Napoleon. He remains throughout a shadowy off-stage presence, entering the action only in the command to send out the decoy vessel with its fake sailing order for the fleet. The imperious demands of the letter and the callous employment of his followers in ordering a boat to fall into the enemy's hands are unmistakable marks of the man. Another light is, however, cast on him from Peyrol's nautical point of view. For the old seaman, the "republican god . . . seems to be some kind of lubber," but Napoleon is a genuine leader: "Under one name or another a chief can be no more than a chief, and that general whom they have been calling consul is a good chief—nobody can deny that" (VI, 76–77). The upshot of his plans to outwit the English fleet was, as Conrad notes, the battle of Trafalgar, but that debacle is not allowed to detract from the image of him as a controlling hand in the destinies of the novel's characters. The portrait is, as it were, truncated at a point which heightens Napoleon's symbolic presence, but does not suggest the wider variety of his Protean forms in his

9. See Oscar Havard, *Histoire de la Révolution dans les Ports de Guerre: Toulon* (Paris, n.d. [1911]), p. 248. This partisan account probably exaggerates the blood-thirstiness of the republicans, but it is the kind of book to which Conrad is likely to have been drawn for its local color. It may be that the name "Réal" was taken from that of Napoleon's police official, Count Pierre-Francois Réal.

contemporaries' imagination. This limitation was to be removed in Conrad's final Napoleonic portrait in *Suspense*.

Nor does the appearance of a historical personage—in this case, of Lord Nelson—impart vivid historicity to the novel, although it fulfills the formal need for a historical personage to be active in the plot. Conrad's long-standing hero-worship of this complex figure is not itself complex enough to impart an authentic tone to his characterization. The language of his soliloquy, on being given the false information, suggests the weakness of conception: " 'And yet who knows!' exclaimed Lord Nelson, standing still for a moment. 'But the blame or the glory must be mine alone. I will seek counsel from no man.' Captain Vincent felt himself forgotten, invisible, less than a shadow in the presence of a nature capable of such vehement feelings. 'How long can he last?' he asked himself with sincere concern" (xvi, 276). The psychic details are chosen to perpetuate the myth of Nelson as an isolated but beneficent hero of the Carlylian type, but are not sufficiently examined to make him a morally-divided hero of the Conradian type.

In addition to its psychology of history, *The Rover* expresses a way of looking at a specific period of the past and, by extension, at historical time. This perspective is rooted in a place, or in personal associations with a place: the Mediterranean coast, especially the strip between Marseilles and Genoa which goes by such names as "Riviera," "Côte d'Azur," etc. For Conrad, this was a scene of youthful adventures and therefore remained replete with colorful mariners and other folk-figures; it is also a place of spectacular beauty and mystery which invited him to indulge his visual imagination. The Mediterranean is, however, not so much a personal or natural as a historical medium in *The Rover* and in *Suspense*. Echoes of its long history recur throughout these last novels, and in *The Rover's* closing paragraph that history forms a frame around the events of the plot: "The blue level of the Mediterranean, the charmer and the deceiver of audacious men, kept the secret of its fascination—hugged to its calm breast the victims of all the wars, calamities and tempests of its history, under the marvellous purity of the sunset sky" (xvi, 286). This vision of the succession of human endeavors, all ending in downfall and death, does not preclude a sense of the value and interest of each event in its turn. The natural setting for historical experience does not mock it by its timeless beauty but rather sets it off in the clear light of esthetic contemplation. Without surrendering his moral or political concerns, Conrad returns in his vision of the past to his earlier esthetic credo: history, too, is part of a "purely spectacular universe."

૪

Suspense: A Napoleonic Novel, actually begun before *The Rover* though published posthumously in 1925, is Conrad's last—and, despite its incompleteness, his most successful—attempt to recreate the atmosphere of the Napoleonic age. The title refers not to the mysteriousness of the story, which is suspenseful only to a normal novelistic degree, but to its subject: Europe's state of suspended animation during Napoleon's exile at Elba, before the Congress of Vienna could agree on its carving-up and before the emperor resolved the suspense by returning to France for his campaign of the Hundred Days, ending at Waterloo. In this situation, the true protagonist is the imperial exile and, in the novel as in history, the observer's attention is drawn to his off-stage presence, even while following the activities of those at the forefront of the action. It is this innovation in the narrative—creating an Eminence Grise of historical dimensions while pursuing the stories of a number of characters caught in the web of history—that gives *Suspense* its power to evoke a specific and crucial period in Western history.

Everyone in the novel holds an attitude toward Napoleon, an attitude which is more like a self-projection. For the servants, keen to detect pretention in their masters and in each other, he is "of no account"—that is, an upstart (Part I, ii, 26). For the recently restored aristocrats, he is a subject to be avoided, as having challenged their existence at its root: ". . . one would have thought, listening to the talk one heard on all sides, that such a man as Bonaparte had never existed" (Part II, iii, 105). For the new-rich bourgeois, he is the model *arriviste* and patron of capitalism; and he, in turn, looks on that class appreciatively—as he says of the villain, Count Helion de Montevesso, "I am grateful to him for giving work to the people. This is the proper use of wealth" (Part II, vi, 146). For the double-agent Doctor Martel, he is the image of the cosmopolitan adventurer, as the Doctor suggests when describing his own stamping-ground: "From one end of Europe to the other. . . . Exactly like that Corsican fellow" (Part III, 1, 178). For the hero, Cosmo Latham, anxious for experience and confused by the complex political and social depths into which he is plunged, Napoleon is an enigma. To the question, what does Napoleon stand for, Cosmo answers, "Many things, and some of them too obvious to mention. But I can't help thinking that there are some which we cannot see yet" (Part I, iii, 38). Finally, to the Italian people among whom he is exiled, Napoleon represents the possibility of national independence, with which he had toyed during his occupation of Italy and other countries. When Cosmo asks his innkeeper, "But what is it that makes you people love this man?" Cantelucci answers, "Signore, it is the idea" (Part III, i, 182).

This set of attitudes creates not a portrait of the man but an image of historical reality. Napoleon was not merely what he was in himself, but a stimulus that brought to expression a range of impulses at work throughout Europe. As one of his modern biographers has put it, "When you tear off the trappings of soldier and ruler, you find, not a frightened and shriveled creature, not even a perverted soul, but a mystery, impenetrable because it is a vacuum. Napoleon is nothing but Napoleon."[10] It is the cultural complex of the national feelings, political ideas, and class attitudes which crystallized around him that is the historical reality of Napoleon—not the mere human, who tended rather toward nonentity —and this Conrad has captured better than the long line of hero-worshippers and devil-exorcisers in previous literature.

The action in the foreground of the novel alternates between the beau-monde Genoa of de Montevesso and his wife, Adèle (the childhood friend of Cosmo), and the popular quarter of town around the harbor. Cosmo's involvement with the de Montevessos fills him with disgust, as he learns about Adèle's miserable marriage and encounters the snobbery and malice of the fashionable world, typified by his chat with Lady William Bentinck. It also, unbeknown to himself, endangers his life, for de Montevesso begins plotting to remove him from the scene, as a possible lover of his

10. Albert Guérard, *Napoleon I: A Great Life in Brief* (New York, 1959 [1956]), p. 67. For the variants of the Napoleonic myth see Guérard, p. 190 ff., and Pieter Geyl, *Napoleon: For and Against* (New Haven and London, 1963 [1949]).

wife. But it is not only a rejection of the upper classes that moves Cosmo to choose his direction on an evening stroll: "In the whole town he knew only the way to the Palazzo and the way to the port. He took the latter direction" (Part III, ii, 196). It is for adventure that Cosmo strikes out, and specifically for adventure among the people, to whom he has been attracted by the figure of the Carbonaro Attilio. In making this personal choice, Cosmo— true to the Scott tradition of the wavering hero—becomes a plaything of large historical forces, is shunted from the hands of the police to those of the revolutionaries, and loses his own will, even his belief in the will as a decisive element of man's activity. On throwing in his lot with the revolutionaries, "After the first few strokes Cosmo felt himself draw back again to the receding shore. But it was too late. He seemed to feel profoundly that he was not— perhaps no man was—a free agent" (Part IV, i, 270).

In the course of taking up the problems of historical engagement, *Suspense* considers one of the strongest passions at work in historical man: the urge to withdraw from history. Cosmo's quest for a community of belief and activity is a quest for self-definition. At the start of his adventure, he feels that "He had nothing to do; and he did not seem to know what to think of anything in the world" (Part III, i, 175–6). But in the adventure itself, he feels a withdrawal from his normal self, a state of personal suspension which is the counterpart for the individual of the state of general suspense in the political realm. He has left behind his money, his servant, his identification papers, so that he can relish the entry into a condition without historical identity: "He surrendered to the soft and invincible stillness of air and sea and stars enveloping the active desires and the secret fears of men who have the sombre earth for their stage" (Part IV, i, 255).

As in the similar scene of *Nostromo*, when Decoud is appalled by the emptiness around him and eventually commits suicide, it is the cutting of ties with one's traditional social commitments that creates the strangeness of the occasion. But for Cosmo, this cutting-off is a desirable, even fruitful, state; he finds himself not alone but organically tied to a human group and its ideals. It is the informing irony of the situation that his breaking of ties with his accustomed life is not a release from the claims of history but a new and intense involvement with them. The implication of *Sus-*

pense is not merely that the wavering hero chooses the revolutionary camp, breaking with his own class and past (he has fought under Wellington in the Peninsular Wars). Its larger burden is that history is an all-embracing medium, in which even he who seeks disengagement from the limitations of his endowed role by casting himself out of society into the stillness of nature, he, too, is to play a role—perhaps his most serious role—in history.

Cosmo chooses, on the strength of Attilio's appeal, to help row out to a ship that will carry messages to Napoleon on Elba. His motives are mixed, to be sure: a desire to see Napoleon, who was already regarded as the prime tourist attraction of Europe; a desire to join with an adventurous mariner, an exemplar of the Cervoni-Nostromo-Peyrol hero in Conrad's œuvre; and a desire to identify himself with a community larger than himself. We do not know how Conrad would have handled Cosmo's almost inevitable meeting with Napoleon or his involvement with the Carbonari, but it is likely—on the basis both of his consistent emphasis on the individual's need for an object of loyalty, and of his characterization of Cosmo as a young man acutely aware of this need—that this adventure would involve a life-commitment for the hero. Some of the possibilities available to Conrad were to engage Cosmo in the movement for Italian nationalism, to show his disillusionment with the world-historical hero on meeting him face-to-face, and/or to lead him to attempt to dissuade the revolutionaries from believing in Napoleon's leadership of the independence movement. To decide among these would be mere speculation, of course, but Conrad's own ideas of Napoleon, if they were to be incarnated in the novel, would have entailed some such alternatives.

Whatever Conrad's political treatment of the denouement was to have been, he had already succeeded in generating a philosophic frame within which to see historical events. The opening and closing pages of the *Suspense* suggest a trans-historical perspective of the kind we have observed in *Henry Esmond* and ascribed to other great historical novels. At the outset (Part I, i, 5–7) Attilio describes a past encounter with an old man of apparently infinite wisdom, but the image, although portentous, is left vague.[11] At the end of the novel an old boatman, who has been requisitioned by the police, is almost drowned in the ensuing

11. Cf. Albert J. Guerard, *Conrad the Novelist* (New York, 1967 [1958]), pp. 289–91.

struggle, and is made helmsman by the escaping conspirators. After Cosmo's meditation on his own and mankind's lack of free will, he notices the old man performing his function without knowing why or even where he steers: ". . . the ancient steersman, the white-headed figure in an unexpectedly erect attitude who, with hardly any breath left in his body and a mere helpless victim of other men's will, had a strange appearance of the man in command" (Part IV, i, 271). When the old man dies at his post, Attilio reflects that it is "strange to think perhaps it had been done for Italy" (Part IV, i, 274), and he answers Cosmo's question, "Where is his star now?" with the enigmatic words that conclude the fragmentary novel: "Signore, it should be out . . . But who will miss it out of the sky?" For this revolutionary fatalist, the loss of an individual is significant only in its contribution to the movement for the common goal—when the individual (star) is lost there are still myriads around it. But the sense of fatality that hovers over these framing images suggests that Conrad was here expressing one of his universal themes with a broad historical reference. The ironic fate that invests life with tragic dignity is here personified in an old-man-of-the-sea who passes blithely through and out of historical engagement. *Suspense*, in its fragmentary state, does not complete its exploration of the relations of personal fate to history, but it moves among them more intimately than almost any other English historical novel.

✌

Despite their success in achieving certain potentialities of historical fiction, Conrad's Napoleonic novels lack the comprehensiveness of social description which could make them high-water-marks of the tradition. The Conrad novel which most fully realizes the spirit of an epoch is not usually thought of as historical because it treats a roughly contemporary situation.[12] Yet *Nostromo* (1904) is

---

12. Ivo Vidan, "The Politics of *Nostromo*," *Essays in Criticism*, XVII (1967), 392–98, makes a brave effort to resist the critical tendency to convert it into anything but a political and historical novel, e.g., in Claire Rosenfield's *Paradise of Snakes: An Archetypal Analysis of Conrad's Political Novels* (Chicago and London, 1967), which sees it in Jungian terms. The dangers of taking the novel in the context of, e.g., the myth of Conn-Eda are illustrated by Dorothy Van Ghent's introduction to the Rinehart edition of *Nostromo* (New York, 1961), which ends by seeing it ahistorically as a "recurrent and resurgent comedy."

more solidly historical than many novels that more neatly fit the definition, directed as it is not only at a specific historical episode—the Colombian civil wars and the secession of Panama—but at the entire course of Latin American history.[13] Moreover, it is not alone its sociological breadth and temporal specificity that make it a novel of history, for these qualities are also present in novels-of-the-recent-past like *Middlemarch* and *Vanity Fair*. Conrad's explorations in narrative method in *Lord Jim* and "Heart of Darkness" enabled him painstakingly to structure *Nostromo* by the movement of time in the consciousness of its several characters. *Nostromo* marks a new movement in English historical fiction by taking as its object of imitation not only a historical period but the experience of historical time itself.

The so-called impressionist method by which Conrad and Ford brought French techniques of expressing subjectivity into English fiction is the basis of Conrad's recreation of historical time. It is a method of narration that follows the sequence of subjective perceptions, deviating from the objective sequence of events to record the course of personal responses to it. By this method, Conrad is able to convey the immediacy of experience and to structure his novels in a manner resembling that in which experience is lived. Beyond this, in *Nostromo*, more than the immediate sense of personal events is impressionistically portrayed. We are given, by narrative shifts from one participant's viewpoint to another's, the kind of data received by the historian in his research—a set of notes recording discrete observations in or on the past, out of which a continuous and coherent sequence must be constructed. This sequence is history, in the sense of a meaningful order of events, but the data themselves are the stuff of history—the facts, which are most frequently mere impressions of what happened. Further, the temporal process of registering the data, i.e., the process of recording history, more nearly resembles the sequence of experiences in history than it does the written revision of the sequence into an intelligible whole. Thus *Nostromo*, by

13. See *Conrad's Politics*, pp. 167–71, for an account of the Colombian-Panamanian background. Recent research on Paraguayan and other sources is summarized in C. T. Watts, ed., *Joseph Conrad's Letters to R. B. Cunninghame Graham* (Cambridge, 1969), pp. 39–42, 206–8, which also gives further details on Conrad's direct source for Colombian affairs, Santiago Pérez Triana, son of a banished Colombian ex-president.

recording the sequences of individual experience and of its registration, is more expressive of historical life than novels which take the posthumous point-of-view of professional histories.[14]

From the first, in Conrad's treatment of Costaguana, history, either as legend or fact, colors every feature of the country's face. The opening parable of the silver-fortune hunters on the Azuera peninsula—against which the modern scramble for silver is set—is placed in an indefinite time which represents a kind of legendary past for Costaguana. In recounting the legend, the origins of the silver itself are placed back in the time of the Conquistadores, and loaded with the crime of its accumulation by means of native slave-labor. Later on, the nineteenth-century history of Costaguana —the source of the political nexus of the novel's action—is given to us under the rubric of extracts from Don Jose Avellanos's work, *A History of Fifty Years of Misrule*. Further details of these years of independence are indicated in the background notes that are cast deftly throughout the first part of the novel. We learn, for example, in Chapter V that the regime of Don Vincente Ribiera, under the auspices of the aristocratic Blanco Party, has existed only some eighteen months, at the beginning of which Ribiera has brought in private capital and a British concessionaire to build a railroad across the Cordillera mountain range. We learn in the same chapter that the new element in Costaguana's history, the Caesarist general, Pedrito Montero, has made his reputation and achieved his power in the same Ribiera regime, rising from an obscure post to become general, minister of war, and the military head of the Blanco Party. Our view of the historical process moves forward as we observe in the novel's present action the military rebel Montero effectively challenging the moribund Ribiera government which engendered him. But the *caudillo* will, we are given to see, lose out to a new force: the separatist tendency crystallized by Decoud.

14. The best descriptions of this technique in *Nostromo* are: Guerard, *Conrad the Novelist*, p. 210 f., and Frederick R. Karl, *A Reader's Guide to Joseph Conrad* (New York, 1960), p. 145 ff. The most useful approaches to reconstructing the sequence of events in Conrad's novels are: Joseph Warren Beach, *The Twentieth-Century Novel: Studies in Technique* (New York and London, 1932), pp. 362–63; and J. E. Tanner, "The Chronology and the Enigmatic End of *Lord Jim*," *Nineteenth-Century Fiction*, XXI (1967), 371–72. Their methods of handling the involutions of "time-shift" narrative would show the temporal consistency of *Nostromo*, if systematically applied.

In maintaining these temporal levels of action, Conrad focuses on the transitions involved in two phases of the historical process: the formation of a capitalist-oriented system in underdeveloped countries, which initiates economic expansion, and the simultaneous growth of class, militarist, and regional interests, which struggle for control of the new or potential wealth of industrial development. We are given a picture of the early stages of imperialism, in which the very backwardness and instability of native governments act as an impediment to the economic dominance of foreign investors. Then follows the beginning of a viable regime and the introduction of the railroad engineers at a memorable dinner party, attended by the president, Ribiera, and the chief British financier, Sir John. When the mine is finally reactivated by Charles Gould— with an influx of American capital from the archetypal capitalist Holroyd—it is for the absurdly naive Captain Mitchell to pronounce with historical accuracy, "This marks an epoch" (Part 1, vi, 68).

When the economic windfall of the mine generates a revolt by the Montero brothers, the only force loyal to the aristocratic ruling class and their capitalist interests is, curiously enough, the urban proletariat—in this case, the stevedores working at the point of contact with imperialism, where the railroad begins and where silver leaves the country. It is Mitchell's role here, too, to pronounce the appropriate clichés: "It was history—history, sir! And that fellow of mine, Nostromo, you know, was right in it. Absolutely making history, sir" (Part 1, viii, 130). Mitchell's further description of Nostromo's role bears a wisdom far beyond his power to conceive —a wisdom that applies equally to the entire nation: "Sir, that was no mistake. It was a fatality." Mitchell is simply referring to the misfortune of the Montero coup, but his words resonate beyond it to cover the career of Nostromo and the history of the country. Fatality is a term equally well applied to the ego-bound life of Nostromo and to the long series of abominations in an underdeveloped nation, of which Costaguana is the type. Fate is conceived here not as a predetermined outcome but as a degenerative tendency that makes *any* outcome bitter; yet *Nostromo* does not end fatalistically.

While the narrative time-scheme of *Nostromo* is as complicated as that of *Lord Jim* or *Chance*, it may be broadly summarized as follows: the historical subject shifts from the middle of the action, the Monterist coup, back to a series of remote pasts—the colonial

period, independence and civil wars, the Guzman Bento dictatorship, and the subsequent "long turmoil of pronunciamentos" (Part
I, vi, 52). The immediate past is then recalled: the Ribiera regime,
the new era dawning at the time of Sir John's visit, the revival of
the mine, and the Monterist attempt to gather that fruit. The
sketching in of these pasts occupies almost half the novel, and is
completed on returning to the debacle in which they have issued.

The precise shift from background to foreground history occurs
when Decoud summarizes the most recent events in his letter to
his sister (Part II, vii, 230 ff.). From that point on we are given
the impression of following present events (the indefinite past
tense serving its time-honored role of conveying ongoing action).
The main events of the plot—the silver shipment, Decoud's suicide,
Hirsch's death, and Nostromo's decision to ride for Barrios's forces,
conclude the dramatic present of the novel. At this point we are
given a series of future anticipations: Barrios's return, the Separatist Revolution, the show of force by U.S. ships, the making of the
Occidental Republic safe for imperialism—and the potential revolutionary forces of the new proletariat. This prediction—it could
only have been a prediction for Conrad in the opening years of
this century (specifically, at the time of the Panama secession)—
is rendered by the narrative device of a tourist commentary imparted by Captain Mitchell to a foreign visitor. Like everything
else in this novel of history, then, even the future is seen as a past,
to be narrated and interpreted by a more-or-less competent historian. It develops that everything is seen from the perspective of
the survivors of history, and that what had seemed in the telling to
be past, present, and future actions are all uniformly reduced to a
historical past. Even the closing events, Nostromo's love and death,
are narrated as a completed action—although it is given enough
afflatus to make it seem like vivid, present drama. To put it
schematically, while it seems that the narrative perspective shifts
from present (o) to remote past (-2) to immediate past (-1)
before its denouement in distant ($+2$) and immediate futures ($+1$),
the entire story is a succession of pasts (P 5, P 4, P 3, P 2, P 1).[15]

15. Both the detailed sequence of narrated events and the perspectives of
the narrators are more complicated than this summary of their effects. Events
in the remote past are filled in periodically in the course of the account
of the narrative present (e.g., Dr. Monygham's sufferings under Guzman Bento).
Action in the "present" (the night on the gulf) is given as Captain Mitchell's
narrative, but at Part III, chapter x it changes from a retrospective to a prospec-
tive view: no longer are events told as having once happened but are sum-

Not only does all time become history, but all the major figures in the novel express themselves and govern their conduct under historical burdens that dominate their imagination. Charles Gould is the most prominent example of a man fully committed to vigorous action in the present, whose conduct is an attempt to revise, relive, or make up for the past—in this case, the miseries undergone by his uncle and father in previous Costaguana regimes. Avellanos is another of the historically burdened political actors who can hardly conceive of a present or future apart from a painful awareness of "fifty years of misrule." By the same token, the personal psychology of Dr. Monygham is dominated by memory, in his case of a more personal and traumatic kind: the tyranny of Guzman Bento, in which he himself was degraded under torture by the terror regime which dominated the entire population of Costaguana. Even the estranged intellectual, Decoud, is motivated largely by his awareness of the long, meaningless farce of Costaguana's mismanaged government. Apart from Costaguana's history, the history of their nations of origin dominates the mind of such immigrants as Antonio Viola. He has been shaped in the crucible of the Italian independence movement, and his subsequent evaluations of men and politics are derived from the heroic standard of the Carbonari. In the same way, the historical imagination of Gould's backer, Holroyd, the San Francisco financeer, is governed by an image of Western history under the supremacy of the Anglo-Saxon nations with a "manifest destiny": "The world can't help it—and neither can we, I guess" (Part I, vi, 77).

Given these historical forces, both in the objective history of the nation and in the consciousness of representative individuals, the present action of *Nostromo* becomes a working out of the données of the past—and simultaneously the opening up of an indeterminate future. The process by which the capitalist entrepreneur becomes an unwilling fosterer of a rising proletariat, which will one day

---

marized as so recently occurring as to be too well known for detailed description. This gives the closing developments of the revolution the effect of a quickly unfolding future, although they, too, are part of the past gathered up by Mitchell. The undoing of Nostromo is also past, but is rendered by the omniscient narrator; this gives it the aura of occurring after Mitchell's historical account, although it is contemporaneous with its closing stages.

make its own bid for political power; the process by which a disaffected intellectual becomes the founding father of a new nation, while remaining alienated from the historical milieu in which he effectively acts; the process by which the United States tends to replace England as the chief economic and military power in Costaguana's imperialist phase; these and other historical ironies are recounted in the novel. *Nostromo* is a great novel of history not only because it is as clear and detailed a fictional embodiment of the great age of imperialism as we possess, but also by virtue of its discovery of an esthetic equivalent for the complex process of historical change. In the action of the novel we trace the circuitous courses by which historical change actually comes about: out of the limited projects of egoistically or economically motivated actors, new social forms emerge, never as they were intended. The controlled disorder of the novel's narrative is the perfect expression of the indirect way in which large historical movements are generated by a plethora of minor personal impulses, which come together in definite shapes, though not determined or permanent ones.

Not only do individuals contribute to the form of the whole in an irrational, if not inchoate, way, but their selection of their own social roles is never quite the same as the roles they come to play. The ultramontane Father Corbelàn becomes the ideologue for the extension of the Sulaco revolution to the rest of Costaguana; the bandit chief Hernandez, who has led the suppressed peasantry into the civil war on the side of the aristocratic and capitalist forces, becomes in the new dispensation Minister of War; and the great loner, Nostromo, who has been an organizer of labor in behalf of his foreign employers, becomes a somewhat passive patron saint of the new workers' party that meets furtively to plan the coming revolution. The sense of history as a relentlessly corrosive force does not commit Conrad to a deterministic view of the historical process. Men shape themselves out of the materials given by the past, or as Marx put it in a famous phrase, "Men make their own history, but they do not make it exactly as they wish." The peculiar power of Conrad's vision of history lies in its simultaneous awareness of freedom and fate; the struggle of heroism and circumstance in tragedy is applied here to the workings of history.

Nostromo's vision of the tragic pattern of history—both in the past and in the present—is expressed by the contemplative Dr. Monygham:

The method followed had been the only one possible. The Gould Concession had ransomed its way through all those years. It was a nauseous process. He quite understood that Charles Gould had got sick of it and had left the old path to back up that hopeless attempt at reform. The doctor did not believe in the reform of Costaguana. And now the mine was back again in its old path, with the disadvantage that henceforth it had to deal not only with the greed provoked by its wealth, but with the resentment awakened by the attempt to free itself from its bondage to moral corruption. That was the penalty of failure. (Part III, iv, 370)

Monygham can see only the futility of any attempt to free Costaguana from its historical tradition of crime and folly—and he predicts the new troubles that will emerge with the formation of a class-conscious proletariat. But Conrad is not imaginatively limited to Monygham's sense of the oppressive weight of the past. In a summary statement, Conrad seems to express a general view of the pattern of Costaguana's history (although speaking specifically of the Monterist revolution): "This will appear less incredible by the reflection that the fundamental causes were the same as ever, rooted in the political immaturity of the people, in the indolence of the upper classes and the mental darkness of the lower" (Part III, v, 387). But with the development of technology and the crystallization of economic roles, the increased self-consciousness and political sophistication of both the upper and the lower classes seem fatally bound for collision with each other. The future of Costaguana will be, then, not a mere repetition of its past, but a struggle for new forms to contain and articulate its human and material energies. It has moved from a known to an unknown history, and the novel's subtlest movement is from a static contemplation of past crimes and follies to an open-ended imagining of the future's potential for change. *Nostromo* does not predict the form of the future, yet it is perhaps the only novel of history to project an anticipation of the future as successfully as it does a sense of the past.

II. WOOLF

Virginia Woolf's two tours de force, *Orlando* (1928) and *Between the Acts* (1941), bring the tradition of the English historical novel to a self-conscious close. It will certainly seem strange at first to consider these iconoclastic works within *any* tradition, let alone that of the historical novel. But if the history of the modern novel has been one of persistent innovation in the technique and range of prose fiction, it is appropriate that these changes be marked in the historical as well as in the so-called "dramatic" novel. Woolf's transformation of historical fiction is of a piece with her renovation—along with Joyce and others—of the traditional novel of character development and personal relations. Moreover, the imaginative impulses which generate the experiments of her historical novels are almost identical to those which create new forms in her other fiction. The changed conception of reality in the age of Freud and Einstein, which expressed itself in a revolution in form not only in literature but in the other arts, has affected historical fiction in much the same way.

Virginia Woolf's idea of history is inextricably entwined with her ideas of personality. *Orlando: A Biography* is almost entirely concerned with the historical formation of the individual and, in turn, portrays history as a series of projections of personal style. An urgent concern with the formation of the private self is by no means the unique possession of Woolf's new form of historical novel. It is an element of the grand theme of historical fiction from Scott down: the relation of personal loyalties, values, and passions to the network of historical forces which surround and condition them. Further, Woolf's interest in both the transitoriness and the continuity of history confronts one of the major dichotomies of traditional historical fiction. This dichotomy has sometimes operated to emphasize the roots of present social conditions in past historical events, sometimes to differentiate a lost, exotic past from the unheroic world of the present. Both these possibilities are exploited in Woolf's fiction; like Scott and other great historical novelists, she maintains the double perspective of past and present. Lastly, Woolf is in tune with the major English historical novelists—and with the major Continental writers in the genre as well—in her acute awareness of the falsity of many of the historical myths on which official historians and lesser novelists thrive. *Orlando* and *Between the Acts* are debunking novels, like *Henry Esmond* or

The Charterhouse of Parma: they focus sharply on the traditional shibboleths by which England has been and, in part, still is governed.

Yet for all its consistency with the tradition, Woolf's historical fiction introduces a new note. It not only reduces entire institutions, such as the aristocracy, to the personal qualities which compose them—and which are subject to various articulations of style by the historical process—but sees the self as an esthetic object related to its historical medium in the manner of a work of art. This personal and esthetic view of history gives Woolf the opportunity to write historical fiction that is both a satire of the foibles of the past and a comic vision of the creative powers of the self which can be salvaged from the detritus of history. *Orlando* and *Between the Acts* are historical novels of the age in which Pound, Yeats, and Eliot emphasized both the cultural indebtedness and the intense individuality of the artist, establishing him as a new type of historical hero.

℘

Critics have been so delighted by *Orlando* as the lone *jeu-d'esprit* by an otherwise tenaciously difficult and somber writer that they have neglected to take the measure of the root idea by which its form is governed: the continuity of cultural tradition, expressed in personal identity, throughout the variations of history and despite the destructiveness of time. It is easy to confuse this idea with a congeries of popular beliefs in the aristocratic virtues as national and racial endowments or family and class traits—a cultural myth fostered with renewed urgency by the aristocracy in its moribund state following the First World War. While Woolf's critical intelligence was not proof against all the popular or snobbish prejudices of her day, it inevitably gave them a peculiar cast. It is possible to trace her special version of the myth by comparing *Orlando* with a number of other books of the previous decades to see how it reflects the anxieties of the age but also transforms nostalgia into art.

Even before and during the war, novelists had begun to exploit the idea of racial continuity amid cultural change. Amid a welter of Teutonists, Imperialists, and Anglo-Saxonists—which included writers of historical fiction like Henty, Rider Haggard, and others—Kipling held pre-eminence in the field. In a collection of children's stories, *Puck of Pook's Hill* (1906), and its sequel, *Rewards and Fairies* (1910), children of the present encounter (apparently in dreams) the men who have inhabited their countryside in the past, and discover linguistic, archeological, or more vaguely spiritual traces of the romantic lives that have been lived there. A series of poems interlarding the stories enforces the movement from heightened consciousness of the past to nationalistic pride in it. The first lyric speaks only of origins:

> *Trackway and Camp and City Lost,*
>   *Salt Marsh where now is corn;*
> *Old Wars, old peace, old Arts that cease,*
>   *And so was England born.*[1]

The final lyric rises to a paean:

> *Land of our Birth, our faith, our pride,*
> *For whose dear sake our fathers died;*
> *O Motherland, we pledge to theee,*
> *Head, heart, and hand through the years to be!*

Besides the standard Kiplingesque traits in evidence here, a notion of history also comes to light. National tradition is not simply a standard for youth to model itself upon, but is already instinct in the character of each successive generation; not only places but persons are marked by their historical forebears.

Yet the sense of continuity is hardly fostered by Kipling's groups of stories. We move from a sequence of medieval tales back to Roman times and forward to the Renaissance, without seeing the past as more than a collection of anecdotes. While there is no claim on a children's book to present a coherent or even a consecutive pattern of history, the tendency of nationalism to seize upon fragmentary and inconclusive nuggets of pastness is already palpable in these early uses of the heritage myth. Virginia Woolf

---

1. R. Kipling, *Puck of Pook's Hill* (London, 1906), p. 4; the quotation that follows is from p. 306. On Kipling, Buchan, and other racialist or imperialist novelists, see Alan Sandison, *The Wheel of Empire: A Study of the Imperial Idea in Some Late Nineteenth- and Early Twentieth-Century Fiction* (London, New York, etc., 1967).

will go beyond this disjointed historical sense, largely by virtue of her stronger interest in the continuity of personality.

During and immediately after the war, two other popular novelists employed the idea of personal continuity amid historical diversity as a means of urging their social and ethical attitudes toward the modern world. These—broadly speaking—historical novels make ingenious efforts to resolve the esthetic difficulties entailed by the idea of persistence of character from age to age. *In a Desert Land* (1915), by Valentina Hawtrey, is a straightforward family chronicle tracing an aristocratic house from the middle ages to the eighteenth century, but its implication for the present emerges only in the epilogue, when a modern woman who has lost a sense of her roots suddenly discovers them in a religious vocation. The movement from the heroism of a Catholic family during periods of persecution to a contemporary's decision to enter a convent is intended to show a continuity of family temperament which gives current significance to the past.

Far more blatant in theme and industrious in its parallel structure is John Buchan's *The Path of the King* (1921). Here the racial implications of the idea of continuity are not stinted: when a heroic trait appears in history, it is to be ascribed to a heroic family line— somewhat democratized by dispersion through the hardier breed of younger sons. Buchan puts the idea in the words of an American interlocutor in the Prologue: "We all of us may have kings' blood in our veins. The dago who blacked my boots at Vancouver may be descended by curious byways from Julius Caesar."[2] This premise is made the focal point of a series of heroic sagas down through the ages, concluding rather incongruously with Abraham Lincoln. It is not the national tradition of Kipling that is celebrated here, nor the family continuity of Hawtrey, but the strain of heroism that distinguishes the élite of the human race.

While there is no evidence that Virginia Woolf learned from the experience of her predecessors, there can be no doubt that she left them far behind in her attention to the esthetic difficulties of ex-

2. John Buchan, *The Path of the King* (London, 1921), p. 2. A later version of the family heritage novel is Norah Lofts, *Bless This House* (London, 1954), in which the continuity of a country house figures as prominently as in *Orlando*, while the diversity of its owners (of various families) is integrated by a series of Interludes between the historical Episodes—a conventional structure reminiscent of the pageant in *Between the Acts*.

pressing a similar theme. *Orlando* boldly addresses itself to the question of inherited traits in family or nation by having an individual personality persist through the centuries. All forms of cultural experience contribute to the making of this character, but the portrayal of history is simplified to converge on one point, the formation of the self. It is the sum of a family's experience—in its genteel and its seamy sides, in its public and its private roles, at its enduring country house and in its widest travels—that constitutes its offspring's character-structure. Historical life of the widest variety enters the novel and vivifies the drama of individual existence amid historical change.

From the outset of her writing career, Woolf was interested in the possibilities of historical fiction. The novelist hero of her first novel plans to write one in a new way:

My idea is that there's a certain quality of beauty in the past, which the ordinary historical novelist completely ruins by his absurd conventions. . . . I'm going to treat people as though they were exactly the same as we are. The advantage is that, detached from modern conditions, one can make them more intense and more abstract than people who live as we do.[3]

What was involved in treating people as though they were "exactly the same as we are" yet "detached from ordinary conditions" was not, however, clear to Terence Hewet, and evolved only gradually in his creator's experiments with form. By taking as its subject neither family, nor nation, nor class, but an individual who incorporates all three, *Orlando* tries to find a historical basis of personality. To place greatest emphasis on the titular hero of *Orlando* is not to question the esthetic tact of personifying a collective hero like the Sackville family. It is to probe towards Virginia Woolf's view of the individual's relation to his culture—that is, her view of history's meaning for man.

In reviewing a book published in the same year as *Orlando* by Woolf's brother-in-law, T. S. Eliot found him "inclined to confound the civilization of a race or an epoch with that of an individual."[4]

---

3. *The Voyage Out* (London, 1965 [1915]), ch. xvi, p. 264. This, the Hogarth Press Uniform Edition, will be cited parenthetically throughout, by chapter and page number for *Orlando*, by page number alone for *Between the Acts*.

4. *The Criterion*, viii (1928), 163. For an excellent commentary on *Civilization*, see Irma Rantavaara, *Virginia Woolf and Bloomsbury* (Helsinki, 1953), pp. 47–57.

That book was Clive Bell's *Civilization*, which may be taken as a summary of the Bloomsbury group's social and historical views (which are expressed nowhere else more distinctly). Based on the ethical individualism and hedonism of G. E. Moore, and continuing the Bloomsburian attack on English esthetic insensitivity, *Civilization* has all the qualities to make it a *bête noire* for partisan critics from Eliot to Leavis. What concerns us here is not the hint of post-aristocratic, esthetic snobbism in Bell, e.g., in the belief that the civilized individual need be free of work to fulfill his potentialities for experience. More to the present point is his selection of historical periods which exemplify the heights of civilization: beyond the Greeks (and after a sneer at the Romans), Bell develops the Renaissance and the eighteenth century as the peaks of England's civilization, while denigrating the Victorians as the precursors of contemporary bourgeois society. Now these are the key periods in *Orlando* and *Between the Acts*, and Woolf's attitude toward them is much the same as Bell's, even to showing wide indulgence toward the sexual tendencies of their freer spirits.[5]

The similarities in their evaluation of historical periods should lead us to a more profound relationship between Woolf's and Bell's works. In his period descriptions, Bell tends to identify the civilized man with his milieu: his qualities are those of the age. Eliot's review raises the question: is there no need for the civilized individual to be in tension with his time, no matter how enlightened, simply because culture is a restrictive as well as a nutritive medium, and must be resisted, if not transcended, by individuals? In *Orlando*, on the contrary, the hero-heroine is a personification not only of his family but also of his time; as one critic has put it, "Orlando is masculine and violent in the dashing Elizabethan age, pensive and morbid in the early seventeenth century, presides at literary tea-parties in the Augustan period, and blushes and swoons in crinolines in the sentimental age of Victoria."[6] Such consistent parallelism im-

---

5. The frankest discussion of Woolf's sexual views and their biographical and ethical implications is Jean Guiguet, *Virginia Woolf and Her Works*, trans. Jean Stewart (London, 1965 [1962]), pp. 273–74; also 67–69, 258–59. The tenor of her feeling for Orlando's original is expressed in the letters asking Victoria Sackville-West for personal and family information to provide the data of *Orlando;* quoted in Aileen Pippett, *The Moth and the Star: A Biography of Virginia Woolf* (Boston and Toronto, 1955), pp. 254–64 *et passim.* This may help to explain why she made her hero hermaphroditic.

6. Bernard Blackstone, *Virginia Woolf: A Commentary* (London, 1949), p. 131.

plies a constant relationship between the individual and his environment which in the esthetic realm functions as symbolism but in the philosophic can only be considered determinism. In contrast, another strain in the novel suggests that the internal dynamics of individual growth are independent of its specific historical forms: Orlando remains the artist-in-growth, fulfilling his personal destiny, which is to write "The Oak Tree" and other poems. He is not a pale reflector of historical periods, but a being with enough vitality to insure his individuality, sometimes in the teeth of the age.[7]

The philosophic roots of Woolf's conception of character will eventually be discovered only after sustained analysis of her intellectual relations with McTaggart, Moore, Bergson, and others.[8] But we can already locate the source of some of her ideas in the original of Orlando herself. In her book on her home and family, Victoria ("Vita") Sackville-West wrote:

Such interest as the Sackvilles have lies, I think, in their being so representative. From generation to generation they might stand, fully equipped, as portraits from English history. . . . let them each stand as the prototype of his age, and at the same time as a link to carry on, not only the tradition but also the heredity of his race, and they immediately acquire a significance, a unity.[9]

This, the program for *Knole and the Sackvilles*, can also stand as the formula for Woolf's novel; indeed, *Orlando* may be read as the fictional form of a family memoir.

The program undoubtedly meets the artist's need for "unity," but what sort of individuality can it project? By reducing the men

7. Woolf's notes on the manuscript reflect the ambiguities of her own conception. At times it emphasizes personal development as organic growth: "This is to tell a person's life from the year 1500 to 1928. Changing its sex, taking different aspects of the character in different Centuries. The theory being that character goes on underground before we are born; and leaves something afterwards also" (MS. of *Orlando* at Knole; page headed *"A Biography"*). On another unnumbered page, the emphasis is on determination from outside the individual: "Everybody has given me everything. *The past has.*"

8. See my article, "Woolf and McTaggart," *ELH: A Journal of English Literary History*, XXXVI (1970), 719–38, for a statement of some of the problems involved.

9. *Knole and the Sackvilles* (London, 1958 [1922]), p. 41; the quotation in the next paragraph is from p. 193 n. Vita also wrote *Pepita* (London [Hogarth Press], 1937), on the seamier side of the family history. The facts about her grandfather's affair with the gypsy dancer who became her grandmother are transmuted by Woolf into Orlando's gypsy exploits.

of the past to "portraits from English history," by making them esthetic objects that can be arranged like pictures in the family gallery, formal composition is achieved at the expense of personal singularity. There is even an intimation in both works of certain constants of physical and mental make-up: the portraits published in some editions of *Orlando* are chosen to suggest that the face remains the same, though the costume and expression vary according to the life-style of each age. The manifestations of the family's character in one age or another seem, then, merely the tincture of the times, while the collective type abides unchanged, like some unalterable germ-plasm.[10] But this is to overlook the novel's view of historical development as the unfolding of personal possibilities rather than as a repetition of fixed characteristics.

Like her aristocratic friend, Woolf is too sophisticated to fall into racial theorizing and snobbish antiquarianism. But another trap yawns before her: the portrayal of the sempiternal, bisexual, omnicompetent Orlando is really an exercise in glorification—most pointedly of Vita, but more generally of the artistic temperament. All the Orlando-figures are one Orlando under different guises, just as each Sackville embodies the abstract title of earl or duke for a time. There is a sense in which the artist, like the family, does not develop at all, but simply expresses his essential nature according to the prevailing style of culture. There is a hint of a profoundly ahistorical view—*plus ça change, plus c'est la même chose*—or as Vita put it on the national scale, "England is always very much the same."

Another side of the question of permanence and change is suggested by the presence of a complex symbol of Orlando's identity, the oak tree. Taken as the great tree on a hill of the family estate, to which the hero retires for poetic contemplation, the symbol is a reworking of the Romantic archetype of organic growth and venerable age. Through all the historical vicissitudes that affect the hero, the tree remains a sustaining presence, its growth being so slow as to imply not change but consistency. On the other hand, the oak tree is not only a tree but a poem: "The Oak Tree" is begun in the Elizabethan age and finally comes to completion in the present—although even now the artist is not content to think it finished. The

10. The pattern of constancy-in-change has been described as "eine zeitlose Wiederkehr kosmischer Energien"; Eric Wiget, *Virginia Woolf und die Konzeption der Zeit in ihren Werken* (Zurich, 1949), p. 68.

progress of the poem toward resolution as an integrated work of art follows the same pattern as the development of Orlando's personality toward the individual whom Woolf is commending to us in this biography. Just as the work of art is conceived as a slow historical creation, the self grows organically into a living whole.

There is some suggestion in *Orlando* that the self changes and grows not merely to exfoliate its potentialities, like a tree, but also to approach an integrated composition, like a poem. While the germ of the book probably came from the aristocratic idea of family continuity quoted above, another, stronger strain in Woolf's intellectual equipment came to the fore in the course of setting it out. This was the idea of the self as a work of art—an idea which in turn depends on the notion that a work of art is an organic unity that comes to completion through a progressive discovery of form. The dominant vision of history that emerges in *Orlando* follows from this view of the progressive formation of the self. It is that of a dynamic interaction with society in which the individual, and even perhaps the society, fulfills its potentialities and becomes itself. The structure of this novel-biography-history is, then, the classic one of idea becoming form, gene becoming person, historical situation becoming esthetic spectacle.

The infinite potentialities of personal expression in history stand, however, as a threat to the orderly fulfillment of the self. On the one hand, Orlando is to be considered the sum of all the Orlandos he has been throughout the novel:

Choosing then, only those selves we have found room for, Orlando may now have called on the boy who cut the nigger's head down; . . . the boy who saw the poet; the boy who handed the Queen the bowl of rose water; or she may have called upon the young man who fell in love with Sasha; or upon the Courtier; or upon the Ambassador; or upon the Soldier; or upon the Traveller; or she may have wanted the woman to come to her; the Gypsy; the Fine Lady; the Hermit; the girl in love with life; the Patroness of Letters. . . . (vi, 278)

It is this additive view of the formation of selfhood that gives rise to one aspect of the novel's form: a series of portraits of the self in its varying historical guises—which could, presumably, be indefinitely elaborated along the way and extended in time. From this standpoint, historical life is a succession of roles which persons (or nations) play as they are required by circumstances.

Alongside this view of the multiple forms of an essentially static self, Woolf insists upon its dynamic unity, its capacity to change and yet remain one: the "true self . . . compact of all the selves we have it in us to be; commanded and locked up by the Captain self, the Key self, which amalgamates and controls them all" (vi, 279). This self is not conceived of as an original possession or genetic root: it is a potentiality that comes into actuality in the process of historical experience. Despite its formal tendency toward serial extension, *Orlando* is a drama of the formation of this essential self out of the myriad experiences of its three-and-a-half centuries of historical living. It is this esthetically unified aspect of the Woolfian world that gives dramatic form to the novel, and does not leave it a mere series of historical pastiches.

In addition to his youthful amatory and political escapades, Orlando is from the outset engaged in a progressive attempt to orient himself toward his historical tradition and his ancestors, as embodied in the great country house which he inherits. This effort is inevitably problematic: "He would have liked to have ended with a flourish to the effect that he would follow in their foot-steps and add another stone to their building. Since, however, the building already covered nine acres, to add even a single stone seemed superfluous" (ii, 99–100). Orlando is reduced to refurnishing the house with all the splendors of the Renaissance, but the problem of becoming an individual when surrounded by such massive structures of family, class, and nation remains.

The extremity of this situation perhaps accounts for the extreme measures to which the hero resorts. In the seventeenth century he undergoes a series of radical transformations in sex, locale, and class-consciousness. She comes to see her culture from a distant perspective and judges it severely, adopting the feminine tendency to escape from history to the personal life:

"Better is it," she thought, "to be clothed with poverty and ignorance, which are the dark garments of the female sex; better to leave the rule and discipline of the world to others; better be quit of martial ambition, the love of power, and all the other manly desires if so one can more fully en-joy the most exalted raptures known to the human spirit, which are," she said aloud, as her habit was when deeply moved, "contemplation, solitude, love." (iv, 146)

This preference for the feminine life—which is, par excellence, the personal life, in place of the public life of men[11]—is confirmed by Orlando's experiences in her career as a woman. She joins a gipsy band in the mountains of Turkey and gains both the gipsies' perspective on the parvenu European aristocrats—whose lineage compares so poorly with their own, which goes back to the Pharaohs—and a still grander, visionary perspective on history, in the course of her contemplation of the Asian mountains under the aspect of eternity.

In the Victorian age, when Orlando is forced by her participation in the domesticating "spirit of the age" to think of taking a husband, she begins to develop further individual characteristics in response to the changing character of modern life. The new shape of Western history is indicated by the heroine's difficulties in adjustment:

> Orlando had inclined herself naturally to the Elizabethan spirit, to the Restoration spirit, to the spirit of the eighteenth century, and had in consequence scarcely been aware of the change from one age to the other. But the spirit of the nineteenth century was antipathetic to her in the extreme, and thus it took her and broke her, and she was aware of her defeat at its hands as she had never been before. (v, 220)

It seems, then, that the development of human personality is presented with a critical challenge in the nineteenth and twentieth centuries, not just another requirement of adaptation. This fall from the relatively idyllic pre-modern state is a fortunate one, however, as it leads to a renewed effort at self-consciousness. Orlando needs to grasp the nature of her tradition and become a distinct self; to do this she must integrate her multiple facets and achieve unity of spirit.

The first phase of her willed creation of the self is a despair of life in history: " 'I have sought happiness through many ages and not found it; fame and missed it; love and not known it; life— and behold, death is better. . . . It is better that I should lie at peace here with only the sky above me—as the gipsy told me years

---

11. See Herbert Marder, *Feminism and Art: A Study of Virginia Woolf* (Chicago and London, 1968), for an account of Woolf's sexual theories that carries historical implications, e.g., "Western civilization has emphasized the (masculine) rational faculties to the exclusion of the (feminine) faculties of intuition. . . . The way to remedy [modern] evils, according to Virginia Woolf, is to let feminine influences act freely, both within society and within the individual" (p. 3).

ago' " (v, 224). It is at this moment that Marmaduke Bonthrop Shelmerdine, Esquire, appears. A parody of Shelley, "whose entire works he had by heart," this male figure is so effeminate as to serve as a foil for Orlando to use in synthesizing her selfhood. Presumably his effeminacy makes a woman's love of him a complementary stimulus to her masculine tendencies. (He also serves the function of presenting her with a child—a necessary stage in the formation of personality, the childless Virginia Woolf would seem to be acknowledging.)

She next acquires the self-definition provided by the settlement of her perennial law suits, which declare her to be indeed a female and which affirm her inheritance of property in a straitened form, consonant with the contemporary restrictions on the British aristocracy. Further, she achieves moments of intense joy derived from her love: in particular, her moment of "ecstasy" while watching toy boats sailing on the Serpentine. These experiences allow her to come to consciousness of herself—to become the person toward whom her entire life has been tending. The moment of meeting or achieving herself is the present moment, "the eleventh of October, 1928"—probably the date on which Woolf expected the novel to be published (it was completed earlier that year). This entry into the present is not a sloughing-off of the past, but a realization of the past's potentialities, a bringing into being of what was before only becoming. This dramatic record of personal formation in history marks a new development in historical fiction, its closest anticipation being *Henry Esmond*.

A vision of promise and fulfillment animates Virginia Woolf's sense of history and gives *Orlando* its stature as comedy. The vision also serves to justify the aristocratic tradition, which enhances the individual's possibilities of achieving selfhood by multiplying his cultural opportunities and by habitually recording the occasions of past experience. Orlando, at the conclusion of the novel, attempts to relate herself to this historical endowment by revisiting her house and reaffirming her connection with her forebears and their artifacts: "She, who believed in no immortality, could not help feeling that her soul would come and go forever with the reds on the panels and the greens on the sofa" (vi, 285). But she is simultaneously aware that the house is an esthetic whole, distinct from herself as a created object: "The house was no longer hers entirely, she sighed. It belonged to time now; to history; was past the touch and control of the living" (VI, 286). Orlando, although the symbol of an entire family, the Earls and Dukes of Dorset, although the product of a long historic tradition, emerges distinct from the process which has made her. She is at last separate from her past, from her family, from her antecedent selves; she is herself alone.

In order to mark this fulfillment she is anxious to perform a rite of selfhood by uniting the two oak trees, the public and the private, the historical and the esthetic, in burying the published form of her poem at the roots of the tree. But she realizes that she has no trowel and that the dogs will dig it up: "No luck ever attends these symbolical celebrations, she thought. . . . 'I bury this as a tribute,' she was going to have said, 'a return to the land of what the land has given me,' but Lord! once one began mouthing words aloud, how silly they sounded!" (VI, 291). So, with indomitable comic spirit, Virginia Woolf sweeps away even the celebration of what her heroine and her tradition have achieved. She does not rest in a vision of created selfhood but reflects on the balance between the historical actor and his age that such selfhood permits:

> . . . the transaction between a writer and the spirit of the age is one of infinite delicacy, and upon a nice arrangement between the two the whole fortune of his works depends. Orlando had so ordered it that she was in an extremely happy position; she need neither fight her age, nor submit to it; she was of it, yet remained herself. Now, therefore, she could write, and write she did. She wrote. She wrote. She wrote. (VI, 239–40)

It is in the act of writing that the processes of historical formation and personal self-creation come together. The making of a work of art becomes a re-enactment of the drama by which individual selves are created in history.

೪

After the formal innovations of *Orlando*, Virginia Woolf went on to elaborate her dramatizing of the esthetic creation of selfhood in *The Waves*. But her next attempt to render the historical process of personal formation, *The Years*, made little attempt to move beyond the form of the family chronicle novel. It is only in her last novel, *Between the Acts,* that Woolf found a consummate means of integrating her notions of selfhood and her historical perspective. This work, connected so intimately with her movement toward death and with the outbreak of a war that threatened the end of civilization,[12] takes a step beyond the tradition of English historical fiction and suggests that the time is past for writing convincingly in the established forms again.

In *Between the Acts,* the foil for history is no longer the self but art: the unity of the novel is achieved not by showing the process by which a unified self is formed out of the fragments of historical experience, but by re-enacting the artist's activity in bringing significant form to the scattered relics of a nation's history. It is not only the art of the novelist or dramatist that is re-enacted but that of the historian as well—both in his shaping of an intelligible record of events and in his critique of explanatory myths and popular conceptions of the past. Whatever the difficulties of following the spectacular transmutations of *Orlando,* that novel was unified by its focus on a hero and on the heroic theme of self-creation. *Between the Acts* has been found more confusing because it takes the experience of history one step back: it is, as it were, a phenomenological reduction of history to its elements. These are not units of history but units of consciousness-of-history: the memories, impressions, and associations by which the past still lives in the minds of the living. The novel proceeds to trace how these data of consciousness are formed into historical attitudes, myths, or theories, and sometimes into works of art.

The two working titles of *Between the Acts—Poyntz Hall* and *The Pageant*—indicate the novel's themes and major divisions. The first (roughly) hundred pages are taken up with the people at the Hall who become the principal characters, with a sketch of a traditional plot (the Olivers' marital and extra-marital affairs), and

12. Cf. Victoria Sackville-West, *Country Notes in Wartime* (London [Hogarth Press], 1940), p. 52: "It is not easy to write these notes amidst the anguish and anxiety of Europe. . . . My only excuse can be that the determination to preserve such beauty as remains to us is also a form of courage." (Woolf used incidents from this book—or from the magazine articles which it comprises—in *Between the Acts,* e.g., a less grotesque version of Giles's killing of the adder with a frog in its mouth.) Woolf may have known that a book of memoirs by Henry W. Nevinson, *Between the Acts* (London, 1903), has a structure similar to that of her novel.

with the cultural milieu of the present. The second hundred are given over to the pageant, with its tableaux of past periods, its exhibition of the artist at work, and its punctuating remarks of incomprehension from the audience. The final half-hundred pages are a synthesis of the two movements, the past being brought into the present when the still-costumed actors mingle with the audience, and the present being conformed to the estheticized past of the pageant by the artifice of mirrors, which add the audience's image to the final scene. At the close, there is a coda, ending with the transforming line, "Then the curtain rose. They spoke." This enforces the repeated suggestion of another phenomenological frame to the novel, in which both the present and the past are seen as artifice, as a grand stage-play enacted in the presence of an ulterior reality which is occasionally invoked by shadowy allusions. The solid world of Pointz Hall is here reduced to another form of play-acting, to which the pageant has been a play-within-the-play —or more literally, an *entr'acte* or interlude—suggesting not only the novel's title but also the pageant's literary status as a masque. The implications of this juggling of illusion and reality have to do with the relations of esthetic form and historical vision, which it is the business of this novel to explore.

Much of the first movement catalogues the various modes by which the past persists in the minds of present-day men. Taken in order of appearance, these are: artifacts (the graves of Mrs. Haines's ancestors, which validate her snobbish claims to deference—p. 7); topographical formations (the marks on the land left by successive stages of civilization, which can be clearly seen from an airplane— p. 8); works of history (the "Outline of History," presumably the most popular of them all, H. G. Wells's, which Mrs. Swithin is reading—p. 13); family chroniclers (Mrs. Oliver's aunts, who purport to trace their descent from the Kings of Ireland—p. 22); literary and antiquarian works (the library of Pointz Hall, which includes the English poets, biographies of Garibaldi and Palmerston, and county histories—p. 26); tourism (the stone medieval barn is seen as a temple by those who have been to Greece—p. 34); place names (given in describing the delivery-route of the fish shop, with a verification of the names' longevity by reference to the Domesday Book—p. 40); paintings (the portraits which record the Western-like habits of an eighteenth-century squire,—p. 46); legend-ridden local sites (the lily pond, which carries a haunted air, as it was the suicide spot of Lady Ermyntrude, whose portrait hangs at the Hall—pp. 54–55); architectural and landscaping art (Pointz Hall and the grounds with their views, as described in Figgis' Guide Book of 1833 and not much altered—pp. 65–66); social class (the old families among the audience and the participants of the pageant: the former of the gentry, the latter of the servant, laboring, and shopkeeping classes—equally old and relatively undisturbed by the passage of time—pp. 35–36, 91–92).

Such a listing, although incomplete, represents an impressive body of evidence for the existence of a historical sense: the characters' unspoken assumption that they have a tradition and that it is operative and valuable. But this is not the only attitude the characters maintain toward the past, and one of the new elements in Woolf's historical novel is a somewhat jaded note of boredom (her own and her characters') with all things English, which overrides traditional nostalgia. For the stockbroker, Giles Oliver, the historical lucubrations of his aunt, Mrs. Swithin, on the view from the house are an irritant. This feeling partly derives from his fears of the impending war and partly from his dissatisfaction with his job and wife, but its effect is to make him reject the sense of the past in favor of a realistic grasp of the present. For his wife, as well, the sense of the past is spoiled by her awareness of the brutal realities of the present, epitomized by the newspaper account of a rape committed by members of that essential British institution, the Guards. Veneration of the past survives, but in a subtler form than regionalism or nationalism: it is present in the sympathetic though confused figure of Mrs. Swithin—who yields herself to the racial memory of prehistoric time. With her homely Anglo-Saxon name, it is no accident that she makes Hastings her place of yearly winter retirement, for with her primeval consciousness she can respond to the palimpsest of history at all its levels. "The Swithins were there before the Conquest" (p. 39), as her brother Bart says.

There is one further sense of the past at work in *Between the Acts*, but—as in the "Time Passes" section of *To the Lighthouse*—it is not clear whose consciousness this is. It is generated by the painting of the Lady Ermyntrude, which fills the room with the past by creating an absence of present things: "Empty, empty, empty; silent, silent, silent. The room was a shell, singing of what was before time was; a vase stood in the heart of the house, ala-

baster smooth, cold, holding the still, distilled essence of emptiness, silence" (p. 47). This consciousness is not ascribable to any
of the characters, and perhaps comes closer to a non-historical
consciousness than to any of the other time-senses in Pointz Hall or
in the pageant.

The subject of Virginia Woolf's view of time has stimulated a
lively critical debate, largely revolving around the degree of prominence in her work of Bergson's idea of *la durée,* an enduring time
in which objects have their existence and which runs independently
of customary, utilitarian clocktime. The only temporal distinction
Woolf makes in *Between the Acts* is the relatively unsophisticated
one of "actual time" and "mind time" (p. 13), but the moments
of silence and emptiness surrounding the portrait of the lady yield
suggestions of a timeless being toward which Woolf is anxious
to point but which she is unwilling to attempt to specify. While
this realm has its attractions—like the siren-call which drew
the author herself into death-by-drowning shortly after the novel
as we have it was completed—it is not allowed to override the
common sense of social life as lived in publicly-shared time: "If it
was painful, it was essential. There must be society" (p. 47).

The pageant that follows conveys the sense of the past through
comedy—although it must be admitted that the humor sometimes
palls. Introduced by a little girl naively representing young England,
and trumpeted by Mrs. Manresa's strident voice—"Scenes from
English history . . . Merry England" (p. 99)—the pageant manages
to convey a commentary both on the past, its subject, and on the
present, its audience. Within this play-within-a-play are four plays-
within-the-play, tableaux of the four main periods of English
civilization, as they were seen in *Orlando*: Elizabethan, Restora-
tion-eighteenth-century, Victorian, and Modern—" 'Let's hope to
God that's the end,' said Giles gruffly" (p. 206). The historical
sketches are not so much satirical as evocative, and are enjoy-
able in themselves as parodies of theatrical conventions and literary
styles. The audience cannot appreciate their purely esthetic qualities, however, and keeps complaining about the lack of pattern,
moral or meaning: it is getting charming vignettes of historical
life but insists on a philosophy of history.

The most complicated of the historical pastiches is, inevitably,
that of the present. The audience muses on the artist's powers:
"But what could she know about ourselves? The Elizabethans yes;

the Victorians, perhaps; but ourselves; sitting here on a June day in 1939—it was ridiculous" (p. 208). Miss La Trobe tries three means: first, "ten mins. of present time. Swallows, cows etc." (p. 209); but this effort at naive realism—an art without art—fails. " 'Reality too strong,' she muttered. 'Curse 'em!' " Nature intervenes to fill the void in art, as it had once before succeeded in doing, by happy accident; then cows, now a rainshower, relieve the tension of silence. The second attempt to represent the present as history is a dumb-show; a journalist has no trouble in reducing it to clichés: ". . . Civilization (the wall) in ruins; rebuilt (witness man with hod) by human effort. . . . Now issued black man in fuzzy wig; coffee-coloured ditto in silver turban; they signify presumably the League of . . ." (p. 212). There is mockery here not only of political symbolism but also of the limits of historical vision: "A painted cloth must convey—what the *Times* and *Telegraph* both said in their leaders that very morning." The third device is to hold the mirror up to nature, the cast literally holding mirrors up before the audience; but this, too, fails as the audience refuses to see more than the visual image of itself. Though nature is available to fill the void when no art prevails, it does so only when uncalled upon; the attempt to mirror nature and assimilate it bodily into the play ends in failure when the audience refuses to see itself as esthetic object.

A fourth image of the present comes about accidentally, but succeeds where conscious design had failed. The costumed cast appears ensemble, mouthing lines from the varied periods of history, then suddenly stops: "And the audience saw themselves, not whole by any means, but at any rate sitting still. The hands of the clock had stopped at the present moment. It was now. Ourselves" (p. 216). The present is seen as a horizon of all experience; it is a compound of the past, yet distinct from it. As at the close of *Orlando*, the historical sequence abruptly ends at the present moment, and history is seen as a collection of disjecta membra, over and done with, yet providing the raw material of esthetic synthesis.

The disembodied voice over the amplifier (obviously Miss La Trobe's) tries to draw these esthetic conclusions, but Reverend Streatfield in his innocence gives them an ethical turn: "we are members one of another," "We act different parts; but are the same," "nature takes her part," "there is a spirit that inspires, pervades . . ." (p. 224). With these phrases, Streatfield generalizes images to universals, and they are not to be dismissed for their pomposity but accepted as expressions of a hope. Woolf does not identify herself with that hope; she merely raises it. Like her surrogate in the novel, Miss La Trobe, she remains anonymous, refusing to appear before her audience.

The cast disperses again into fragments of history, and the audience disperses into its fragmentary present. But there is a means by which this atomization is at least symbolically arrested: a collective point-of-view emerges out of the snatches of the audience's remarks. This running commentary, which so often during the pageant reveals the incomprehension and absurdity of the middle-class English audience, now serves to integrate it: "He said she meant we all act. Yes, but whose play? Ah, that's the question! And if we're left asking questions, isn't it a failure, as a play? . . . Or was that, perhaps, what she meant? . . . that if we don't jump to conclusions, if you think, and I think, perhaps one day, thinking differently, we shall think the same? (p. 233). This is the vision of Bernard at the end of *The Waves*; it is the vision of Mrs. Swithin during the pageant. After portraying the flux of past phenomena, and the inability even of art to master the present's shifting senses of the past, Virginia Woolf expresses a faith that never quite left her amid her (and Miss La Trobe's) increasing despondency: the faith in the collective imagination of mankind to create a harmonious consciousness—which we may call a vital culture—out of its members' disparate private experience.

It is a prefiguration of this ultimate synthesis (akin to McTaggart's ideal of a union of selves in universal love) that the conclusion of the novel offers us. The artist has intuited the realm of personal experience and can now become the audience of her audience. Imagining a play she wants to write, she sees "two scarcely perceptible figures" behind a rock in a primeval domestic drama, and "heard the first words" (p. 248). At the same moment Giles and Isa Oliver speak, to begin their private drama in the "night that dwellers in caves had watched from some high place among rocks" (p. 256). (Similarly, Mrs. Swithin, reading the Outline of History, returns to prehistoric man, reads of his rise from a semi-crouching position, and then herself rises in an act of sympathetic repetition of the progress of the race.) The artist has not mastered past or present but can anticipate the future; she has not integrated the artifices of the pageant but can move beyond it to intuit the play-world of ordinary life. There is no mysticism here: only a conviction of the esthetic power to put men in touch with the eternal patterns of experience and, more important, with other minds.

From this faith in esthetic union derive the novel's numerous images of harmony in man and nature, e.g., the interlude of in-activity during the pageant in which "The view repeated in its own way what the tune was saying" (p. 158); the procession of the cast, singing, *"All passes but we, all changes . . . but we remain for-ever the same . . ."* (p. 164); the poetasting of Isa Oliver on some Elysian field where "all's equal" and "change is not" (p. 181). Pre-eminently, the faith gives rise to the character of Mrs. Swithin, who accepts fully the pageant's implications of the unity of man's consciousness ("I could have played . . . Cleopatra!"—p. 179), and who is accused, perhaps accurately, of not believing in history (p. 203). It is she who is capable of the synthetic view par excellence:

Mrs. Swithin caressed her cross. She gazed vaguely at the view. She was off, they guessed, on a circular tour of the imagination—one-making. Sheep, cows, grass, trees, ourselves—all are one. If discordant, producing harmony—if not to us, to a gigantic ear attached to a gigantic head. And thus—she was smiling benignly—the agony of the particular sheep, cow or human being is necessary; and so—she was beaming seraphically at the gilt vane in the distance—we reach the conclusion that *all* is harmony, could we hear it. And we shall. (p. 204)

Although Woolf did not enjoy this serenity, lacking a Christian or other firm ground of belief, she did make the "circular tour of the imagination"—the phrase can stand as a descriptive motto for *Between the Acts.*

If we ask for the pattern of Woolf's vision of history in her last novel, we find it cannot be based entirely on that of *Orlando,* in which the growth of personality was closely related to changes in national culture. The idea of English history presented on and off stage in *Between the Acts* is more subtle than any of the philosophi-cal theories of history taken up in previous historical novels. It might be called a post-theoretical idea, for it is in tune with the attitudes toward the past that dominate the modern historian's craft. Here we are no longer presented with broad causal relation-ships of events derived from prophetic visions of the shape of history. Neither the liberal view of progress, which was part of Woolf's intellectual heritage, nor the cyclical views of eternal return, which so many of her contemporaries embraced, is identifiable in the novel's world.

Some of her Bergsonian critics fall into the trap of taking the religious interpretation of Streatfield and the intuitive responses of Mrs. Swithin as expressing the doctrine of the novel,[13] but Woolf will not be contained by the limited perspectives of any of her characters. Another Bergsonian critic, James Hafley, brings us closer to her sense of history by considering the novel's conclusion:

Just as the actors, annihilating their own identities in the English past, attain freedom, so the present moment, itself inseparable from the past, becomes free; so also Isa and Giles at the conclusion of the novel begin a free act, after the irresoluteness that has characterized them during the day. . . . Here the Bergsonian prerequisites for free will have been attained: the whole past is in the present, so that the present moment is no longer spatialized; the past is a purely temporal past, so that the present moment will be a creation, a unique achievement—this act will be the first act ever to have been done; Isa and Giles have shed their immediate identity and have become "enormous."[14]

There is much to be questioned in this interpretation, but Hafley's perception gets us to the core of Woolf's notion of history: it is a machine for the production of novelty. The artist emulates the historical process itself when he mechanically arranges the often trivial data to produce something that freely leaps beyond the patterns of the past—and even beyond the pattern he constructs.

The pageant is a reduction of the past to caricature: history is something already done, rather stale, and inevitably absurd when seen from a later perspective. As the audience discovers, we can learn very little from watching the spectacle of the past, but we have a great stake in remembering it, reliving it in esthetic form, and making it part of the present in a ritual performance. In the dual process of laughing at and acting out the past, we discover ourselves alive in the present in a way we had not before known.

13. E.g., Margaret Church, *Time and Reality: Studies in Contemporary Fiction* (Chapel Hill, N. C., 1963), p. 72. See the bibliography of this book for a listing of the Bergsonian critics and their antagonists.

14. James Hafley, *The Glass Roof: Virginia Woolf as Novelist* (New York, 1963 [1954]), p. 151.

Our present becomes historical: it is not merely the given world, an immediate flow of sensation, but one of a number of historical possibilities that happens to be present, temporarily. The men of the present are enabled to give historical stature to their actions, to add a new act in the pageant, to discover—like the man who finds he has been talking prose all his life—that they have been living in history all their lives.

David Daiches has said that in *Between the Acts* the hero is England, but from his description it seems rather an anti-hero: "History flowering into the present is no story of happy fulfillment of heroic promise: the past has made the present fragmentary and the present has made the past petty."[15] This is so in the sense that all reality is both petty and fragmentary for Woolf; but both history and private life are shown by this mutual reduction to partake of the same reality and thereby to be continuous. It is this continuity that makes England the hero of the piece: England is the continuity of personal experience, unheroic in itself but compacted of the enduring stuff of historical memory, esthetic imagination, and popular mythology. England is thus one of the class-names for the collective experience which Woolf pursued all her artistic life. That is why this historical novel includes both a pageant of the past and a dramatic present; the novel is not the equivalent of the work of art that Miss La Trobe creates, but that creation as it is experienced by the men of England, unprepared and petty, historically limited but also historically engaged. This most detached and artificial of novels may be said to build its audience into its form, becoming an image not of art but of art-in-history.

The total reality symbolized by the novel is, then, universal: it is not simply history, which is always with us, nor nature, which is intercalated with history in the pageant, nor consciousness, which experiences them either as artist or audience, but all three orders overlapping and made temporarily harmonious by art. The dispersion of the audience into isolated fragments is not the only devolution at the close; the precarious harmony of the three orders of reality is broken into its elements—and we feel an inevitable let-down on being left with the Olivers' banal quarrel and coupling.

15. David Daiches, *Virginia Woolf* (Norfolk, Conn., 1942), p. 123.

But for a while in *Between the Acts* we have been given a comprehensive vision not of history, but of a reality more comprehensive than history, which only poems like *The Divine Comedy* and Shakespeare's history plays attain to. In this work, the historical novel transcends its origins and may well have achieved a limit of the genre's resources.

❧

Between the Acts is not a novel about history but a novel about consciousness-of-history, which includes historiography and historical fiction itself. This incorporation of its own tradition—and the exercise of a widely assimilative formal power—make it the last historical novel of the old school, or the first of the new. It is now no longer possible—whether in historiography or in historical fiction—to write convincingly about the past without building the interpretive process into the structure of the work. Despite the considerable learning of many recent historical novelists, their lack of methodological self-consciousness leaves them amid the conventions of the realist novel, and the critical reader will persist in seeing their best efforts as costume flummery. The historical novel of our time will probably join the experimental movement of the modern novel or retire from the province of serious literature. Like history itself, the historical novel must be more than its past, passing freely into new possibilities, or remain a sterile repetition of the forms doled out to it from tradition.

Two liberating trends in post-Woolfian historical fiction can be discerned. The first of these derives from the new approach to classical civilization that grew in the wake of the Cambridge school of anthropology. Perhaps the first and certainly the most energetic attempt to make historical fiction out of the ritual patterns of *The Golden Bough* is Naomi Mitchison's *The Corn King and the Spring Queen* (1931), in which Plutarch's life of Agis and Cleomenes is subsumed under the Frazerian rubric of the sacrifice of the sacred king for the renewal of the tribe. Whatever the novel's literary limitations, the dark side of Greek civilization—especially in its relations with its Scythian and Egyptian neighbors—emerges as forcefully into historical fiction as it did into historiography with the writings of Fustel de Coulanges. The failure of Robert

Graves, with the authority vested in him by *The White Goddess*, to enter this field partly accounts for its neglect until recent years. (Graves preferred to write two brilliant pseudo-court-memoirs of the Emperor Claudius, and two revisionist versions of the American Revolution as seen from the eyes of a British soldier, Sergeant Lamb.[16])

With the emergence of Mary Renault (Eileen Mary Challans) into historical writing, after a string of indifferent contemporary novels, the resources of the archaic period are coming to be tapped. It is not in her only (strictly speaking) historical subject—the Peloponnesian War, in *The Last of the Wine* (1956)—that her strength as a novelist of antiquity emerges, for her attempt to write up Socrates, Plato, and other classical figures within the family romance of an Athenian aristocrat never loses its statuary pallor. But her sequence on the Theseus myths—*The King Must Die* (1958) and *The Bull from the Sea* (1962)—succeeds in making historically plausible a legend-ridden past. One has only to compare her use of her scholarship with that of Mitchison, Graves, or lesser writers on classical themes (e.g., Alfred Duggan or Bryher) to sense the difference between a genuine artist and a learned entertainer. For Renault, modern knowledge is not an instrument for exposing the anthropological imperatives or political motivations of the men of the past. For the very reason that she treats Theseus as myth as well as man, she is able to rewrite his legendary exploits as history—speculative history, to be sure, but more readily approachable than the politically reduced or anthropologically expanded visions of man we are given by Graves and Mitchison, respectively.

The power to convey human depths can be a two-edged sword: the impressive characterizations of H. F. M. Prescott's *The Man on a Donkey* (1952) are not matched by a historical grasp of institutions, which would allow it to take the growth of Renaissance monarchy under Henry VIII with the seriousness with which it takes the loyal Catholic martyrs. Renault's imaginative sympathy

16. Robert Graves, *I, Claudius* (1934); *Claudius the God* (1934); *Sergeant Lamb of the Ninth* (1940); *Proceed, Sergeant Lamb* (1941). Graves has also written novels on Jesus, Milton, and other figures. An American follower of Graves is Gore Vidal; in an introductory note to *Julian* (1964)—and in his treatment of Roman politics—Vidal expresses his debt to Graves's method as scholar and novelist.

extends to institutions, and allows us to find our way into the cultural climate of the past—to recognize the ritual drama of the Cretan bull-dance in the way we recognize our own myths and communal passions. And then, Miss Renault can write English prose of studied simplicity and rhythmic beauty:

> It was dolphin weather, when I sailed into Piraeus with my comrades of the Cretan bull-ring. Knossos had fallen, which time out of mind had ruled the seas. The smoke of the burning Labyrinth still clung to our clothes and hair.
> I sprang ashore and grasped both hands full of Attic earth. It stuck to my palms as if it loved me. Then I saw the staring people, not greeting us, but calling each other to see the Cretan strangers.[17]

This, the opening of *The Bull from the Sea*, is not a bravura stroke but strikes a note that is maintained throughout, enhancing the legendary past by giving it a luster unlike history, yet conveying the concrete reality of things as they might have affected historic (or pre-historic) heroes.

The only other post-Woolfian phenomenon in historical fiction worth building hopes on is William Golding. It is still too early to assess Golding's stature and achievement as a novelist—now that the rage of *Lord of the Flies* has subsided, the issue may be confronted more coolly—but there is no denying that *The Inheritors* (1961) and *The Spire* (1964) represent significant innovations in the treatment of historical themes. That the earlier of these novels is concerned with pre-history—with pre-humanity, for the most part—diminishes its status as historical fiction only on strict theoretical grounds.[18] It is an attempt to extend the genre's range by stretching the imagination to conceive what it felt like to be alive at a special historical moment: the emergence of man. *The In-*

17. Mary Renault, *The Bull from the Sea* (London, 1964 [1962]), p. 9. I quote the English paperback edition, as most readily available.

18. On the propriety of a historical work's inclusion of prehistory, cf. J. H. Huizinga: "The historian tries to re-experience what was once experienced by men like ourselves, and stops short of saurians. . . . Attempts to enliven the story with word-pictures of the primeval scenery or the peculiar lineaments of Neanderthal man do not help—the whole remains a hopeless hybrid" (*Dutch Civilization in the Seventeenth Century and Other Essays*, trans. A. J. Pomerans [London and Glasgow, 1968], p. 192). It is possible to draw quite opposite conclusions for the historical novel, although we can never achieve verifiability of the novelist's imaginative entry into the Neanderthal mind.

heritors is, however, inevitably a *tour de force*: it evokes amazement not because it is done well but because it has been done at all.

The Spire needs no such qualifications: it is not only an effective projection of the past through the mind of a culture-hero, the unknown creator of the magnificent spire of Salisbury Cathedral, but it takes up a theory of the role of the hero in history and thereby attains philosophic stature as a historical novel. The theory —and much of the detail—is Carlyle's: Dean Jocelin of Salisbury is a version of Abbot Samson as he is portrayed by Jocelin of Brakelond in *Past and Present*. His struggle against his cathedral chapter—who resist the upset of their lives which the enormous building program requires—follows the lines of the Abbot's efforts to reform his monastery. The authorial attitude toward the creative power of the medieval church is similar in these two writers: *Laborare est orare* becomes ". . . what is the point of all this brooding? I have too great a work on hand. Work! Work!"[19]

But Golding takes up Carlyle's heroic theme only to question it; his hero is a sex-obsessed fanatic, whose personal sacrifices for his cultural vision are tainted by the gross human inadequacies they involve: "When I threw myself down and offered myself to the work, I thought that to offer myself was the same as to offer everything. It was my stupidity." The novel is a critique of the gigantic pride that accompanies the historical innovator, but its psychological realism does not in the end undo Carlyle's hero-worship. After all is said about the hero's inadequacies, there looms his spire as his permanent justification. The presence of Carlylian themes here suggests that the modern historical novel at its best remains in touch with its tradition. Both the psychological penetration and symbolic force of *The Spire* demonstrate the continuing possibility of a renewal of stylistic and conceptual growth in historical fiction.

19. William Golding, *The Spire* (London, 1965 [1964]), p. 100; the quotation below is from p. 194.

Index

THE JOHNS HOPKINS PRESS

Designed by James C. Wageman

Composed in Baskerville text and display
by Monotype Composition Company

Printed on 55-lb Lockhaven Offset
by Universal Lithographers, Inc.

Bound in Holliston Roxite C 56565
by L. H. Jenkins, Inc.